PROCEEDINGS

OF THE

FOURTH CALVINISTIC CONGRESS

HELD IN

EDINBURGH

6th to 11th July 1938

*Printed for the Congress Executive and published
by them at the Congress Office*

15 N. BANK STREET, EDINBURGH 1

1938

EDITORIAL COMMITTEE

Rev. Professor J. H. S. BURLEIGH, D.D. (Convener), Edinburgh.

Rev. W. H. HAMILTON, M.A., Edinburgh.

Rev. S. LEIGH HUNT, London.

W. ROUNSFELL BROWN (Hon. Secretary), Solicitor, Edinburgh.

Note—The Committee, and not Speakers, are responsible for all matter given only in Summary.

PRINTED IN GREAT BRITAIN BY
MORRISON AND GIBB LTD., EDINBURGH AND LONDON

CONTENTS

CONTENTS

INTRODUCTION

THE Third Calvinistic Congress, held in Geneva in 1936, concluded with a Resolution that a Fourth Congress be held in Edinburgh in 1938. It naturally fell to Rev. Professor Donald Maclean, D.D., of the Free Church College, Edinburgh, who had from its outset been associated with the movement, to take the initiative in promoting the Edinburgh Congress. Early in 1937, at a meeting convened by him of ministers and elders likely to be interested, arrangements were entered upon. An Executive Committee was named, of which Rev. Professor Daniel Lamont, D.D., Edinburgh, then Moderator of the General Assembly of the Church of Scotland, was elected Honorary President. Dr. Maclean was appointed President, with three Vice-Presidents, viz. : Rev. D. E. Hart Davies, D.D., minister of St. Thomas's Congregation of the Church of England in Scotland; Rev. Francis Davidson, D.D., Professor in the Original Secession Theological College, Glasgow; and Rev. W. J. Moffett, B.A., Clerk of the Synod of the Reformed Presbyterian Church in Scotland. Mr. Walter Rounsfell Brown, B.L., Solicitor, Edinburgh, was appointed Honorary Secretary.

The basis of the Congress, as expressed by Dr. Maclean and accepted at the initiatory meeting, was as follows :

The Congress is not an *open forum*; nor is it to impose binding resolutions on any taking part; rather to facilitate discussion towards pooling concepts of the Reformed Faith as applicable to present-day life. The participating Churches, as heirs of the Reformation, have a care for, and a duty to examine lovingly, their tradition in the light of Scripture, which is the anchorage of the Faith.

The General Topic of the Congress, as agreed upon at Geneva, was " The Reformed Faith and its Ethical Consequences." A Sub-Committee arranged for a series of papers dealing with the various aspects of this subject, for speakers to initiate discussion after each paper, and for leaders of Opening Devotions each morning of the Congress. Two Evening Public Meetings were also arranged.

Other Sub-Committees were entrusted with the arrangement of hospitality for members coming from abroad, and with the raising of a Congress Fund to meet the cost of printing and other necessary expenses. In both of these undertakings the

Sub-Committees were generously supported by friends of the Congress. The Corporation of Edinburgh graciously agreed to welcome delegates to an Evening Reception in the City Chambers, and the B.B.C. granted facilities for a short Sunday afternoon Congress Broadcast.

By cordial invitation of the Divinity Faculty of the University of Edinburgh, the Congress met within New College, the Divinity School of the University. The closing session was held in the Free Church of Scotland Presbytery Hall, and the two Public Evening Meetings were held in the Assembly Hall of the Free Church.

LIST OF MEMBERS OF THE CONGRESS

THIS " Who is Who " of the Congress contains the names of (1) Originators of, and Executive Committees for, the Congress, and (2) those who supported and encouraged the holding of, and intimated their intention of attending, the Congress. Many of these found it impossible to fulfil their purpose of attending ; numbers varied from session to session. The highest attendance at any session was one hundred. The capital letters at the end of some items indicate as follows :

> **C**=Member of Committees.
> **P**=Author of a Programme Paper.
> **D**=Having taken part in Discussions.
> **M**=Took part in one of the Public Meetings.
> **B**=Took part in the Broadcast.
> **E**=Gave Exposition at Morning Devotions.

> *C. of E.=Church of England.
> C.F.=Chaplain to the Forces.
> C. of S.=Church of Scotland.
> F.C.=Free Church of Scotland.
> U.F.=United Free Church of Scotland.

1. BAIN (Rev.) John, Min. (1911) C. of S.,* St. Paul's (Edinburgh) Congregation.
2. BAXTER, John William, B.Com.(Edin.), Elder, F.C. ;* Treasurer, F.C., Edinburgh. ACTING TREAS. CONGRESS FUND.
3. BAXTER (Rev.) William J., M.A., Hon. C.F.,* Min. (1912) C. of S., Dowanhill (Glasgow) Congn. Pres. Scottish Refor. Socy. **C.**
4. BESSELAAR, G., M.A., Litt.D., Prof. Univ. of Amsterdam. Elder, Ref. Ch. of Holland (*for 36 years office-bearer Dutch Presb. Ch., S. Africa*).
5. BEATON, Rev. Donald, Min. Free Presb. C. of S., Oban Congregation. **C.**
6. BLAIR, Duncan M'Callum, M.B., D.Sc., Regius Prof. of Anatomy, Glasgow Univ. Elder F.C. **C.**
7. BRADING (Rev.) Francis C., B.D., F.R.C.S., Min. C. of E.,* Ditton, near Maidstone, Kent (*late Secy. Scrip. Gift Miss. and Naval and Military Bible Socy.*).
8. BREED (Rev.) Charles, Min. Strict Baptist Ch., Manor Park Congn., London. *Vice-Pres. Sov. Grace Union.*

9. BROWN, George Graham, F.R.G.S., etc., 19 Mayfield Gardens, Edinburgh, 9. Secy. (Edin. dist.) China Inland Miss. (*late Missionary in China*). **C.**

10. BROWN, Walter Rounsfell, B.L. (Glasgow, 1882), 6 Grange Terrace, Edinburgh, 9. Solicitor (1883) ; Lt.-Col. Territorial Army (retired). Elder, F.C. (late Gen. Treas. F.C.). HON. SEC. and (Joint) HON. TREAS. CONGRESS EXECUTIVE. **C.D.**

11. BURBRIDGE, William B., Accountant. Hon. Secy. Sov. Grace Union, 31 Imperial Bldgs. Ludgate Circus, London, E.C.4. (*Convener, First Calvinistic Congress, 1932.*)

12. BURLEIGH (Rev.) John H. S., D.D., Min. (1924) C. of S., Prof. (1931) Eccl. History, Edinburgh Univ. CONVENER EDITORIAL COMMITTEE. **C.P.**

13. BYRNE, Frederick, 2 Blessington Place, Dublin. Member of Ch. of I., St. Mary's, Dublin. Theological Student.

14. CAMERON (Rev.) William J., M.A., B.D.(Edin.). Min. (1932), F.C., Burghead (Morayshire) Congn. **C.**

15. CAMERON (Rev.) Thomas, M.A., Min. (1900) Presb. C. of E., Westmoreland Road Congn., Newcastle-on-Tyne.

16. CARRUTHERS, S. W., M.D., Ph.D., 50 Belvedere Road, London, S.E.19. Elder Presb. Ch. of E. Convener Bus. Com. Gen. Assem., 1931. Secy. Bus. Com. World Presb. Alliances, 1929, 1933, 1937.

17. CHRISTIE (Rev.) J. G. L., M.C., M.A. Min. (1925) C. of S., Rodger Mem. (Coldstream) Congn.

18. COLLINS (Rev.) Geo. N. M., M.A., B.D. Min. (1928), F.C., St. Columba (Edinburgh) Congn. Editor, F.C. Mag. for Young.

19. CRAIG (Rev.) James, B.D.(Glasgow). Min. Presb. C. of S. Africa, 34 Nicolson Road, Durban, South Africa.

20. CZABA, Joseph, Sopron, Hungary. Teacher of English, Academy at Sopron.

21. CURTIS (Rev.) William A., D.D., D.Litt., D.Theol. Min. (1903) C. of S. Regius. Prof. of Biblical Criticism, Principal of New College and Dean of Faculty of Divinity, all in Univ. of Edinburgh. Joint. Conv. C. of S. Com. on Inter-Church Relations. Past. Pres. Gen. Presb. Alliance.

22. DAVIDSON (Rev.) Francis, M.A., B.D.(Glasgow), D.D.(Aberdeen). Min. (1909) United Orig. Sec. Ch. Prof. (1928) Biblical Criticism, U.O.S. Ch. Div. Hall. Principal (1938) Bible Train. Inst., 64 Bothwell Street, Glasgow, C.2. Author of *The Faith that Lives*. VICE-PRES. of CONGRESS EXECUTIVE. **C.D.**

23. DAVIES, Lt.-Col. L. Merson, 8 Garscube Terrace, Edinburgh, 12, M.A., F.G.S., F.R.S.E., F.R.A.I. Late Royal Artillery. Director, and Lecturer in Geology, Inst. of Anthropology. **C.D.**

24. DRUMMOND (Very Rev.) Robert J., D.D., Chaplain to H.M. the King. Min. (1883), C. of S. Senior Pastor, Lothian Rd. (Edinburgh) Congn. Ex-Mod. (1918), U.F. Gen. Assem. **C.B.**

25. EDWARDS, T. Tweedale, Artist, 52 Queen Street, Edinburgh, 2. F.R.H.S., Member Martyrs and St. John's (Edinburgh) U.F. Congn.

26. ENYEDY (Rev.) Andrew, D.Theol., Palocy U.88, Miskole, Hungary. Min. (Notary in Chief of dist. referendony of Home Miss. Com.) Reformed Ch., Hungary.

27. FISHER, Matthew George, 25 Northumberland Street, Edinburgh, 3. K.C., M.A., LL.B. Elder, St. Cuthbert's (Edinburgh), C. of S. Congn.

28. FORRESTER (Rev.) David M., M.A., B.D.(Edin.), D.D.(St. Andrews). Min. (1886), U.F., Broughton (Peeblesshire) Congn. Late Principal Clerk U.F. Gen. Assem. Ex-Mod. (1933) U.F. Gen. Assem. **C.**

29. FORRESTER (Rev.) W. R., B.D., Min. (1922) C. of S. Professor (1935) Christian Ethics, Univ. St. Andrews. **D.**

30. GILLON (Rev.) R. Moffat, M.A., Ph.D., Min. (1911) C. of S. Bruntsfield (Edinburgh) Congn. Secy. Scottish Reformation Society. **C.**

31. GILMOUR (Rev.) William James, B.A. Min. (1932) Reformed Presb. C. of S., Loanhead (Midlothian) Congn. **C.**

32. GRANT (Rev.) Angus, M.A.(Glasgow)., Min. F.C., Lochfyneside (Minard, Argyll) Congn.

33. GREGG (Rev.) A. C., B.D. (Edin.). Min. Reformed Presb. C. of S., Greenock Congn. Editor, *Church Magazine*, also *The Bulwark*.

34. GUTHRIE (Rev.) William Alexander, J.P., M.A., D.D.(Edin.). Min. (1924) C. of S., Fountainbridge (Edinburgh) Congn. Member Church and Nation Com. C. of S. Member Town Council of Edinburgh.

35. HAGAN (Rev.) Edward James, O.B.E.(Mil.Div.), B.A.(Queen's, Belfast). Min. (1907) C. of S., Warrender Park (Edinburgh) Congn. **C.**

36. HAMILTON (Rev.) W. H., M.A., Min. (1914) C. of S. Gen. Secy. (1927) Alliance of Refd. Chs. holding Presb. System, 44 Queen Street, Edinburgh, 2. Ed. Mag. and Pubns. of Alliance. **C.M.**

37. HART-DAVIES (Rev.) D. E., D.D., Min. (   ) C. of E. in Scot., St. Thomas (Edinburgh) Congn. VICE-PRES. CONGRESS EXECUTIVE. **C.**

38. HAXTON, Mrs. David, 5 London Road, Seapoint, Capetown, South Africa. Member Women's Assoc., St. Andrew's Presb. Ch., Capetown.

39. HEIJLMAN, J., Klopperhingel 53, Haarlem, Holland. Elder Reformed Ch., Evangelist.

40. HENDERSON (Rev.) George D., M.A., B.D., D.Litt., D.D., F.S.A.(Scot.), F.R.H.S. Min. (1916) C. of S. Prof. (1924) of Ch. History, Univ. Aberdeen. **C.M.**

41. HENDERSON (Rev.) John, M.A. (1926), Edin. Studied Tübingen (1929–30), Bonn (1930). Min. (1931) C. of S., St. Margaret's (Juniper Green, Edinburgh) Congn.

42. HENDRY (Rev.) George S., B.D., Min. (1930) C. of S., St. Andrew's (Bridge of Allan) Congn. **C.**

43. HIRST (Rev.) F. M., M.A., B.D., Min. Baptist Ch. (1914), Coventry, (1917) Leicester, (1920) Serampore Col. India, (1924) Morningside (Edinburgh) Congn. **D.**

44. HORNSBY (Rev.) John T., M.A., Ph.D.(Edin.), Min. Cong. Ch. Pastor (1910) Bristo Place (Edinburgh) Congn. Treas. Scot. Ch. Hist. Socy. **C.**

45. HUNTER (Rev.) Adam Mitchell, M.A.(Hons.), D. Litt., F.R.S.E. Min. (1897) C. of S. Librarian New Col. Univ. Edinburgh. **C.**

46. INNES (Rev.) T. Christie, M.A.(Aberdeen), M.R.A.S. Min. (1933) Presb. C. of E., Camden Road Congn., London ; (1935) Min. U.F. Ebenezer (Leith, Edin.) Congn. ; (1938) Min. C. of S., 121 George Street, Edinburgh 2. **C.E.**

47. IRWIN, James, 5 Dumbreck Road, Glasgow, S.1. Merchant ; Member and Hon. Treas. of Synod Funds, Refd. Presb. C. of S. **C.**

48. JAKUBENAS (Rev.) Paul, D.Theol. Traku 5, C. 13, Kaunas, Lithuania. Prof. of Theology, Refd. Ch.

49. JOHNSON, Douglas, B.A., M.R.C.S., L.R.C.P., Secy. Inter. Varsity Fellowship of Evangel. Unions, 39 Bedford Square, London, W.C.1.

50. KELLER (Rev.) Adolf, D.D., Professor Refd. Church. Palais Wilson, Geneva. Vice-Pres. Presb. Alliance.

51. KENNEDY, Mrs., 33 Fountainhall Road, Edinburgh. Member C. of S. **C.**

52. KNIGHT (Rev.) George A. F., M.A., B.D. Min. (1935) C. of S. Missionary Scottish Mission, Budapest.

53. KNOX (Rev.) Robert M. Min. (1910) F.C. Buccleuch (Edinburgh) Congn. Ex-Mod. (1930) Gen. Assem. **C.**

54. KOLFHAUS (Rev.) William, D.D., Vlotho, Wesser, Germany.

55. KROMSIGT (Rev.) P. J., D.D. (Retired Minister, late of Amsterdam), Riouw Str. 5, The Hague, Holland. **D.M.**

56. KUYPER (Miss) Catherine M. E., 22 Madoerstraat, The Hague, Holland, Member Refd. Church.

57. LAMONT (Very Rev.) Daniel, M.A., B.D., D.D. Min. (1900) C. of S., Prof. (1927) Practical Theol., New Col. Univ. Edinburgh. Ex-Mod. (1936) Gen. Assem. HON. PRES. CONGRESS EXECUTIVE. **M.D.**

58. LANG (Very Rev.) Marshall B., T.D., D.D. Min. (1895) C. of S. Whittingehame (East Lothian) Congn. Ex-Mod. (1935) Gen. Assem.

59. LANGENHOL (Rev.) W. A., Kirchestrat 1, Rheydt, Rhine Provence. Pastor, Evangel. Ch.

60. LECERF (Rev.) Auguste, D.D., D.Theol., 54 Rue des Saints Pères, Paris, Min. Église Réformée, Prof. of Theology, Faculty of Paris. **D.B.M.**

61. LEIGH-HUNT (Rev.) Stephen, "Dunbay," 15 Windsor Avenue, Edgemore, Middlesex. Presbyter, Free. Ch. of E., Editorial Secy. S.G.U. **D.**

62. LIGHT (Rev.) Alfred W., 31 Imperial Bldgs., Ludgate Circus, London, E.C.4. Min. Particular Baptist Ch. Lecturer, S.G.U.

63. LOUDEN (Rev.) R. Stewart, B.D.(Edin.). Min. (1938) C. of S., St. Mary's (Old Aberdeen) Congn.

64. LUSK (Rev.) D. C., M.C., M.A. Min. (1911) C. of S., West Coates (Edinburgh) Congn.

65. MACALPINE, George, O.B.E., Elder, C. of S. Joint-Secy. C. of S. Committee on Christian Life and Work, 121 George Street, Edinburgh, 2. **C.**

66. MACAULAY (Rev.) Hector, M.A.(Classics, St. Andrews). Min. (1909), F.C., Strathy (by Thurso) Congn.

67. M'CLYMONT (Rev.) A. W., D.Litt., 62 Belgrave Road, Corstorphine, Edinburgh. Min. C. of S. Joint Scottish Secy., United Socy. for Christian Lit.

68. M'CONNACHIE (Rev.) John, D.D., Min. (1902) C. of S., St. John's (Dundee) Congn. **C.**

69. M'CRACKEN (Rev.) Joseph, Min. (1936) Irish Evangelical Ch., Belfast.

70. MACDONALD (Rev.) Duncan, M.A., Min. (1910) F.C., Milton (Glasgow) Congn. Ex-Mod. (1934) Gen. Assem.

71. MACDONALD, George H., Bank Agent, Dingwall, Elder, F.C. **C.**

72. MACDONALD (Rev.) William C., M.A., Min. (1919) C. of S., Palmerston Place (Edinburgh) Congn. **E.**

73. MACDOUGALL (Rev.) David, M.A.(Glasgow), Ph.D.(Edinburgh), Min. (1915) C. of S., Dalry (Edinburgh) Congn.

74. MACEWAN, William C., M.A., M.D., Walford Lodge, Prestonpans. Elder, C. of S. Chairman *Monthly Visitor* Tract Socy. **C.**

75. MACFADYEN (Rev.) Archibald, R.S. of Lit., London. Min. (1911) Gorgie (Edinburgh) Baptist Church. Author of *The Conversations of Christ*, etc. etc. **C.E.**

76. MACINTYRE (Rev.) Neil, Min. Free Presb. C. of S., Gilmour Place (Edinburgh) Congn.

77. MACKAY (Rev.) Hugh G., M.A. (1930), B.D. (1936) Edinburgh. Min. (1934) F.C., Kinglassie (Fife) Congn.

78. MACKENZIE (Rev.) David, M.A.(Hon.), Min. (1921), F.C., Nairn Congn. **C.**

79. MacKinnon (Rev.) Donald, B.Ped., F.S.A.(Scot.), Min. (1923), F.C., Portree (Isle of Skye) Congn. Author of books on Scottish History and Celtic Literature.

80. Mackenzie, Kenneth, 19 Braidburn Crescent, Edinburgh, bank agent (retired). Elder, C. of S.

81. MacKnight (Rev.) R. I. G., A.B. (1896), B.D. (1900), Ph.D. (1907). Studied Johns Hopkins Univ. ; Leipzig ; Chicago. Min. (1909), Prof. (1929), Refd. Presb. Ch., N. America, Walkinsburgh Pa, U.S.A. Author of *Kenosis in the Incarnation*, etc. **P.**

82. MacKnight (Rev.) W. J., D.D., Min. Refd. Presb. Ch., N. America, Syracuse Congn.

83. Maclean (Rev.) Donald, D.D., Min. (1897) F.C., Prof. (1920) Church History, F.C. College, Edinburgh. Ex-Mod. (1919 and 1937) Gen. Assem. Pres. Scot. Ch. Hist. Socy. Pres. Internat. Com. of Calvinistic Congresses. Editor *The Evangelical Quarterly*. PRES., CONGRESS EXECUTIVE. **C.D.M.**

84. Macleod (Rev.) John, D.D., Min. (1897) F.C., Principal (1927) and Prof. (1930) Apologetics, F.C. College, Edinburgh. Ex-Mod. (1920) Gen. Assem. **C.P.D.**

85. Macleod (Rev.) John, O.B.E. (Mil. Div.), late C.F., Min. (1904) F.C., Hope Street (Glasgow) Congn. Ex-Mod. (1917) Gen. Assem. **C.**

86. Macleod (Mrs.) Una, 8 Lansdowne Crescent, Glasgow, N.W. **C.**

87. Macpherson (Rev.) Hector, M.A., Ph.D.(Edin.), Min. (1916) C. of S., Guthrie Mem. (Edinburgh) Congn. Author of books on Astronomy, History, etc. **C.D.**

88. Mactavish, Duncan, M.A., Castleton Cottage, by Lochgilphead, Argyll. Member F.C.

89. Manson, Roderick, Elder, C. of S. Secy. *Monthly Visitor* Tract Society (inst. 1832), 4 York Place, Edinburgh, 1. **C.**

90. Martin (Very Rev.) Alexander, D.D., LL.D., 17 Grange Terrace, Edinburgh, 9. Min. (1884) C. of S., Prof. and Principal (*emeritus*) New Col. Univ., Edin. Ex-Mod. (1920 and 1929) Gen. Assem. U.F.

91. Marwick (Rev.) William, 10 West Mayfield, Edinburgh 9. Missionary (retired). Secy. The Carlyle Society.

92. Matthew, Thomas, Solicitor, Kilwinning, Ayrshire. Deacon, U.O.S. Ch. **C.**

93. Matyas (Rev.) Ernest, D.D., Rector of High School ; Director of Theol., Serospataki Reformatus Fuiskola Igazgatoi, Hivatala, Hungary.

94. Maxwell (Rev.) Thomas, B.D., Min. (1934) C. of S., Millhill (Musselburgh) Congn.

95. Mekeel (Rev.) Herbert, Min. First Presb. Church (209 Union Street), Schenectady, New York.

96. Merriweather (Rev.) Alfred, Min. U.F., Martyr's and St. John's (Edinburgh) Congn. Ex-Mod. Gen. Assem.

97. MIKLOS, Balint, Szentesin, Hungary, student of Divinity, F.C. Col. Edinburgh.

98. MOFFETT (Rev.) W. J., B.A., Min. Refd. Presb. C. of S., Airdrie (Lanarkshire) Congn. Clerk of Refd. Presb. Synod. VICE-PRES. CONGRESS EXECUTIVE. C.

99. MUSCULUS (Rev.) Paul Romane, Pasteur de l'Église Réformée de France, Pouzanges (Vendée), A.E.M. de l'Ecole Nationale Supérieure des Arts Décoratifs de Paris.

100. NAGY (Rev.) Alexander, Ph.D., Min. Refd. Ch. ; Secy. of Danubian Dist., Budapest, Hungary. Studied New Col., Edin., was assistant (14 years) in Scot. Miss., Budapest. B.

101. NICOLAS, Albrect, Essen, Germany, Theol. student, Confessional Ch.

102. NIESEL (Rev.) Wilhelm, Berlin-Lichterfelde Gardeschu renweg 126, Lic. Theol. (1930, Munster).

103. PAGE, W. M., 31 Queen Street, Edinburgh, 2; Solicitor Supreme Courts. Elder, C. of S. ; Hon. Sec. C. of S. Com. on Public Worship and Aids to Devotion ; Hon. Treasurer The Hymn Society.

104. PARKER (Rev.) William Joseph, B.A.(Manchester and Ridley Hall, Cantab.), Min. C. of E., Albert Mem. (Manchester) Church.

105. PATERSON (Very Rev.) W. P., D.D., LL.D., 17 South Oswald Road, Edinburgh, Min. (1887) C. of S., Prof. (emeritus) Univ. of Edinburgh.

106. PEARS (Rev.) Thomas Clinton, Junior, B.D., Litt.D., Min. Presb. Ch. in U.S.A. ; Manager, Dept. of Hist., and Secy. Presb. Hist. Socy., 520 Witherspoon Bldgs. Philadelphia, Pa.

107. PERINS (Rev.) Gerard M. van., Min. Refd. Ch. in America, late Missionary to N. American Indians ; Editor, Christian Cynosure, etc., Clifton, New Jersey, U.S.A. D.

108. PHILP (Rev.) Horace R. A., M.B., Ch.B., Min. (1921) C. of S. in England, Newcastle Congn., formerly Supt. C. of S. Mission, Kenya. Author of God and the African, New Day in Kenya. D.

109. PLATTS (Rev.) H., Min. Ind. Ch. in Sheffield ; Member S.G.U.

110. POLSON (Rev.) John, M.A., B.D., Min. (1923) C. of S., St. Andrew's (Berwick-on-Tweed) Congn.

111. PORTEOUS (Rev.) Norman W., Min. (1929), C. of S., Prof. 1931–35), Heb. and Oriental Lang., Univ. of St. Andrews (1935–37), O.T. Lang. and Lit., Univ. Edin. (1937), Heb. and Semitic Lang., Univ. Edin.

112. PRIOR, Arthur, New Zealand, c/o New Zealand House, 415 Strand, London, W.C.2. Journalist and student Theol. ACCOMPANIED BY MRS. PRIOR.

113. RAMSAY (Miss) Mary Paton, M.A. (Aberdeen), Doct. de l'Univ., Paris ; Officier de l'Instr. Publique, 11 Saxe-Coburg Place, Edinburgh. Authoress ; Member C. of S. C.M.

114. READ (Rev.) David H. C., M.A., B.D., Min. (1936) C. of S., West (Coldstream) Congn. **M.**
115. RIDDELL (Rev.) J. G., M.A., Min. (1924) C. of S., Prof. (1934) Univ. Glasgow. **C.**
116. ROBERTSON (Rev.) Thos. R., M.A.(Hon.)(Glasgow), Min. (1934) F.C., Bishopbriggs (Glasgow) Congn.
117. ROBINSON (Rev.) Stewart M., M.A., D.D., Min. Presb. Ch., N. America. Editor *The Presbyterian* (founded 1831), Philadelphia, Pa., U.S.A., B.M. ACCOMPANIED BY MRS. ROBINSON.
118. ROBINSON (Rev.) William Childs, A.B., D.D.(Roanoke), A.M., B.D.(Columbia), Th.M.(Princeton), Th.D.(Harvard), Prof. Columbia Theol. Sem., Decatur., Ca., U.S.A. **P.**
119. ROCH, William, 104 Florissant, Geneva, Calvinistic student.
120. ROODENBURG (Rev.) J., N.H.V., D.Theol., Parkineg 231, Voorburg, The Hague, Holland. Min. Nat. Reformed Ch.
121. Ross (Rev.) Alexander, M.A., B.D.(Aberdeen), Min. (1913) F.C., Prof. (1937) N.T. Exegesis, F.C. Col. Edin. Ex-Mod. (1935) Gen. Assem. **E.**
122. ROWAN (Rev.) Thomas, M.A., Grad. Theol. (Princetown), Min. Presb. Ch. of Ireland, Benburb Congn.
123. RUTGERS, Victor Henri, LL.D. and Theol.D. (h.c. Paris), Professor of Law at the Free University of Amsterdam, late Member of Parliament, late Minister of Instruction, Arts and Sciences, sometimes Dutch Delegate at League of Nations meetings, President of the " Nederlandsche Bond van Gereformeerden (Calvinisten)," de Lairessestraat 117, Amsterdam, Member Reformed Church (Gereformeerde Kerk) of Amsterdam. ACCOMPANIED BY MRS. RUTGERS.

124. SAUSSURE (Rev.) Jean de, Min. Nat. Prot. Ch., Geneva, Pastor of Cathedral Ch. Publications : *Les Contradictions de la pensée religieuse* (1926) ; *A l'École de Calvin* (1930) ; *La Doctrine Calviniste des Sacraments* (*paru dans Études sur Calvin. et le Calvinisme* (1935) ; *Crois tu cela ?* (1938). **P.D.**
125. SAWLE, William John, B.C. and M.T. Col., Clifton, Bristol, 8. Theol. student.
126. SCHELVEN, A. L. Van, B.A., Beeklaan 624, The Hague, Holland. Student Theol.
127. SCOTT, John, " Burnside," George Street, Stevenston, Ayrshire. Assoc. Chart. Inst. of Secretaries. Elder, and Synodical Treas., U.O.S. Ch.
128. SCOTT (Rev.) John, M.A. (ordained and inducted on 26th December 1926), U.O.S.C., now Min. C. of S., 121 George Street, Edinburgh, 2.
129. SEBESTYÉN (Rev.) E., Raday Utca 28, Budapest ix, Hungary, Ph.D., D.D.(*Hon. Causa*) Free Univ., Amsterdam), Prof. System. Theol., Refd. Theol. Sem., Budapest. Editor *Magyar Kalvinizmus*. Pres. John Calvin Socy. of Budapest. **P.**

130. SHAND, John Harvey, 48 Northumberland Street, Edinburgh, 2, Writer to the Signet, F.S.A.(Scot.), Member of C. of S. **C.**
131. SHAW (Rev.) John, M.A.(Edin.), Min. (1923) F.C., Leith (Edin.) Congn. Principal Clerk, Gen. Assem. ; Lecturer Relig. Instn., Moray House Training Col. for Teachers.
132. SKENE (Rev.) A. L., M.A., 52 Spottiswoode Street, Edinburgh, 9. Min. (1892) F.C., thereafter U.F. (now C. of S. retired list).
133. SLOAN, David T. C., 200 St. Vincent Street, Glasgow, Shipowner, Elder and Secy. Congn. Ch., Helensburgh.
134. SOUCEK (Rev.) J. B., D.D., Jungmannova 15, Praha II, Czechoslovakia. Min. Evang. Ch. of Czech Brethren. **M.**
135. SPARK, J. Brown, Southlea, Barnton, Edinburgh. Merchant, office-bearer Charlotte Chapel (Baptist), Edinburgh. **C.**
136. STAP, I., Koninginnelaan 15, Amersfoort, Holland. Office director, Netherlands League of Refd. Y.M. Societies.
137. SWANTON (Rev.) R., 16 Kerma Avenue, E. Melvern, S.E.5, Vic. M.A., B.D.(Melbourne), Min. Presb. Ch. of Australia (Postgrad. Student Theol., Univ. Edin.).
138. SZABO (Rev.) Imre, Min. Refd. Ch., Budapest. Mod. Presb. of Budapest.

139. THOMAS (Rev.) Richard, Schiviglerstrasses 39, Vienna. D.D., Min. and Prof. Theol., Zwinglikirche, Vienna.
140. THOMSON (Rev.) G. T., B.A.(Oxon.), D.D., Min. (1920) C. of S., Prof. (1936) (formerly Syst. Theol. Univ., Aberdeen) of Christian Dogmatics, Univ. Edin. **C.P.D.**
141. THOMSON (Rev.) T. B. Stewart, M.C., B.D., Sen. Chaplain (T.A.), Scot. Command, Min. (1919) C. of S., St. Stephen's (Edin.) Congn. **D.**
142. TOROK (Rev.) Stephen, D.D., Prof. Refd. Col. (Zwinglikirche), Papa, Hungary.
143. TORRANCE (Rev.) T., F.R.G.S., 12 Chalmers Crescent, Edinburgh, 9, late of Changtu, Szechuan, W. China, missionary. Author of *The Beatitudes and the Decalogue; China's First Missionaries—Ancient Israelites; Exp. Studies in St. John's Miracles.*
144. TORRANCE (Rev.) T. F., M.A., B.D., 12 Chalmers Crescent, Edinburgh. Lectures (1938–39), System Theol., Auburn Theol. Sem., U.S.A.
145. TRAILL (Mrs.) Grace R., 8 Palmerston Road, Edinburgh, 9. Member C. of S. **C.**

146. VISCHER (Rev.) Wilhelm, Lic.Theol.(*Hon. Causa*), 1928 (Basel), Pastor, ten years, Refd. State Ch.; Tutor (1928–34) Heb. and O.T. Theol. Bethel. Germany ; Now Min., St. James Parish Congn., Basel ; Privat Docent in O.T. Univ., Basel. **P.**
147. VOLF (Rev.) Rudolf, Rodgyvy 13, Naksou, Denmark, Min. Lutheran Ch., Naksov.

148. WATSON (Rev.) William A., M.A.(Belfast), B.D.(London), D.D., Min. (1895) and Gen. Secy. (1926) Presb. C. of I., Church House, Belfast.

149. WEBB (Rev.) William H. S., Min. Congn. Ch., Hope Park (Edin.) Congn.

150. WEBSTER (Rev.) J. Macdonald, D.D., Min. (1897) C. of S. ; Secy. Overseas Dept., C. of S., 121 George Street, Edinburgh, 2. C.

151. WENDLAND (Miss) Ruth, Gethsemane Str. 3, Berlin, N.58. Student Theol.

152. WENHAM, John W., Portley Wood, Whyteleafe, Surrey, B.A. Ridley Hall, Cantab.), appointed Tutor, St. John's Theol. Hall, Highbury, London.

153. WENCELIUS (Rev.) Léon, 16 Rue Sleidan, Strasbourg, Bas-Rhin, France, Bes.L.(Nancy), Les.L., B.Theo., Lic. Theol. (Strasbourg), S.T.M., S.T.D.(New York), Des.L. (Paris), Assoc. Prof. of French, Strathmore Col., Pa., U.S.A. ; Assist. Min. French Ch. du St. Sauveur, Philadelphia, Pa, U.S.A. Author of *L'Esthétque de Calvin; Calvin et Rembrandt*, etc. etc. P.

154. WILSON (Rev.) J. R. S., M.A., B.D., Min. (1906) C. of S., North Leith (Edin.) Congn. C.

155. WYLIE, James, Accountant, Gen. Treas., C. of S., 121 George Street, Edinburgh. HON. (JOINT) TREAS., CONGRESS EXECUTIVE.

156. NEILL (Miss) Dora, B.A., Assistant to Secy. of General Presbyterian Alliance, 44 Queen Street, Edinburgh (*acted as Assistant to Hon. Secy. of Congress*).

FRIENDS OF THE CONGRESS

In addition to contributions towards the Congress Funds, and of personal hospitality to members from beyond Scotland, given by not a few of the before-named, there were generous contributions from, and in some instances most friendly hospitality on the part of, the undernoted friends, although otherwise they did not take part in the Congress.

J. G. Williamson, Rothesay.
Rev. Ken. Cameron, Inverness.
J. H. Macdonald, London.
Dr. W. U. Urquhart, Glasgow.
P. M'Kinnon, Helensburgh.
J. Maclennan, London.
Rev. W. H. Cameron, Resolis.
Rev. Prof. A. Main, Glasgow.
Rev. W. MacQuarrie, Artafallie.
Roderick Cameron, Inverness.
John Macdonald, Glasgow.
Miss Sinclair, Edinburgh.
John Fraser, Inverness.
Donald MacArthur, Glasgow.
W. M. Mackay, Dundee.
Rt. Hon. Lord Maclay, Glasgow.
Rev. A. A. Macdonald, Strontian.
Miss Elsie Campbell, Kilsyth.
James Sinclair, Latheron.
Wm. R. Anderson, Glasgow.
W. R. Rycroft, Lima.
Miss Balfour Ogilvie, Edinburgh.
Mrs. Sanderson, Edinburgh.
Rev. Rod. H. Macleod, D.D., Edinburgh.
J. H. Stevenson, K.C., Edinburgh.
Miss A. B. Bruce, Edinburgh.
Rev. J. A. Macleod, Kiltearn.
Rev. W. R. Mackay, Carrbridge.
Rev. A. M. Renwick, D.Litt., Lima.
Walter R. Brown, Beverley.
Anonymous (F.C. source) for hospitality.
Anonymous (F.C. source), for travel of Continental members.

Mrs. Philp, Edinburgh (for hospitality).
Mrs. J. B. C. Neilson (for hospitality).
J. P. M. Anderson, Bloemfontein, South Africa.
Miss Campbell, Kingussie.
Miss Macleod, Carrbridge.
Free Church College, Edinburgh.
Finance Committee, F.C., Edinburgh.
Rev. J. Mackay Maclennan, Lairg.
Edmund K. Simpson, Ipswich.
Hope Trust, Edinburgh, per D. & J. H. Campbell, W.S.
J. D. Walker, Aberdeen.
Misses Howie, Kilmarnock.
P. A. Walker Browne, M.B., Nethybridge.
Col. H. L. Warden, Edinburgh.
Jas. B. Shields, Edinburgh.
Mrs. W. Harvey Carson, Ottawa, Ontario.
J. B. M'Neill Fraser, Edinburgh.
Miss Paul Matthews, Dundee.
Miss Gray, Edinburgh.
Anonymous (per C. of S.).
G. W. Service, Glasgow.
Sir Thomas Henderson, Hawick.
Geo. W. Macfarlane, Glasgow.
Misses Shand, Edinburgh.
Friend, per C. of S.
Mrs. R. S. Duff, Glasgow.
Miss C. Smith, Edinburgh.
Mrs. Boyd, Edinburgh.
Douglas I. Gray, West Cults.

2

Dr. Robert Aird, Glasgow.
Miss Fraser, Aberdeen.
D. Norman Sloan, Glasgow.
J. D. Rose, Kirkcaldy.
Mrs. Wm. Falconer, Aberdeen.
A. C. Waugh, Edinburgh.
J. F. Fairweather, Edinburgh.
Misses Campbell, Helensburgh.
Mrs. Macqueen Ferguson, Edinburgh.
David M'Call, Edinburgh.
Sir Henry Keith, Hamilton.
Sir Wm. Henderson, Hawick.
D. Maclaren, Dunsandel, New Zealand.
Very Rev. Prof. Daniel Lamont, D.D., Edinburgh.

Sir Geo. A. Mitchell., Glasgow.
Miss E. A. Scobie, Pollokshields, Glasgow.
W. R. Davidson, Esq., Dess, Aberdeenshire.
" Anon."
Sir Harry Hope, Bart., Kinnettles, Forfar, Angus.
Lady Russell, Priorsfield, Edinburgh.
Geo. D. Gibson, Esq., Galashiels.
Fred L. L. Moir, Esq., Glasgow.
Rev. Adam Philip, D.D., Edinburgh.
Very Rev. J. Harry Miller, C.B.E., D.D., St. Mary's College, St. Andrews.

"A SPEAKING LIKENESS."

Three Notables in an Interval between Sessions.

REV. PROFESSOR DONALD MACLEAN, D.D.
VERY REV. R. J. DRUMMOND, D.D.
REV. AUGUSTE LECERF, D.D.

PROCEEDINGS OF THE
FOURTH CALVINISTIC CONGRESS

Wednesday, 6th July 1938

The Congress opened with an Evening Reception in the Martin Hall, New College. Members were welcomed by the Rev. Principal W. A. Curtis, D.D., D.Litt., D.Theol., Principal of New College and Dean of the Faculty of Divinity, who expressed the lively interest of the Faculty in the subject of their coming conference. Dr. Lamont and Dr. Maclean having suitably replied, the members spent some time in fellowship, and in using the opportunities afforded them to inspect the College and its new Library.

Thursday, 7th July

The Congress assembled at 9.30 a.m., Dr. Lamont presiding. After the singing of Psalm 121, and Prayer by the Chairman, Rev. Alexander Ross, B.D., Professor of New Testament Exegesis, Free Church College, Edinburgh, read a passage of Scripture (Eph. ii. 1–10) and gave the following Devotional Address :

SALVATION BY GRACE

" Back to Christ " used to be a favourite watchword with New Testament scholars : perhaps it still makes an appeal in some quarters. It has often been used in a mischievous fashion, with the implication : " Back to Christ, ignoring Paul, who grievously misunderstood Jesus, obscured His simple religious and ethical message, and led the whole Christian world off on a false scent." The true standpoint is : " Back to Christ through Paul, who, inspired by the Spirit of truth, gave to the world an inexhaustible exposition of the deepest meaning of the Christian revelation."

St. Paul's Epistle to the Ephesians has been called " the Switzerland of the New Testament." If there are depths in it that baffle the profoundest searchings of our finite minds, there are also spiritual Everests in it that men find hard to scale. Consider, for example, this great pronouncement : " By grace are ye saved through faith ; and that not of yourselves ; it is the gift of God " (Eph. ii. 8). Let us gaze at some of the wonders in the far-reaching vista of spiritual truth which is spread out before us here.

19

I. *Think of the Ultimate Source of our Salvation.* This is a text with which Calvinists must feel thoroughly at home, for it traces the salvation of sinful man to the sovereign grace of God alone. " By grace are ye saved . . . not of works." Dr. G. G. Findlay said very truly : " The opposition of gift and debt, of gratuitous salvation through faith, to salvation earned by works of law, belongs to the marrow of St. Paul's divinity," and we might add that it belongs to the marrow of Calvinism, which is just a fresh publication and exposition of Paulinism. All the glory of man's salvation must be given to God. *Sola gratia.* " Salvation is of the Lord " ; it does not " leave up nor down one spot for the creature to stand in." Salvation is not *of* works, but *unto* works. The good works of the child of God are the result of salvation, not the efficient cause of it. " We are His workmanship, created in Christ Jesus unto good works," and there can be no good works in man apart from His justifying, regenerating, sanctifying grace.

" Grace " is a great New Testament word which is not so frequently heard on the lips of preachers as once it was. The grace of God means His love, looked at from one specific standpoint. It means His love as lavished on the utterly unlovely, the love of the King of heaven for the beggar on the dung-hill and the hopelessly lost in the pit of corruption, the love of the altogether Holy One as it goes out to the totally depraved, the unutterably vile. Really to appreciate such love, we need such a vision of ourselves, in the merciless searchlight of the Word of God, as will force us to acknowledge that " love so amazing, so divine " is so utterly unexpected, so startling, that it will require eternity even to begin to understand it.

Elsewhere Paul writes : " Ye know the grace of our Lord Jesus Christ, that, though He was rich, yet for your sakes He became poor, that ye through His poverty might be made rich " (2 Cor. viii. 9). That verse suggests four ways in which we can endeavour to think of the grace of God in Christ. We may try to measure it by thinking of the *height* from which the Lord of glory looked down on us in our sin and misery. " He was rich," rich in the possession of all divine attributes, rich in glory and in power, " dwelling in the light that no man can approach unto," " the King all-glorious above, pavilioned in splendour and girded with praise." So rich was He in His essential being that He thought into existence whatever is. That is the New Testament doctrine of Christ, and no other Christ will ever meet man's desperate need. That He should think of people like us with such love, with that " great love with which He loved us," is the mystery of mysteries.

Again, we may try to measure the grace of our Lord Jesus

Christ by thinking of the *depths* of guilt and degradation in which He saw us lying. What He did, says St. Paul, was done " for your sakes," for the sake of men and women who, as he reminds them elsewhere (1 Cor. vi. 9, 10), had been adulterers, thieves, drunkards, extortioners. That God should love the holy angels is not so wonderful, perhaps, but He loved a world of sinners lost and ruined in the Fall, even men and women like those to whom Paul wrote, who were the objects of divine love when they were dead in trespasses and sins, when they were by nature the children of wrath even as others. That God should love men and women like that proves that His love is gracious love. " He did not wait till I loved Him, but loved me at my worst."

Again, we may try to measure this grace by thinking of the *sacrifice* which He made. " He became poor." The purely humanitarian view of the Person of the Lord Jesus Christ completely fails to do justice to a statement like that : when that view dominates the mind, our interpretation of a statement like that must needs be hopelessly shallow. We must trace the mystery of our Lord's Person back beyond Golgotha and Nazareth and Bethlehem, to the glory which He had with the Father before the world was. For us, being born means enrichment, for it means coming out of nothingness into conscious existence, but for Him being born meant impoverishment. So the Westminster Shorter Catechism reminds us that the first step in the humiliation of Christ was His " being born." The full statement runs thus : " The humiliation of Christ consisted in His being born, and that in a low condition, made under the law, undergoing the miseries of this life, the wrath of God, and the cursed death of the cross, in being buried, and continuing under the power of death for a time."

When Paul wrote that one pregnant word, " He became poor," he meant all that. He who is the eternal Son of the Father, the Son of His bosom, who is clothed with honour and majesty, who covers Himself with light as with a garment, became a baby in a woman's arms, and she " wrapped Him in swaddling clothes and laid Him in a manger." He who is the Creator of the ends of the earth, who fainteth not, and is never weary, sat weary with His journey by Sychar's well, and slept in tired exhaustion through the howling of the hurricane on the Galilean lake. He who opens rivers on the bare heights and fountains in the midst of the valleys, is heard asking for a drink of water from a Samaritan woman, and on the Cross cries : " I thirst," so that, as Archbishop Alexander said in a striking line : " The fountain wails, ' I thirst,' " He who is the eternal object of the Father's love endured the hiding of the Father's

face, when God " made Him who knew no sin to be sin for us,"
when He was made a curse for us, when the Lord made to meet
upon Him the iniquity of us all, when, suffering the uttermost
penalty due to sin, He cried : " My God, My God, why hast
Thou forsaken Me ? " The grace that brought our sin-bearer
there is the grace by which we are saved.

Once more, we may try to measure the grace of our Lord
Jesus Christ by thinking of the *height* to which He raises us.
Through His poverty we become rich, rich in possession of all
spiritual blessings in heavenly places (Eph. i. 3), rich in
possession of redemption, which we have in His blood, the
forgiveness of sins, according to the riches of His grace (Eph.
i. 7) ; rich through the indwelling of the Holy Spirit of promise
(Eph. i. 13) ; rich because Christ has made His home in our
hearts through faith (Eph. iii. 17) ; rich in the enjoyment of
fellowship with the Father, to whom we have access through the
Son, in one Spirit (Eph. ii. 18) ; rich in faith and heirs of the
kingdom which God has promised to them that love Him
(James ii. 5).

II. *Think of the Manner in which this Salvation becomes ours.*
" By grace are ye saved through faith ; and that not of yourselves : it is the gift of God." That is to say, as I understand it,
the faith as well as the salvation is the gift of God. And thus,
as we Calvinists affirm, salvation in every stage of it, beginning
middle and end, is of the Lord. To understand Paul as merely
saying again what he has said already, namely, that the salvation
is a gift of God, is to think of him as indulging in what seems
to be a rather flat tautology. The faith that unites us to Christ
has no merit in it ; that faith itself is a gift of God. " The Holy
Spirit applieth to us the redemption purchased by Christ by
working faith in us, and thereby uniting us to Christ in our
effectual calling." As the Westminster Confession of Faith
says : " Those whom God effectually calleth He also freely
justifieth ; . . . not for anything wrought in them or done by
them, but for Christ's sake alone ; not by imputing faith itself,
the act of believing, or any other evangelical obedience, to them
as their righteousness ; but by imputing the obedience and
satisfaction of Christ unto them, they receiving and resting on
Him and His righteousness by faith ; which faith they have not
of themselves ; it is the gift of God."

We are saved by grace, *dia pisteōs*, not *dia pistin*, as though
our faith were in any sense whatever the procuring cause of our
salvation. We are saved *through* faith instrumentally.

Faith has no merit in it, for it gives nothing to the God of
salvation. It is only a taking. Calvin says that " faith brings a
man empty to God that he may be filled with the blessings of

Christ." Thomas Goodwin says : " All other graces are working graces, but the hands of faith are merely receiving hands." Faith makes us aware of Christ, and unites us to Christ, who saves. " Nothing in my hand I bring, simply to Thy cross I cling." Or, better still, perhaps, simply unto Thee I cling. " Thou must save, and Thou alone."

III. *Think of the Salvation itself.* We have seen already that this salvation enriches us with priceless spiritual blessings Let us consider three further points in connection with it.

The salvation of which our text speaks is an accomplished salvation, a lasting salvation. Note the remarkable emphatic Greek tense which Paul here uses : *este sesōsmenoi.* I once read of a Salvationist who found himself travelling one day in a railway carriage with a bishop of the Church of England. This Salvationist was an ardent soul, who did not believe in hiding his light under a bushel, so, greatly daring, he suddenly addressed to the bishop the question : " Are ye saved ? " He replied : " Do you mean *sezōmenos,* or *sōtheis* or *sesōsmenos* ? " That was, perhaps, rather hard on the Salvationist, yet that sudden little lesson in Greek tenses may have reminded him of what, no doubt, he knew well enough already, that the New Testament makes use of a variety of tenses when dealing with the great theme of salvation.

Sometimes Paul uses the present participle when he writes of " the saved," as, *e.g.,* in 1 Corinthians i. 18 ; xv. 2 ; and 2 Corinthians ii. 15. Salvation, from one point of view, is a process which advances from more to more, in the sanctification of the child of God. But here Paul looks at salvation from another angle : here he emphasises the fact that the salvation of the believer is an accomplished fact. The salvation of the Lord is not something that we possess to-day and may lose to-morrow. " Once in Christ, in Christ for ever, thus the eternal Covenant stands." Paul does not lose sight, indeed, of the fact that these Ephesians had their battle to fight (Eph. vi. 10-13). But, though the battle is fierce, and though it will last so long as they draw this fleeting breath, the issue of it is certain. " You are saved men," he says to them, " saved in the Lord with an everlasting salvation."

And he adds this thought, that the one sure and certain proof that we really possess this salvation is a holy life. Those who are saved are regenerated persons, " created in Christ Jesus unto good works." Those who used to walk " according to the course of this world " now walk in these good works, they walk " in love " (Eph. v. 2). Those who used to be " the children of wrath " are now " beloved children " (Eph. v. 1), and they wear the family likeness which proclaims them to be the new-born sons and daughters of Him who is the " Holy Father." That is the best evidence that they were chosen in Christ before the foundation of the world " (Eph. i. 4).

Once again, in the final clause of our text, Paul seems to lay emphasis on this thought, that when a man has been loved with everlasting love, and has been led by grace that love to know, the humbling and exalting experience makes him realise that, however commonplace his life may sometimes seem to be, and however drab its circumstances may often appear, he is fulfilling the eternal purpose of God, and about his dreariest moments there lies " the light that never was on sea or land." To quote the great words of Browning :

> " Ere suns and moons could wax and wane,
> Ere stars were thundergirt, or piled
> The heavens, God thought on me His child ;
> Ordained a life for me, arrayed
> Its circumstances every one
> To the minutest ; ay, God said
> This head this hand should rest upon
> Thus, ere He fashioned star or sun."

Facing life in that spirit, we shall be " more than conquerors through Him who loved us."

OPENING ADDRESS

By the Very Rev. Professor Lamont, D.D.

My Dear Friends,—I exercise the privilege of chairmanship by extending once more to you all a very cordial welcome to this Congress. I am in no mood to offer any apology for the holding of a Calvinistic Congress. If a man's greatness is to be measured by the quality and strength of his influence upon history, then John Calvin was a very great man. It is an historical fact that Calvinism made strong men and women and strong nations. There must have been something in it which was sufficient to account for this fact, and there is no difficulty in fastening upon what that something was. The central principle of the Calvinistic system is the Sovereignty of God, and it was Calvin's emphasis upon this principle and the widespread and deep-seated acceptance of it by the religious thought and life of his time that brought about, under God, that mighty spiritual movement which has persisted, at least in its effects, for four centuries until this hour.

When it is said that the *Bible* is the best instruction on the Sovereignty of God, we must agree. It is one of the things which

Calvin himself said with emphasis. But we must add that, in point of fact, the Church and theology needed Calvin to restore the doctrine of God's sovereignty to the fundamental place which it holds in the Bible. How easily the acids of this world corrode the Truth until, since it is no longer the Truth, it ceases to have power over the minds of men ! And these acids have been insidiously at work in recent generations, with the result that the very existence of God is being questioned or denied over large tracts of the world. With the decline of Calvinism has come the decline of the central principle of Calvinism which is also the central principle of the Bible. The sense of God is deplorably feeble in the world to-day, with the disastrous consequences which are all too apparent in the life of men and nations. No wonder many earnest thinkers are calling the Church back to that vital truth in Calvinism which we have allowed to grow dim and which must shine out again if God is to put right what man has put wrong.

It is the fundamental fact of our existence that it is in God that " we live and move and have our being." It is precisely in an age like ours, so busy here and there, that this ground of the Truth loses its proper contact with the minds of men. But, while *men* may ignore *it*, *it* does not ignore *men*. Our very existence depends from moment to moment upon the Will of God. The one thing which puts man above the animals is that he, when empowered by the Holy Spirit, can acknowledge the secret of his existence and live in the light of it. Where men do *not* acknowledge it, in the way which God Himself has made so plain, they prove themselves to be alienated from the life of God, straining against *Him* Who keeps His Omnipotent Hand upon them at every moment. This is the essence of human sin, straining against God, and whether it is done deliberately or thoughtlessly it is fatal to the life of man. To acknowledge the Sovereignty of God and to order one's life by that acknowledgment is man's chief end, and the missing of his chief end is man's last and sorest loss.

The acknowledgment of the absolute Sovereignty of God is the only foundation upon which a moral life can be securely built. If a man has the notion that the sanctions of morality are only in himself, or in his social group, or in the human race, he will, at the pinch, reject these sanctions. Even at the best, they are only relative. The sanction must be absolute if it is to provide an immovable basis for morality, and such a sanction can have but one Source, the God of righteousness and of the stars. God is He " with whom " we and all men " have to do." The absence of the sense of God as Creator, Sustainer and Judge of men, if that absence were sufficiently widespread, would turn this world into a shambles. And is not that the way which the world is taking at the moment ? Pray God that the last folly of mankind may be arrested before it is too late.

It is true that the word " sovereignty " does not *define* the gracious relation of God to us men. That is why so many shy at the word and rest content with the assurance that God is Love. But the *Love* of God detached from the conviction of His *Sovereignty*, is bound to be misunderstood. In the Epistle in which the saying " God is Love " occurs twice, the fact of God's Sovereignty is everywhere assumed. It is always in the context of His Sovereignty that the Bible tells of His Love. John is careful to define the Love of *God*. It is not to be measured by the standards of human love, even though the highest human love is the nearest earthly analogue to Divine Love. " Herein is love, not that we loved God, but that He loved us, and sent His son to be the propitiation for our sins." It is as if he said : " To know what the Love of God is, you must gaze into its depths in the Cross of Jesus."

A few weeks ago I attended a two days' Conference on Evangelism in the city of Philadelphia in the U.S.A. It had two immediate purposes. One was to serve as a preparation for the meeting of the General Assembly of the Presbyterian Church in the U.S.A. The other was to celebrate the bicentenary of the " heart-warming " of John Wesley—that heart-warming which meant so much for England and indeed for the world. The combination of these two purposes was highly significant. And I observed that when a paper was read on the *Sovereignty of God* there was one point at which the great audience—Methodists, Presbyterians and many of other denominations—seemed to catch fire. It was when the speaker, in the culmination of his message, echoed the simple Gospel truth that God's Sovereignty is most plainly and passionately defined in the Cross of the Lord Jesus. There, in that wondrous Cross, God has wrought reconciliation for men, and there he invites, entreats, commands " all men everywhere to repent," receive the reconciliation and be adopted into the family of God. No entreaty is so passionate as this and no command so imperious. The Sovereign God has opened up for men the Way to Himself and now commands all men to take that Way. There God's Sovereignty and His Love meet at the one turning-point. And there Presbyterians and Methodists, in the Conference to which I have referred, met and learned from one another and from God.

What of those who obey not the Gospel of God ? Next to the wonder of the Redemption itself is the wonder of its rejection. We can explain neither of these two wonders, nor ever shall till our minds take on a new dimension on the other side. They are hidden deep in the counsels of the Godhead. The greatest of Christian thinkers, like Paul and Augustine and Calvin, have tried, not to probe the mysteries of the Divine Will, but to find a resting-place for their minds in the presence of these mysteries. And we are wise if we find *our* rest where, after all their thinking, *their* minds rested : " O the depth of the riches both of the wisdom and knowledge of God ! . . . How unsearchable are His judgments, and His ways past finding out ! . . . For of Him, and through Him, and to Him, are all things : to whom be glory for ever. Amen."

Paper No. 1

THE REFORMED FAITH AND ITS ETHICAL CONSEQUENCES TO THE INDIVIDUAL

By J. Sebestyén, Ph.D., D.D.

Principal of the Reformed Theological Academy at Budapest (Hungary)

THE central theme of the Calvinistic Congress in Geneva—held in 1936—was a great Calvinistic doctrine, namely, the doctrine of the everlasting predestination of God and its different aspects. It is well, therefore, that this conference, on the other hand, puts the emphasis on the ethical consequences of our Reformed Faith.

There can be no doubt that every religion, even the heathen religions, have ethical consequences, for every religion has some type of life-forming power. The ethical consequences of the various religions are very different, since their religious content differs widely from each other. So we may classify religions according to the purity and value of their doctrines as well as their ethical importance.

The ethical effect of a religion may be very valuable and useful or, on the other hand, very harmful. A religion may inspire life with the highest ideas and cause it to grow and develop with its greatest possibilities. At the same time religion may impede the progress of life and prevent its development, or may ruin it completely. Thus the stiff and rigid conception of God in Islam, for example, puts its mark on the Muslim's life, or the spirit of Buddhism and Hinduism determines

decidingly every phase of the Hindu's life. The statement of
Ribot has therefore firm ground : " If two peoples do not
believe in God in the same way, they will not cultivate their
land in the same manner."

The dependence of practice on doctrines may be seen not
only in the realm of the heathen religions. The case is the same
with Christianity itself and with the lives of the different
Christian denominations. There is a possibility of classifying
even Christian denominations and parties according to their
ethical life. They have not the same ethical values.

Roman Catholicism had and still has an enormous ethical
and social effect on its adherent's life and on the world. This
ethical life, however, shows a definite ecclesiastical mark and
is under the tutelage of the Church. The Greek Orthodox
Church is also not without ethical and social influence on the
life of its members, but that influence is entirely negative. It
hinders the development of society and impedes any reform
in conditions of living. The Mystics of the Middle Ages, on
the other hand, had no ethical and social force at all. They
had no ethical programme for life as a whole. Later on, the
Anabaptists had an exclusive and deformed ethical programme.
Lutheranism represents a stronger and sounder ethical system
than those mentioned above, though it is far from being
satisfactory. The different sects of Protestantism show again
great divergencies in the value of their ethical and social
effects.

It is our conviction, which is justified by the results of the
most modern sciences, that of the different Christian Churches
and denominations, *Calvinism* has had from the beginning
the highest ethical ideas and the best ethical programme for
life as a whole. The ethical and social influence of Calvinism
has not only been the greatest and the most many-sided upon
the different nations of the world until now, but this form of
Christianity proclaimed and bestowed all those high ideas on
our whole social life. These ideas represent the real—the
life-creating values in our day. This ethical and social effect
was, and is, especially the real power of Calvinism. It was its
distinctive character that this faith could regenerate not only
individuals but even societies. For this reason Troeltsch, the
great and unprejudiced critic of Calvinism, declared : " To-day
this (*i.e.* Calvinism) is the real Great Power of Protestantism."
Further he said : " While, for example, Lutheranism, in spite
of all its valuable content, was left unfinished and it was unable
to organise itself fundamentally or to exercise any reasonable
influence on politics, Calvinism was moved by some wonderful
driving power to get out to the common life, and in Calvinist-

individualism it gained a special stimulant to activity, that is, to throw its personality into the struggle for the solution of the problems of the world and of society, that it should work unceasingly, thoroughly, yet constructively."

We should lay proper stress on the fact that the great and sound ethical and social power of Calvinism is directly dependent on its doctrinal content, on its theology. Calvinism never has known or accepted a free morality. On the contrary, we have the right to say that the greatest characteristic power of the Reformed Churches was ever that Calvinistic doctrines became ethical truths, that is, principles of a definite way of living. The doctrine was ever " the word of life," as Paul expressed it in Philippians ii. 16. The Calvinist Theologians of old used to say accordingly : the *dogmata morum* or *dogmata vitæ* are founded on, and originate from, the *dogmata veritatis* or *fidei*. Therefore they took it for granted that the System of Theology has two parts : doctrinal and practical. The first place was always given to the doctrines of Dogmatics from which are derived the precepts and doctrines of Ethics.

This method of thinking is based on the teaching of the Bible. It is not an arbitrary creation of the Reformed theologians. The Bible tells always not only what to *believe* but what to *do*. Doctrines and precepts are often mixed in it. This is the reason why the Calvinistic Confessions and Creeds call the Bible a norm for our faith and for our works. The Word of God reveals what He is, and how the sovereign God wishes Himself to be served. It is clear from this, that religion is not doctrine, not self-redemption by works, not romantic pathos, not æsthetic ecstasies of the human soul, nor a spiritual ornament of human nature. Religion is something much more and higher than all these taken together. Religion is the *service of God, cultus Dei*, with all our mind, with all our soul, with all our strength (Bavinck). Religion is a living sacrifice which is holy and acceptable unto God (Rom. xii. 1). It is, therefore, a matter not only of the heart, but also of the mind and of the hands. Man is in the service of God with his heart, with his mind and with his hands, but only because he believes in Him ! Faith and practice go together, and the second is dependent on the first.

In a word : our privilege is not more nor less than to speak, in connection with Calvinistic Ethics, about the moral realisation of Christ's life in the life of the individual believer. This moral realisation of Christ's life is the chief requirement of the Reformed Faith in practice, because there is no other way for the individual believer to become a Christian (Christlike) personality and character. This means that Calvinism is to create a new type of man—as Lord Morley puts it. " Nothing less than to create in man a new nature "—says Lord Morley in his *Oliver Cromwell*—" was his (Calvin's) far-reaching aim, to regenerate character, to simplify and consolidate religious faith."

By new men to create a new life—this is the ethical programme of Calvinism. New men are created by living and heroic, courageous faith in God. From this faith, on the other hand, all the ethical forces spring forth. This was the idea in the Calvinistic philosophy of life even in old times : " Sound doctrine applied by the Spirit of God must be the foundation of a sound life," and further : " Principles regulate practice." For this reason it was emphasised : " There can be no sound life and character based upon scriptural doctrine without correct views of God and man. Those two subjects go together. Our view, regarding man, will fashion to a great extent our ideas concerning God and will have a direct and far-reaching effect upon character, life and influence. Only as we get a true vision and see man from the right point of view can we understand his condition, his position, his knowledge and his standing before God " (Talbot).

The interdependence of faith and practice was always strongly emphasised by the Calvinistic theologians. Calvin himself laid particular stress on the thought that the knowledge of the right doctrine and the practice of piety are inseparably bound together. Voetius, the greatest theologian in the seventeenth century, was another champion of this thought, and so his inaugural oration in the University of Utrecht was : " De pietate cum scientia conjugenda," that is, " Concerning piety, that it is to be bound up with knowledge."

According to the Calvinistic view all this is reasonable, because the right knowledge of God always means life. The proper knowledge of God leads always to the revelation of it in the Christian's life. As Calvin says about the knowledge of Christ : " It is a doctrine not of the tongue but of the life : and is not apprehended merely with the understanding and memory, like other sciences, but is only received when it possesses the whole soul, and finds a seat and residence in the innermost affection of the heart " (Inst. III. vi. 4).

This statement with others shows the great mistake of those who often charge Calvin with one-sided and dry intellectualism. For though Calvin often speaks about " doctrine " and " dogma " he never takes it for some intellectual abstraction. He simply emphasises that there must be thought in every sphere of life. And so great was his genius even in this, that he could infuse life into each of his thoughts. This was because he believed that the Word of God was given for the reformation of life. He thought that the chief duty of the Church is to apply the commandments of the Lord upon the practical life and so to make them " the Word of Life " in the community of believers. From these it is clear that in Calvin's view religion and piety, faith and practice, can never be separated from each other (Inst. I. ii. 1 ; III. ii. 9).

The knowledge of Gospel, therefore, necessarily should find its realisation in a righteous life, that is, in a definite style of life (John xiii. 17 ; Ps. xxxii. 1, 2). For man was created by God to *praxis pietatis*, that is, to the practice of piety. This is the reason that Calvinistic mysticism is so sound. It is founded on two pillars : the one is the right doctrine, the other is the true *praxis pietatis*, and both are founded on the Word of God. In this way Calvinistic mysticism never drifts into pantheistic subjectivism nor sinks into morbid sentimentalism, but continues to be active, productive and courageous in the life of the individual as well as of the Church.

There is a generally accepted view according to which the values of Christianity are only for the individual. The importance and significance of Christianity is measured on the ground of what it gives to the individual soul. Someone thinks that if he has realised the Father's grace in Christ, has accepted it and so been converted, his goal is reached. Then he enjoys the peace of the relieved soul and his peace is disturbed only when he gazes at the evil world around him. He is convinced that, seeing the wickedness of this world, the best he can do is to sigh or to pray for it. With this he has finished all that a gentle Christian soul can do. He thinks he is not responsible for anything in this world. He believes—but he remains passive, and leads a secluded, withdrawn life. The end of such a Christian life is to find the Father. Outside of this everything is unimportant.

This passive view of life is dominant to a more or less degree in many forms of Protestantism. Even Luther belongs to some of its classes, and there is truth in Troeltsch's assertion that Luther was especially lacking in ethical and social principles which are highly developed in Calvin's system. Calvin not only accepted all the best ideas of his predecessors and contemporaries in this respect, but proceeded much farther, saying that the chief end of life is not the happiness of the individual soul, not a sacro-egoism of men, but the glory of God. This glory should shine in the world with the greatest splendour and this glory should be restored in all the spheres of life.

This main thought kept Calvinism away from passivity or

mysticism ; from a one-sided sentimentalism or secluded Christianity. The most classical expression of the characteristic of Calvinism in this respect I ever read is the following sentence : " Thus for Calvin the Gospel was not only the power to save those individuals who believe in Him, not only comfort for the afflicted heart, not only the overpowering of the dangerous heresies of the soul : but at the same time the remedy for common troubles, the purificatory and regenerating factor for great social communities and the foundation on which all these should be built " (Hundeshagen). This magnificent definition clearly and decisively reveals for us the *active character of Calvinism.* This religion should be called appropriately a piety revealed in action. If the Gospel is truly not restricted to the quiet moments of our meditations, if its profits are not limited to our secret prayers, if it is a remedy for the public and common troubles : then it is clear that a real Calvinistic Christian cannot rest until the forces of the Gospel penetrate the very life cells of our society and until the life of our human community is governed by the ethical precepts of our God.

This determined and decisive activity does not take its origin in some exterior and unimportant source. Its dynamic energy is not from humanism as some think ; nor from the racial and active character of some people, as others believe. The power-house from which these ethical effects are derived is nothing else than a deep theological thought : the doctrine of the sovereignty of God. This doctrine brings and pursues Calvinism into the life of this world and of our society, and for this reason it always works for purification in the life of individuals as well as that of societies and human communities. Thus the final end as well as the ultimate purpose in Calvinism is never the salvation of the individual, nor the peace and happiness of the person in his isolated state, but always something higher and more magnificent, namely, the assurance of the sovereignty of God, the assertion of the glory of the everlasting Father, Son and the Holy Spirit not only in Nature but in the lives of men.

It is proper to note, that Calvin's " Cathecismus Genevensis " and the " Westminster Shorter Catechism " after asking about the chief end of man give the simple answer : Man's chief end is to glorify God and to enjoy Him for ever. But we may say of the other reformed Creeds and Confessions that they also strongly emphasise the theocentric view of man and life and they do not forget the ethical consequences of the Reformed Faith which culminate in the service of God.

This chief end of Calvinism prepares for man an exalted position in the grace of God. This finds a classical expression in these words : " Man is represented as standing at the apex of all the created orders.   He is crowned as king of the lower creation, and is given dominion over all the lower creatures. As such, it was his duty and privilege to make all nature and all the created beings that were placed under his rule, subservient to his will and purpose, in order that he and his whole dominion might magnify the almighty Creator of the universe " (Berkhof : Gen. i. 28 ; Ps. viii. 4, 9).   In this way man became the " lord of creation."

.   .   .   .

Now after these general introductory notes let us see what are the ethical consequences of the Reformed Faith *in the life of the Christian individual in things fundamental* ?   Our answer may be summed up in four points, which are as follows :

1. Firstly : the Reformed Faith by its right teaching of God leads man to the right service of God.   The restoration of man's covenant with God by the Holy Spirit brings with itself a committal to the right service of God and a deep thirst after it.

2. Secondly : the Reformed Faith forms a Christian character and personality, able to do the work of this service according to the requirements of the general priesthood.

3. Thirdly :   the Reformed Faith makes complete the consciousness of the vocation of the Christian personality concerning the whole earthly life and its duties.

4. Fourthly : the Reformed Faith represents also a certain Christian Ideal of life and a certain Christian view of life and by that creates a special Calvinistic *style of life*.   This is what enables the Christian to perform all those Christian activities which are for the glory of God.   This is the fulfilment of Paul's idea :   " we are labourers together with God (1 Cor. iii. 9).

1. As the first point of the four we should emphasise that the driving power of the service of God works in all forms of religions and in every Christian denomination.   But this power has never had so great an effect as in Reformed Christianity, because the chief end is nowhere so clear and definite.   The right knowledge of God leads man to *cultus* and *obœdientia*, that is, to service and obedience at the same time. In this way the theocentric purpose of the creation of man in the image of God ripens and is unfolded.   This purpose means that man ought not only to know and pray to God but to live and walk and work *coram Deo*, *pro Deo* and *cum Deo*—before the face of God, for God and with God.

2. The second ethical effect of the Reformed Faith is the formation of the Christian character and personality out of

3

the believing soul.   This means that the man, who by the grace of God has become a " perfect man," as Ephesians iv. 13, requires it, must have acquired at a full mature age a Christian character and an ethical personality.   Such a man should be able to do the work of the service of God, not only in the Church, but outside of it, in life according to the requirements of the general priesthood.

The establishment of this thesis proves the fact that the sovereignty of God does not annihilate the ethical personality and morality of the believer, but on the contrary the knowledge of this sovereign God trained and formed the highest type of Christian personalities which the world has ever seen.   So the charges against predestination that it paralyses the moral energies, that its effect would be lethargy, fatalism, passivity, antinomianism or a lack of responsibility, have never had any real foundation whatsoever.   The truth is quite the contrary. For the Reformed Faith is characterised by its ethical heroism. This faith creates in the souls of its possessors the consciousness of the responsibility to work unceasingly for the glory of God. So the faithful and heroic Christian personalities who are full of energy and aspiration are directly dependent on the spirit of the Reformed Faith.   The same view is held by Irwin when he says :   " It is sometimes urged against those who hold Calvinistic views of predestination and election, that these views tend to antinomianism.   In other words, it is said, that men who regard themselves as elect, tend to consider themselves safe, no matter how they live.   Whatever may be the theory . . . in actual fact this has not been the case.   The Reformers who denied justification by works were the most zealous in insisting upon good works as the fruit and evidence of faith. The Calvinist who emphasised election, emphasised also the fact that it was an election unto holiness (see Eph. i. 4)."

The history of mankind proves that this ideal of character produced a whole gallery of heroes in the civil and social life of the reformed peoples, of whom the world was not worthy but of whom we can boast in Jesus Christ for ever.   As Carlyle says :   " Calvinism has produced, in all countries in which it really dominated, a definite type of character and conception of morals which was the noblest that had yet appeared in the world."

" We might say then—may we repeat with Irwin ?—that the two great lessons of Calvin's teaching are God's sovereignty and man's responsibility.   Both have an elevating and inspiring influence upon the mind and character."   His statement is expanded by Professor Williston Walker when he says :   " A personal relation of each man to God, a definite divine plan for each life, a value for the humblest individual in the God-appointed ordering of the universe, are thoughts which, however justly the social rather than the individual aspects of Christianity are now being emphasised, have demonstrated their worth in Christian history.   Yet perhaps the crowning historic significance of Calvinism is to be seen in its valuation of character.   Its conception of the duty to know and to do the will of God, not indeed as a means of salvation, but as that for which we are elected to life, and as the only fitting tribute to the ' honour of God ' which we are bound to maintain, has made of the Calvinist always a representative of a strenuous morality."

" To be a Christian is to be committed to a career whose goal is the Christian character (Rom. viii. 29)," says T. B. Kilpatrick.   This character is best formed by the Reformed Faith.   The Christian character and personality is the most wonderful fruit of the Reformed Faith.

The Reformed ideal is represented in a higher synthesis when the Christian character and personality is taken as the outcome of the fullness of faith in Christ.   This fullness of character and personality is revealed in the three offices of man, namely that of the prophet, the priest and the king which is known as the General Priesthood of Believers.

The ethical consequences of the Reformed Faith in the life of individuals are most beautifully expounded and realised in the spheres of these three offices of the Christian in connection with God, with our neighbours and with this world.

The investigation and exposition of the immeasurable importance of the prophetical, priestly and kingly offices of believers in their personal, ecclesiastical and universal aspects would be the subject of many other lectures.   The *John Calvin Society*, which was organised in Hungary in the 1936 jubilee-year, held a conference of two whole days to discuss these aspects.   This was done by this Society because to-day " it is to be feared that many of God's people are but very partially instructed in the fundamental truth which is attached to the exclusive mediatorial priesthood of Christ, and the ministerial priesthood of all His quickened followers."

3. If the Reformed Faith creates such Christian person-alities, it is natural to suppose that these personalities should execute all their works with the definite consciousness of their vocation.   The ethical consequences of the consciousness of this vocation are very great and important.   This means to take hold of the real meaning of life, to fulfil obediently the destiny and mission of our life and of the world's life as God wishes it to be fulfilled.

It is clear from this, that besides the call of salvation

the Reformed Christian has another vocation that is the Calling by which he works and moves in this world for the glory of God. Those who believe in the free will do not like to speak about vocation—says Professor I. D. du Toit. But for those who walk in the footsteps of Calvin this expression is inestimably valuable. This expression supposes real obedience toward the Word of God which calls us (1 Samuel xv. 22).

The vocation in the ethical sphere of life is, of course, the direct consequence of the vocation of God about which we hear in Dogmatics. The vocation of God is revealed in the earthly life and work of the Christian believer and the call is always for the service of God in this life.

4. The living Reformed Faith is not restricted to the service of God in general, nor to the formation of Christian personality, nor to the fulfilment of the vocation. This faith prepares a sure programme for the whole of this life of the world. The Reformed Faith gives a special view of life, a peculiar conception of its destiny, and so, some philosophy of life. This follows from the fact that God revealed for us not only truths for salvation, not soteriological teachings alone, but He gave us directive precepts for the world, life, man, etc., that these all should serve His everlasting Glory. The panorama of the universality of Calvinism becomes more and more disclosed from century to century as generation after generation searches after the richness of God's magnitudes (*magnalia Dei*) and ordinances. Therefore, there is every reason for the optimism of Dr. Henry Beets when, regarding the future of Calvinism, he justly says: " And we need not be ashamed of this Calvinism. Its teachings, properly understood, are based upon the Word of God. Its principles are the very warp of the Holy Writ. Every true Christian, even though not professedly accepting our Creed, is a Calvinist on his knees in utter dependence on free grace. It still holds good and will as long as the world endures, as Watson said in 1811, after Bishop Tomlinson called Calvinism " dead "—" such doctrines do not die, they only sleep,"—and as Froude expressed it : " Calvinism has appeared and re-appeared, and in due time will re-appear again, unless God be an illusion and man be as the beasts that perish."

From all these it becomes evident that the ethical consequences of the Reformed Faith in the lives of individuals (and through them in the life of communities) are of paramount importance because this form of Christianity prevails in men's lives, not only as a mere religion, but as a world-view and as a philosophy of life. By this distinctive characteristic Calvinism changes and transforms all its truths and principles into life and action. So these principles and doctrines are not to be seen as ideals in metaphysical regions, but as real and practical powers and forces which are leading and governing the believer's life and filling it with ethical content.

The final result in the ethical consequences of the Reformed Faith is a most special type of life—though it is a much-debated question in our times whether this Calvinistic mode of life is discernible or not and, what is more, whether this mode does really exist at all. Raising this question is too late now, because after four hundred years of the existence of Calvinism it is a settled question. There is a characteristic Calvinistic mode of life, as history proves.

A special manner of life is the direct consequence of the faith of the different churches, denominations and parties. Though they should live geographically in the same place, economically under the same conditions, the style of their life is different from each other. The Calvinistic manner of living is not only radically different from any other type of life but, in its educative and propagative values it stands far above all others. This is naturally so because the mode of life is nothing else but the realisation of the ethical consequences of the great Christian principles. Because the ethical ideas of Calvinism are of the highest value on account of their doctrinal basis, the practical expression of these ideas in the form of a certain manner of living should be also the highest and best. This mode is what the Bible calls, " the word of life."

The monumental " style of life " of Calvinism is such an irresistible testimony before the world from generation to generation that even the unbeliever and the sociology founded on atheistic principles are compelled to acknowledge its high value, though they would refuse to accept its religious and theological principles. This fact is demonstrated by the statement : " Calvinists have been the highest honour of their own age and the best models for imitation for every succeeding age " (*Encyclopædia Britannica*).

It is worth noting that the ethical consequences of the Reformed Faith appear and prevail not only in the whole realm of life of the Christian man, but these consequences show a great variety of form in the different spheres of life. As the gifts of divine grace are different and have various relations, so the ethical consequences of these divine gifts differ from each other. So the energies of the Reformed Faith find different expressions according to the ages, situations, professions, sexes, family circumstances, etc., which determine the life of its followers. We are not able to go into details concerning these questions, because that would require the working up

of all the spheres of life from this point of view. That is, however, the task of the other lectures of this conference.

One sphere of life is, however, very remarkable from the
point of view of the individual. This is the sphere of the
different sexes : of the male and the female. It is not only the
most interesting but even the most important task to investigate
the ethical consequences of the Reformed Faith separately
in the life of the male and of the female. The peculiarity of
the sphere of sexes is in this : Regarding to the personal
relationship to God, and in the saving power of the Reformed
Faith, there is no difference between male and female. There
is, however, a greater difference with regard to the ethical
consequences of the Reformed Faith in the life of the male and
female, when these are applied and realised in it. All this is
because when God determined the ordinances of life and divided
up the tasks and duties of life, He appointed in many respects
different missions and destinies to the male and to the female.
Thus the service of God will be revealed in different ways in the
life of the male and also in that of the female. Calvinism took
it as a privilege to respect God's ordinances even in this sphere,
and made every possible effort that the male should be a real
man as God wishes him to be, and that the female should be a
real woman as God wishes her to be. Calvinism could present
such wonderful men and women for more than four hundred
years that, seeing them, the unbelieving world might use the
exclamation of Libanius the orator tutor of Julian the Apostate—
" Oh these Calvinists ! What men and women they have ! "

The ethical consequences and practical effects of the
Reformed Faith in the life of the individual believer have
disclosed themselves with immeasurable richness. The responsibility toward God and neighbour, the activity and heroism
of the service of God, the conscientious Church-membership,
the love of work, the accomplishment of all works with a
consciousness of the vocation, the struggle against sin, the
growth of character and personality, etc., are all such characteristics which should be counted as the ethical consequences of
the Reformed Faith in the soul and life of the believer. All
these exclude any fatalism or indifference towards the matters
of life. Such phenomena would stand in contradiction to the
object of the Calvinist's faith, which teaches that the sovereign
God, by His grace, prepared and made communion with man,
for He was not only man's Creator, but became man's Father
through Jesus Christ our Lord. The attitude of a son can
never be that of fatalism or indifference toward the father.

From the sonship of the Calvinist rises the wonderful
trust in God. The trust is the foundation of that magnificent

attitude of the Calvinist in the greatest storms of life which may be called steadfastness and the peace of the soul, and which is typified and described with great power in the Forty-sixth Psalm. The deep trust in God furnishes the believer with the strength which is able to suffer all the afflictions of life, which is able to struggle through all the conflicts of this world and is able to complete every task.

In a word, the believing Calvinists were men of action ! It was a distinctive mark of the Calvinists that they were always ready to do their duty. They always knew their vocation and call, and they always obeyed God. Thus the Calvinists were always particularly the men of strength and activity (J. D. Kestell). This is the reason why Tydeman could say : " In modern times no system has had a more potent practical influence than Calvinism."

Calvinism became a real blessing to the life of nations in spite of great persecutions and many martyrdoms. This fact should never be forgotten : Calvinism worked up the energies of Christianity for real life when the lives of its believers were daily in danger and peril. Just imagine *what* Calvinism could have achieved, *if* it had had fifteen hundred or seventeen hundred years for an undisturbed and peaceful development of his spirit and of his forces, as Rome had or the Greek Orthodox Church had ! In that case world-history would have been something quite different, and the Kingdom of God would have been realised in the life of the nations a thousand times more than it is to-day !

Let us beseech God to grant to our Calvinistic Christianity such a wonderful age, and such a long period of time, that this purest form of Christianity may unfold itself in its entire richness and power so that its truths may captivate and conquer the whole human life for the greater glory of God !

" If Calvinism regenerated the world in the past, it can do so again. May we have a greater regard for its principles and a strong determination to declare in these ominous days the whole counsel of God " (Atherton).

RÉSUMÉ DU DISCOURS

Fait par Le Professeur I. Sebestyén, Ph.D., D.D.

Le Congrès calviniste de Genève en 1936 affirma la doctrine de la " prédestination perpétuelle de Dieu." Il est maintenant convenable de considérer les conséquences morales de cette vérité.

Les conséquences morales de toutes les religions varient pour le bien ou pour le mal, selon la vérité ou l'erreur de leur doctrine. Parmi de différentes présentations de la vérité chrétienne, le calvinisme s'attribue l'idéal moral le plus élevé et le meilleur programme pour la vie dans sa totalité. " Le calvinisme est la vraie grande puissance du protestantisme "— cette revendication est basée sur sa théologie. La morale n'est ni libre ni spontanée ; mais elle est la suite d'un commandement divin et d'un pouvoir donné par Dieu—en d'autres termes, de la conduite de la Bible.

La foi et la pratique sont, au concept calviniste, inter-dépendantes. L'on se trompe grandement lorsqu'on considère Calvin comme ayant oublié la vie pour exposer le dogme. Ses pensées étaient pénétrées de la vie ; ce ne fut ni un rêveur mystique ni un reclus égoïste qui ne s'occupait que de sa propre âme. Le chrétien calviniste écoute la parole de Dieu, et se met à être le serviteur de Dieu afin de faire la volonté de Dieu. Dieu est souverain ; c'est le but principal de l'homme que de glorifier Dieu."

Il en découle quatre conséquences morales :

(1) La foi réformée, par un bon enseignement, conduit au bon service de Dieu.

(2) Cela aboutit au caractère et à la personnalité chrétiens.

(3) Il en résulte une conscience claire d'une vocation divine.

(4) L'on s'aperçoit d'un idéal chrétien de la vie—d'une " manière de vivre calviniste."

En détaille : Le premier chef correspond à la prophétie ; la découverte et la révélation de la volonté de Dieu.

Le second chef correspond au sacerdoce des croyants. La foi réformée développe le caractère—l'a déjà développé en élevant de petites gens à des hauteurs héroïques.

Sous le troisième chef la foi réformée reconnaît la vocation chrétienne, laquelle est une idée ou conscience, en dehors de la doctrine de ceux qui prêchent le libre arbitre. La vocation de Dieu veut dire l'abandonnement de la vie quotidienne à l'exercice de la volonté de Dieu.

En dernier lieu (chef IV) une foi réformée vivante envisage la totalité de la vie dans ses différentes activités—comme on va le discuter dans les autres sujets du congrès, plus tard.

Le calvinisme a été démontrée depuis plus de 400 ans par des hommes et des femmes merveilleux qui ont doué le monde de richesses morales ; qui ont récompensé la persécution par la bénédiction ; qui ont témoigné dans le monde de la puissance de la parole de Dieu par un exemple de constance dans le devoir spirituellement soutenue, par une tranquillité d'esprit intérieure.

Le calvinisme peut faire tout cela encore.

Paper No. 2

THE LAW OF GOD

THE TOUCHSTONE OF A CALVINISTIC ETHICS

By Professor W. CHILDS ROBINSON, D.D., Columbia
Theological Seminary, U.S.A.

IN the Sermon on the Mount, our Lord and Saviour, Jesus
Christ, brought the whole moral life and ethical conduct under
the eye of the heavenly Father. According to the high theism
which He taught, the standard and the promise is the Father's
perfection, the motive His glory and the reach of the Divine
requirement as far as the all-seeing eye of God can penetrate.
Our Lord so completely subsumed ethics under religion that
certain of the Formgeschichte teachers have said that He
taught no ethics. Their statements serve to emphasise the
fact that He did not teach men to measure their conduct by
human values or tribal customs, but by the revealed will of
God. Indeed, the Saviour removed the law of the Lord as
far as possible from mere custom, norm, or abstract legality,
and presented God Himself at its every point of impact upon
the human soul. Moreover, both undergirding and overarching
this penetrating exposition of God's holy will are those assur-
ances of His grace which make His yoke easy and His burden
light. For those who are destitute of spiritual wealth there
is the blessing of Heaven's Kingdom ; for those who hunger
and thirst for righteousness the promised fullness, " Ye shall
be perfect."

John Calvin apprehended the Saviour's point of view and
gave ethics a definite place in his systematic presentation of
Christian doctrine. He accepted the Ten Commandments in
the rich content which the Lord gave them in the Sermon on
the Mount. Calvin insisted on a life as well as a faith Reformed
by the Word of God. For him doctrine meant any teaching
of the Word, duty as well as dogma, promise as truly as
precept. In thus recognising that " the dogmatic itself is
ethics and the ethics is dogmatics " he receives high commendation from Barth.[1] Calvin used the law of God to define duty
and included it in the Genevan Confession and the *Institutes*.
As a result expositions of the Commandments received a large
place in Calvinistic catechisms and frequently in Reformed
worship. In recognition of this phenomenon, B. B. Warfield

[1] K. Barth, *Kirchliche Dogmatik*, i. 2, 876, 888.

declared that Calvin's study of Christian ethics constituted one of his three distinctive contributions to the history of Christian doctrine.

Hence, in a day when the permanence and validity of the law of the Lord are being challenged on every hand, when the attractions of the world and the treacheries of our own hearts are continually betraying us into a disregard for God's revealed will, we can state the relationship of Calvinism and Ethics to the life of the individual no better than by showing how Calvinism presents theonomy and rejects the systems which contradict or impinge upon this position.

I. In Distinction from Antinomianism, Calvinism maintains Theonomy, that is, the Sanctity of God's Law.

In differentiation from current misrepresentations, your last two congresses have clearly shown that Calvin did not teach a Scotist doctrine of God as arbitrary or bare omnipotent will (*Institutes*, III. xxiii. 2 ; I. xvii. 2). Calvin did not exalt the power of God above His goodness or His wisdom. He held that God can no more fail to do good than He can fail to be (II. iii. 5). Further, every act of the Divine Being is the expression of infinite wisdom, which is diametrically opposed to arbitrariness. " We represent God as a law unto Himself, not as *ex lege* " (III. xxii. 2). The will of God is the revelation of His character as loving, holy, just, wise, good and true. And the law is a transcript of the will of God, " an efflux of the Divine Being " ; hence it is " the highest standard of perfection " and " the law of all law." Thus, the precept of the Lord is permanent and stable. *The law is holy, and the commandment holy and righteous and good.*

Moral creatures are as truly subject to the law of God as nature is to the law which the Creator has ordained for her. For Calvin the *summum bonum* is not some general truth or universal rule of conduct that man originates and applies ; but " the chief good consists in the practice of righteousness in obedience to the commands of God ; and the ultimate end of a happy life is to be loved of Him " (II. i. 4).

Our sinful minds seem to have a propensity toward antinomianism. Again and again in handling justification by faith alone, the dispensations of God's covenants, the experience of a vital relationship with God, dialectors have been wont to question the permanence or the present authority of the law of God. In an effort to avoid legalism we too easily become antinomian. We forget that the will of the superior is always law for the inferior, and that this is always properly, profitably and graciously true when God is the superior.

Calvinism seeks to steer a straight course between antinomianism and neo-nomianism. Or, to change the figure, " the Gospel, like its blessed Master, is always crucified between two thieves—legalists of all sorts on the one hand and antinomians on the other ; the former robbing the Saviour of the glory of His work *for* us, and the other robbing Him of the glory of His work *within* us." [1] Calvinism understands that the situation of fallen man is so serious that he cannot be saved by any evangelical obedience or other legal requirement exacted of him ; and also so grave that he cannot be saved without an inward work of regenerating and sanctifying grace, in which the law of God measures his conduct and stimulates his endeavours. Our sinful nature is such that we must examine ourselves often by the law of God lest we forget our need of the righteousness of Christ for justification and of the power of the Spirit for sanctification. The righteousness of Christ, the grace of the Holy Spirit, and the goads of the law—each in its proper Scriptural place and relation—are all used by God for the justification and sanctification of the sinner. " Being destitute of all things in himself, he is justified by the righteousness of another, and sanctified by the Spirit of another." [2] Or, in the words of current Calvinism, " There is no antinomy between believing the Gospel and loving the law. For the two acts are formed by the very same obedience to God. It is the same prayer which is practically destined for the one as for the other . . . the prayer of Augustine, ' Command what Thou wilt, and do Thou in me what Thou commandest.' " [3]

The law is like a mirror in which we behold our impotence and iniquity so as not to presume on our counterfeit righteousness. Even when treating of Christian Liberty, Calvin is careful to show that the law leaves no man righteous ; hence " the question is not how can we be righteous, but how though unrighteous and unworthy, we can be considered as righteous." Thus, before the tribunal of God " Christ alone must be proposed for righteousness " ; and we must " turn our eyes from ourselves and fix them solely on Christ " (III. xix. 2). The law works such a terror of eternal death that sinners betake themselves entirely to the Divine mercy as the only port of salvation (II. viii. 2) and to the end of their lives the faithful

[1] *Thornwell's Collected Writings*, ii. 385.
[2] *Ibid*. p. 394.
[3] A. Lecerf, *Revue d'Histoire et de Philosophie Religieuses*, janvier–février, 1937, p. 33.

have no other justifying righteousness than that obtained from the Mediator (III. xiv. 11).

According to Calvinism there is no justification apart from regeneration, since the faith which is the condition or instrumental cause of justification is the work of the Holy Spirit. And at the same time as He works justifying faith in the soul, the Spirit writes the law of God upon the heart. Or, as Calvin puts it, " By the Holy Spirit Christ dwells in us so that we are sanctified, that is, consecrated to the Lord by real purity of heart, having our hearts moulded to obey His law, so that it is our prevailing inclination to submit to His will and to promote His glory by all possible means " (III. xiv. 9). " The state of Christians under the law of grace consists not in unbounded licence, but in being engrafted into Christ, by whose grace they are fundamentally delivered from the curse of the law, and by whose Spirit they have the law inscribed on their hearts " (II. viii. 58). The law of God is inscribed and engraved by the finger of God on the hearts of those in whom the Spirit lives and reigns (II. vii. 12).

This doctrine is not that the law written on the heart exempts a Christian from the external Word of the Lord. Rather the law within causes one to delight in the objective law of God. Calvin is not among those who substitute love, consecration, conscience, or inferences—even in regenerated hearts—for the law of God. " Man has fallen as a totality, and we must remind the naturalistic moralist that his *conscience* has fallen, as we remind the Arminian that his will has also." [1] Thornwell has well written, " In our present fallen condition it is impossible to excogitate a standard of duty which shall be warped by none of our prejudices, distorted by none of our passions and corrupted by none of our habits. . . . It is only of the law of God contained in the Scriptures that we can justly say, *It is perfect*." [2] Calvin expressly teaches that " the law exhibits a perfect model of righteousness " (II. vii. 13).

And neither the advent nor the appropriation of Christ has detracted from the observance of the law. The Saviour said that *He came not to destroy the law but to fulfil it*, that *till heaven and earth shall pass, one jot or tittle shall in no wise pass from the law till all be fulfilled*, and that *if ye love Me ye will keep My commandments*. " Thus the law has received no diminution of its authority," rather, " the doctrine of the law remains therefore inviolable, which by tuition, reproof and correction forms and prepares us for every good work " (II. vii. 14, 15). God's call places us " with the comfort of

---

[1] John Murray, *The Sanctity of the Moral Law.*
[2] Thornwell, ii. 457.

the Gospel under the discipline of His law," [1] under the *obedience of faith*. Indeed, Calvin holds that the third work of the law, which is to regulate and guide the lives of the faithful, is its principal use. When excited and animated by the Spirit they desire to obey God, they derive a twofold advantage from the law. First it gives them a better understanding of the Divine will and confirms them in the knowledge of it. A servant animated by the strongest desire to gain the approbation of his master carefully inquires for and observes the orders of his master in order to conform thereto. In the second place, the law not only instructs, *it also exhorts*. Meditation thereon excites to obedience and restrains from transgression. The indolence of the flesh deters even regenerate souls from proceeding with due promptitude in the path of piety. " To this flesh the law serves as a whip, urging it like a dull and sluggish animal forward to its work ; and even to the spiritual man, who is not yet delivered from the burden of the flesh, it will be a perpetual spur that will not permit him to loiter " (II. vii. 12). Thus Calvinism echoes the doctrine of the Psalmist (Ps. xix. 7–8 ; cxix. 8–10), as that of the Saviour and of the Apostle to the Gentiles (Rom. vii. 12 ; xiii. 8–10) ; and holds that " the praise of the Law of God, as it sounds in the one hundred and nineteenth psalm, will never through all eternity become obsolete." [2]

Professor John Murray has well summarised the matter : " The believer is not redeemed by obedience to the law, but he is redeemed unto it. He is not free to sin but to righteousness, and righteousness is simply conformity to the law of God. The moral law is the reflection or expression of the moral perfection of God and is therefore the immutable standard of obligation, norm of righteousness and rule of life. To deny the permanent authority of the moral law is to deny the holiness of God. God has declared, *ye shall be holy for I am holy*." [3]

The Statue of Liberty holds in her hand the Book of Law. Liberty is not licence ; but grace to wish to do what He commands, grace which makes His yoke easy and His burden light. And this great Scriptural doctrine illumines every duty with God's own light, elevates every task and sanctifies every vocation.

> " A servant with this clause
>   Makes drudgery divine ;
> Who sweeps a room as for Thy laws,
>   Makes that and th' action fine."

---

[1] K. Barth, *Gottes Gnadenwahl*, p. 31.
[2] Barth, *Evangelium und Gesetz*, p. 12.
[3] Murray in *Daily Manna*.

II. In Distinction from the Autonomous Ethics of
Philosophy, Calvinism proclaims Theonomy, that
is, the Necessity of Scripture for an Adequate
Ethics. Or otherwise put, the Reformed hold that the
Gospel is the power of God unto salvation, " the ethical
system of the universe."

(a) *The Rule of Conduct*

Man's desire to be his own lord led to his fall from a life
of obedient fellowship with God into sin.   In contradiction to
the very concept of the creature man is continually seeking
to give the law to his own being.   This claim to autonomy is
characteristic of human philosophy.[1]   The current Aryan
ideology substitutes honour, courage and fidelity for love and
humility, virtues which God commands.   The *Bekennende
Kirche Theses* affirm that " the law reminds man that he is
not autonomous, but is accountable with his whole existence
to the Creator " and that " the standard by which every life
situation will be measured is the law." [2]

This does not mean that we disregard the ethical studies
of the great philosophers.   That which we have learned from
philosophy may often be used as tools for the better construction of what we have to say from the Bible.[3]   The moral nature
of man properly invites the researches of every thinker.   Paul
speaks of the work of the law written in the hearts of men
(Rom. ii. 14–15).   Calvin recognised a " light of truth " in
heathen writers and was careful to state the psychological
views of Plato, Aristotle and Cicero (II. ii. 15 ; I. xv. 6 ;
II. ii. 2–3).   American Calvinists—Thornwell, Hodge and
Shedd—acknowledged conscience or the elemental principles
of right as the birthright of man's being.   Theologians have
often been called to a deeper study and a fuller appropriation
of the truth of the Word by the vigorous ethical probing of
great philosophers.

However impressed by the darkening effects of sin, neither
Paul nor the Reformed theologians maintain that it is possible
for man to deduce from conscience a perfect system of natural
morality.   Psychological studies in rationalisation show how
difficult it is for one to reproduce in reflection the spontaneous
processes of conscience, or to apprehend from his own nature
the fundamental moral laws in their integrity and completeness.

[1] K. Heim, *Ethics*, i. ; E. Brunner. *Der Mensch in Widerspruch*, pp. 90 *et al.*
[2] *Bekennende Kirche Theses*, 1933, I.
[3] So Brunner, *ibid.*, p. 328 ; in citing this book the speaker is not assenting
to everything therein.

Nor can the heart, which, according to the Word, is deceitful above all things and desperately wicked, be trusted to apply laws resting on fallible deduction to concrete cases. It is all too easy by foolishly measuring ourselves by ourselves and comparing ourselves with ourselves to justify any act which we may wish to perform by some test of evolution, pragmatism, or dramatic completeness. On the other hand, the Scriptures " prescribe the law in its fullness and integrity, illustrate its application by description and example, indicate the prejudices which are likely to pervert us, and signalise the spirit which will always ensure obedience." [1] We seek to profit by the great ethical studies, but in the clear realisation that our moral philosophy must be subject to the Word of God, the only adequate rule for life.

Kant's ethics have aroused more than one theologian from his dogmatic slumbers. His attacks upon heteronomy, or the purely objective character of duty, have led men to recognise that the law of God cannot be rightly understood apart from the living Law-giver. The Kantians teach that man stands in independence of God, of a Divine will and law, that all theonomy must be regarded as heteronomy and simply rejected.[2] Bavinck replies : " This philosophy is right in its opposition if this heteronomy be thought of as a moral law which comes to us from without, is imposed upon us from above, and finds no echo in our own spirit. Such a merely external law may be, perhaps, a natural law, but in no case can it be a moral law. Such a view accords with those who think of man merely as an animal become man by external influences, but it is not Christian ethics. For Scripture teaches that man was originally created after God's image, and bore the moral law in the inmost recesses of His heart ; and that even in the state of sin he is still bound to the ideal world by his reason and conscience ; and that the dissension which now exists between duty and inclination, according to all experience, is, in principle, reconciled in regeneration and conversion. As Jesus said that it was His meat to do the will of His heavenly Father, so Paul testified that he delighted in the law of God after the inward man ; and all sincere Christians humbly speak the same words. To do good is a duty and a desire, a task and a privilege, and thus the work of love. Love is, therefore, the fulfilling of the law. Thus the true, and the good and the beautiful, which ethical culture means and seeks, can only come to perfection when the Almighty Divine will not only prescribes

[1] Thornwell, ii. 458.
[2] Frank-Grutzmacher, *Geschichte und Kritik der Neueren Theologie*, 1908, p. 43.

the good in the moral law, but also effectually works it in man himself.   The heteronomy of the law and the autonomy of man are reconciled in this theonomy." [1]   And epigrammatically " Rabbi " Duncan writes : " What is man's creation ? *Being* like God.   What is the law ?   Surely a very reasonable one.   *Be* like God."   The Scriptures presuppose man as originally made in the image of God, and when they command him to be like God they are not demanding something essentially foreign to his moral nature, but the exercise of his energies in God, an exercise re-established and sustained by God's grace.

Christ not only reconciles us as our Priest, legislates for us as our Prophet, and goes before us as our Example, He also dwells within us by His Holy Spirit as the power of a new life and the hope of glory.   The soul of man cannot properly be subject in the ultimate sense to the will or command of any other human being.   But the Infinite Person sustains such multiple relations to the soul that man can and should obey His Will and seek His likeness.   Or better, as the Lord, God calls man to the obedience of faith and, in responding to this call, the believer finds that slavery to Christ alone is the true and only freedom of the soul.

Those who reject theonomy in the interest of human freedom generally end by substituting some form of heteronomy for the authority of God.   In place of the infinite wisdom of Heaven many are setting up the arbitrary will of an economic or political idol.   A recent inquiry into Christian missions [2] rejected the finality and sufficiency of God's Word at the same time that it gave dogmatic sanction to the particular type of philosophy taught by its authors, namely empirical idealism.

The current American movement for a new or progressive education affords an interesting concrete example of this difference between human heteronomy and true Theonomy. For some time the new educators have been decrying any imposition of the teacher's views upon the pupil.   According to the pupil-centred curriculum, the purpose is not indoctrination, but the leading out of the natural talents and interests of the students.   Too much of this reasoning has been taken over into religious education by those who have forgotten that Christianity being a historical and a supernaturally revealed religion can never be merely led out of the child, or for that matter, out of the adult.   As a result in many places the use of the catechism is *taboo*.   However, one of these new educators became interested in the bringing in of a socialistic economic order, and immediately urged the schools to reject

---

[1] H. Bavinck, *The Philosophy of Revelation*, pp. 261–263.
[2] *Re-thinking Missions*, a Laymen's Inquiry.

the bogies of imposition and indoctrination, to reach for power and impose a new social order.[1]

Calvinism opposes this Dewey-Counts programme in both its tenets. We object to the heteronomy which imposes any merely human ideology. No man has the right to impose principles, customs, morals or beliefs, resting on no better foundation than his own opinions, as ultimate authority upon students or children. On the other hand Calvinists will continue to accept, indoctrinate and impose the truth of God upon as many as possible ; for, while man is imperfect, arbitrary and external in relation to his fellows, God is infinite in His perfections, wisdom and relations to His creatures. And, though the method of inculcating Divine truth may vary, the Calvinist, in the opinion of the speaker, will not hastily dispense with the Heidelberg or the Shorter Catechisms which magnificently summarise, expound and apply the moral law as given in the Word, and which have been so effective in moulding individual ethical conduct.[2]

He that hath the words of eternal life calleth the sinner unto Himself in order that his inner life may be made conformable to that outer law, that his aims may be ennobled and his motives purified, that temptation may find him armed with the Sword of the Spirit, which is the Word of God.[3] Christ came to establish the law as a rule for a holy life (*Institutes* IV. xvi. 15).

(b) *The Path of Virtue* [4]

In his *Stones of Venice*, John Ruskin has called attention to an interesting illustration of the levity with which the virtues were treated by the pagan spirit of the Renaissance. Writing about the capitals of the façades on the Ducal Palace in Venice, he says : " The point I have here to notice is in the copy of the ninth capital, which was decorated . . . with the figures of the eight Virtues—Faith, Hope, Charity, Justice, Temperance, Humility (the Venetian antiquaries call it Humanity !), and Fortitude. The Virtues of the fourteenth century are somewhat hard-featured ; with vivid and living

[1] G. S. Counts, *Dare the Schools Bring in a New Social Order ?*

[2] The Greek word *katecheo* occurs nine times in the New Testament, six times in the sense of primitive religious instruction. The question and answer method is encouraged in Deuteronomy (vi. 7), was used by the best of uninspired thinkers, Socrates and Plato, and by the rabbis in Judaising Galilee.

[3] So J. W. Burgon, *Inspiration and Interpretation*, pp. 21–22.

[4] In this section on the Path of Virtue the writer wishes to acknowledge his indebtedness to his friend, the Rev. G. T. Preer, pastor in Oakdale, Louisiana, for valuable help.

4

expression, and plain everyday clothes of the time. Charity has her lap full of apples (perhaps loaves), and is giving one to a little child, who stretches his arm for it across a gap in the leafage of the capital. Fortitude tears open a lion's jaw ; Faith lays her hand on her breast, as she beholds the Cross ; and Hope is praying, while above her a hand is seen emerging from sunbeams—the hand of God (according to that of Revelation, ' The Lord giveth them light ') ; and the inscription above is, ' Spes optima in Deo.'

" This design, then, is, rudely and with imperfect chiselling imitated by the fifteenth-century workmen : The Virtues have lost their hard features and living expression ; they have now all got Roman noses, and have had their hair curled. Their actions and emblems are, however, preserved until we come to Hope : she is still praying, but she is praying to the sun only : *The hand of God is gone.*"

Modern paganism rejects the virtues inculcated by the Redeemer and substitutes might for right, success for justice, force for love, *Mut* for *Demut*. Ancient paganism correlated the virtues with the soul and with society, but being unable to rise above the human plane found no unifying principle, no sanctifying grace. Aristotle's trichotomy and the three classes in Plato's Republic offered ready foundations for three primary virtues, one applicable to each soul and to each class in society, namely, temperance, courage and wisdom. Then presiding over the whole is justice. Other classical philosophers list truth, justice and benevolence as the cardinal virtues. The Peripatetics and the Stoics realised the need for a unifying principle among the virtues, but were unable to find it.

That unity is only discovered when holiness, likeness to God, is made the foundation of virtue. The Bible presents the whole path of virtue in its brief admonition, *Be ye holy for I am holy.* J. H. Thornwell pointed out that the Bible is distinguished from all other ethical systems by the prominence which it gives to the moral character of the object of worship. The Scriptures stress the holiness of God as the fundamental nature of the Divine character. Consequently the holiness of God is the standard of right and the ground of virtue. The sacred writers point beyond conscience and ground our love of holiness in our love for the Holy One of Israel. The light of the knowledge of the glory of God as it shines in the face of Jesus Christ is used by the Spirit to evoke our love, devotion, and praise. In loving God we love what is right and good, we embrace in principle the whole plenitude of virtue. The very essence of a holy nature in man is love to God, sympathy with the Divine perfection, a state of soul which harmonises with the Divine character. And the effectual call of the Holy Spirit brings one into union and communion with God and so produces the new man which after God is created in righteousness and true holiness (Eph. iv. 24). The everlasting contemplation of the Lord is used by the Spirit to motivate our wills and draw out our energies toward the good and the right. The action and reaction of God's grace upon us and of our souls upon Him is thus the source of virtue and the cause of blessedness.

In the Mediæval Church the emphasis fell upon the Virtue of Knowledge, first as a means of understanding the Virtue of Faith. But Knowledge was separated from Faith when Thomas Aquinas recognised two separate domains of Knowledge—Divine and Secular. Then the latter set up for itself over against the former as sufficient in itself, and so was born the humanistic spirit of modern philosophy. Thus separated from God, the Virtue of Knowledge was corrupted and terminated in humanism. However, Calvin destroyed the gap between Faith and Knowledge by defining Faith as Knowledge Revealed and so returned to the Augustinian view of God's Wisdom as the Judge of the human mind. Moreover, the Reformers regarded the Divine Knowledge revealed in Scripture not as an end in itself, but as a means to the other virtues. Reading, meditation, prayer and the preaching of the Word were in order to a pious life. Knowledge is the instrumental, piety the generic, virtue.

Calvin wrote the *Institutes* to " lay down some elementary principles by which inquirers on the subject of religion might be instructed in the nature of true piety." Therein the essence of piety is presented as the consecration of the whole self, including the bodily appetites and desire to God (Rom. xii. 1–2), which consecration involves " self-denial " and " cross-bearing." The former does not mean the wanton denying of the blessings of life. We are to receive not only those good things which meet our needs, but also those that give us pleasure with thankful acknowledgment to God, the Giver thereof. But when we are hindered in securing these things we are likewise to see the guiding hand of the Heavenly Father and have patience in pain and fortitude in disappointment. Self-denial is, thus, the acknowledgment of God rather than of self in the whole area of our experience. It is living continually out of the Father-hand of God.

The painful side of piety, " bearing one's cross," is God's way of exhibiting in His children the several virtues which are manifestations of piety; somewhat as the First Epistle of Peter exhorts us not to regard sufferings as strange things,

but as means which God uses to separate us from our sins.
" But if God Himself acts justly, when, to prevent the virtues
which He has conferred on believers from being concealed in
obscurity and remaining useless and perishing, He furnishes an
occasion for exciting them—there is the best of reasons for
the afflictions of the saints, without which they would have
no patience." [1]   Similarly, Piety generates Obedience and
Charity.   " How extremely difficult it is for you to discharge
your duty in seeking the advantage of your neighbour ! Unless
you quit all selfish considerations, and as it were lay aside
yourself, you will effect nothing in this duty.   For how can
you perform those which Paul inculcates as works of charity,
unless you renounce yourself and devote yourself wholly to
serve others ? "

Further, Courage or Fortitude results from Piety.   " It is
a source of peculiar consolation when we suffer persecution
' for righteousness' sake.'   For then we ought to reflect how
greatly we are honoured by God, when He thus distinguishes
us with the peculiar characteristic of His service."

The certitude, which the very gift of faith conveyed, that
God was eternally for the believer, and the realisation that
God's glory was the end of one's being, supplied the dynamics
of a fortitude which enabled Calvinists to organise churches
in spite of civil persecution.   To the handful of Protestants
who gathered in the home of Stephan de la Farge, Calvin
insisted that if God be for us none can be against us, and
ere long the banner of the Reformation was lifted over the
University of Paris by Nicholas Cop, and despite dungeon, fire
and rack, continued to float over Huguenot, Dutch " Beggar "
and Scottish Covenanter.   In the crucial tests of life the heart
that is directed to the honour of God has more fortitude than
one that is sustained by the desire for self-glory.   As this is
being written, the daily papers are recording the list of suicides
in connection with a great turn-over in a Central European
power.   The fortunes of the nation shifted, and when there
seemed no place for the affirmation of self or the realisation of
national aims many leading figures took their own lives, and
in some cases the lives of members of their families.   But God
implants a fortitude that supports His people when the fortunes
of life have gone against them, so that His servant Job sings,
Though He slay me yet will I trust Him.   " It is Gospel humility
that makes the true patriot, the friend, the man who is superior
to every form of physical and temporal ill."   The day calls
for men who can live as seeing Him that is invisible.
We need the Word of God as it was preached by Calvin

[1] *Institutes* III., vii, and viii.

that we may again have those who do not fear the face of man.

In the portrait representing England, St. George is accompanied by Fortitude and Purity, carrying his armour and bearing his banner. The former of these Virtues we have just studied. Accordingly we may close this survey of representative Virtues by pointing out the deeper reach of the God-affirmation of Christianity than of the self-affirmation or the self-realisation of paganism in reference to the Virtue of Purity. As long as the eye of the world is on the natural man, pride prompts him to act properly ; but the Word of the Lord reminds one that His Presence is in every place, in the house of Potiphar, in the mill and the counting-house, as truly as in Bethel. Nay more, the Sermon on the Mount throws the searchlight of Heaven farther than any modern psycho-analysis has ever gone into the darkest recesses and foulest corners of our souls. The more one realises that one lives every moment under the eye of the Heavenly Father, the more the *coram Deo* makes for purity in life and word and thought.

(c) *The Key to Happiness*

Non-Christian ethics have commonly regarded happiness as synonymous with pleasure or the gratification of the desires either of the individual or of society. This desire for, and mad pursuit of, pleasure obsesses the interest of the day and obstructs the road to real happiness. A current study in anthropology gives this account of the working of lawless *Begehren* in the individual :

" The self-will which ought to be imbedded in God's will, now steps out naked. Man puts the I in the place of God, he makes himself the final purpose and directing point of all desires and activities ; it is the self-glorification, the *cor incurvatum in se ipsum* in its concrete, direct manifestation. But since the human I is constituted not for the I but for God, the man who no more seeks God, but himself, seeks ever in emptiness. He must, therefore, do one of two things : either fantastically raise himself, blow himself up for a god, or fill out the empty I, so to say, with world stuff. The first happens in all forms of metaphysical, religious, mystical self - deification. The desire to be like God becomes the concrete contents of the life, not merely, as in the Fall itself, the ultimate presupposition lying behind (the sin). More often it is the second : the empty I throws itself upon the

world. First of all this also occurs in religious forms :
nature and world deification—Paganism. The honour
which is withheld from the Creator is carried over to the
creature (Rom. i. 21 f.). But this world deification
becomes again the same common world greed. This is
so much the usual thing, that the natural man generally
knows sin only in this form. However, in consequence of
this greed for the world the I loses itself in the world,
above all it loses there its freedom. What is one in the
Divine Love comes here into opposition : the having
oneself and the losing oneself. Therefore, the man
who has thrown himself upon the world or is prepared
to throw himself there, must ever again take himself
back from the world—and that is the content of all
natural ethics : self-glorification and self-affirmation as
over against the world, up to the point of forsaking the
world—asceticism. So the man is torn from one side to
the other between two opposing tendencies, the contraction
upon himself and the expansion into the world, between
the desire for independence and the throwing of himself
away and entangling himself in the things of this world,
especially in those things that serve his pleasure, between
haughty egotistical isolation and wasteful self-abandon." [1]

To this picture of the sinful soul one perhaps need only add
that the better each one knows himself the less reason has he
for finding the key to happiness in the enjoyment of his
evil self.

Moreover, society as well as the individual needs to be
reminded that she that liveth in pleasure is dead while she
liveth. What Thornwell wrote years ago is more dangerously
true to-day, " This fundamental error, that happiness is
pleasure, pervades society." " It is the animating spirit of the
eager and restless quest for wealth, honour and power."
" Philosophy projects upon it its visionary schemes for the
benefit of the race, and, forgetting that all real improvement
must begin within, directs its assaults upon the outward and
accidental—aims its blows at the social fabric, and seeks to
introduce an order of things which shall equally distribute the
sources of enjoyment." [2]

Surely Calvinism has come to the kingdom for such a
time as this, if it can ease the tension between conflicting
ideologies for securing happiness through increasing the
pleasurable enjoyments of a greater number, by showing that

---

[1] E. Brunner, *Der Mensch in Widerspruch*, pp. 232–233.
[2] Thornwell, ii. pp. 465–466.

real happiness is not in the pursuit of worldly pleasures, but in
the enjoyment of God, here and hereafter. Man's whole
personal, moral and spiritual nature was made in the image of
God, and hence his happiness consists in the virtuous exercise
of his whole being in devotion to God. Jesus declared, *My
Father worketh hitherto and I work.* Adam was placed in the
Garden to dress and keep it. The sentence in Revelation, *His
servants shall serve Him* was regarded by Thomas Aquinas as
the great promise in the Bible. " Inactivity is no part of
bliss."

The Bible reveals God as at once the subject who initiates
and the object who elicits man's virtuous energies and sustains
them in a course of unimpeded action. Or, to return to the words
of our leading Columbia theologian, " we cannot think without
thinking something, we cannot love, we cannot praise, we
cannot exercise any virtuous affection, without exercising it
upon something. An abstraction wants life, and finite objects
limit, condition and obstruct our energies." Further, " the
fundamental force of our being is love, and love implies the
existence of a person with whom we can be united in intimate
fellowship and who can draw out the most intense affecion of
which we are susceptible."

Accordingly, the Calvinistic key to happiness is the great
message which for three centuries the Shorter Catechism has
taught the oncoming generations, " Man's chief end is to
glorify God and to enjoy Him forever." " This and this only
is happiness : that we enjoy as we glorify ; that the very
going forth of our energies upon Him, the ever-blessed, is
itself blessedness—this is the doctrine which lies at the basis
of the ethical system of the Bible."[1] And, referring to the
enjoyment of God forever, " Rabbi " Duncan declared,
" Every fibre of my soul winds itself around that with un-
utterable, sickening, fainting desire. Oh, that the Beloved
may be mine, and I His, and I His, *and I His.*"

III. In Distinction From Heteronomy Calvinism Maintains Theonomy, in its Doctrines of the Completeness of Scripture and of the Sole Headship of
Christ over His Body the Church.

Since the development of this third thesis lies outside of
the ambit of the assigned topic the speaker would state rather
than amplify the position presented.

This thesis does not constitute an insurrectionary or
revolutionary principle. Calvin recognised that God had

[1] Thornwell, ii. pp. 464–465.

established two governments, encouraged obedience to the constituted authorities for the sake of the Lord, and in his exposition of the fifth commandment inculcated respect for everyone in their several stations in life. But no one can read the record of Calvin in Geneva, of Presbyterianism in Scotland, of the origin of the speaker's own denomination, or of the Bekenntniskirche in Germany without realising that Calvinism stands opposed to the effort on the part of any state or ideology to conform the Church to any rule other than the Word of God.

Furthermore, though Calvinism recognises with the Apostle the propriety of having a " pattern of doctrine " (Rom. vi. 7), good forms of sound words (2 Tim. i. 13), concerning faith, morals, church praxis and eschatological hope,[1] she has offered satisfaction from " the mouth of God," that is from the Holy Scripture for those things she has thus set forth.[2] Presbyterian and Reformed Churches have given dogmatic sanction to their respective Calvinistic standards because they were convinced that these presented the teachings of the Word of God. Exercising an ecclesiastical authority which is ministerial and declarative (rather than magisterial and legislative), the Calvinistic Church requires the observance of the principles and practices of the Word of God as interpreted in her standards which set forth that Word. But accepting the teachings of Scripture (Isa. xxix. 13 ; Matt. xv. 6–9 ; Acts iv. 19 ; v. 29), she has testified in Calvin's Letter to Emperor Charles V, in the Petition of the Westminster Divines to Parliament, in the Confession drawn up by these Divines (xx. ii ; xxxi, iii ; i. vi, x.), in the Preliminary Principles which that great Scotsman, John Witherspoon, set forth for American Presbyterianism, in the Barmen and other declarations of the Bekenntniskirche [3] against any church authority making its own " laws to bind the consciences of men by virtue of its own authority."[4] In the Barmen declaration the *Bekenntnissynode* rejects the false doctrine which says there are provinces of our lives, in which we are to own not Jesus Christ, but some other Lord ; in which we do not need justification and salvation through Him." In declining to accept the oath prescribed for ministers, the Bekenntniskirche holds that, " That which is demanded by him, going in fact beyond,

---

[1] From the New Testament A. Seeberg, R. Seeberg and A. D. Heffern find indications of a *Catechism of Primitive Christianity*, containing teachings on these four themes.

[2] *Scots Confession of* 1560.

[3] Of course, only a part of the Bekenntniskirche are Reformed.

[4] John Witherspoon in Preliminary Principles of *the Constitution of the Presbyterian Church, U.S.A.*

above the Scripture, is, in reality, in contradiction against the Scripture." [1]

RÉSUMÉ DU DISCOURS

Fait par Le Professeur W. CHILDS ROBINSON, D.D.

(La Foi réformée: sa consequénce morale pour l'individu)

LA PIERRE DE TOUCHE D'UNE
MORALE CALVINISTE

Le sermon sur la montagne toucha la vie morale entière et mesura la conduite éthique par la norme de la perfection divine. La doctrine du Christ implique une morale d'un niveau ni moins élevé ni différent que la volonté révélée du Père.

Jean Calvin, en suivant le Seigneur insista sur une vie, ainsi qu'une foi, conforme à la parole de Dieu.

I. Le calvinisme maintient la sainteté de la loi divine. Il n'est pas arbitraire ; il n'est que juste et bon, étant une transcription de la volonté de Dieu. Par conséquent la rédemption n'est pas une délivrance de la domination de la loi. Dans une vie renouvelée l'obéissance de la foi se fait voir.

II. L'évangile postule la morale essentielle. 1° C'est une meilleure règle de conduite pour l'homme que celle de la nature ou de la philosophie. Il n'est pas déraisonnable d'exiger de l'homme qu'il soit parfait, puisqu'il a été créé à l'image de Dieu. L'évangile ne se moque pas de ce besoin, plutôt c'est par l'évangile que l'on est poussé à l'atteindre, que l'on découvre le chemin qui y mène. 2° L'évangile signale le sentier de la vertu. Les philosophies anciennes ne pouvaient pas trouver un principe unifiant parmi les vertus. L'esprit humaniste de la philosophie moderne y échoue également. L'évangile révèle la vertu suprême, recommandée par les apôtres, reconnue et rétablie par Calvin—la piété, la dévotion pour Dieu, le service devant Dieu avec obéissance, l'expression active de la foi. 3° Suivre cette régle de conduite, pratiquer cette haute vertu c'est trouver le bonheur. D'autres pensées de plaisir sont des chimères et leur pourchas est vain. " Le but principal de l'homme est de glorifier Dieu, et de jouir éternellement de Lui."

[1] A. Frey, *Der Kampf der Evangelischen Kirche in Deutschland*, p. 134 ; Basel, *National-Zeitung*, 28th to 29th May 1938, p. 2, *Der Eid auf den " Fuhrer " und die Bekenntniskirche.*

III. Les Écritures sont une loi autoritaire pour l'Église et Jésus-Christ est son seul chef et souverain.

Ce dernier chef enchevanche sur d'autres subdivisions du sujet devant le Congrès. L'auteur n'a fait qu'affirmer, sans élaborer l'assertion.

Paper No. 3

THE REFORMED FAITH IN ITS ETHICAL CONSEQUENCES IN THE FAMILY

By Rev. Principal JOHN MACLEOD, D.D., Free Church College, Edinburgh

The family as an institution belongs to the natural order. Its welfare tells on that of the community, and of the State, and of the world. So also what affects it to its hurt has an injurious influence on all the constituencies that reap the benefit of its well-being. There is a bond of nature that binds together husband and wife, parent and child, brother and sister. And the bond of kinship alike by way of blood and by way of affinity helps to bind into one the larger units of the local community, the State, and the race. Thus nature itself teaches us to aim at the furthering of the well-being of our flesh and blood who are our kith and kin. What belongs to the order of nature is taken up into the sphere of grace and all that is good in it is guarded and confirmed and intensified. The godly discipline of the Church is meant to defend the home.

When we face the question of how the specific Reformed Faith has told on the ethical good of the family we do not mean to make exclusive or monopoly claims on behalf of either the Faith in general, or the purest exhibition of the Faith in particular, as if in no sense and to no extent the good of the Family were attained outside the range of Christian, or the highest, influences. There is such a thing as common grace which keeps the world from being all that the unchecked wickedness of mankind would make it. Nature itself bids us seek the good of our home. Every Christian society acknowledges this. And however seriously some exhibitions of the Christian Faith may diverge from the final norm of apostolic truth yet, in so far as the element of Christianity is at work in appropriate practice, it tells in the direction of ennobling and purifying the life of the households of the Church. That form, however, of the Christian Faith which does fullest justice to the claims of God and His Christ is fitted to do the greatest service in giving to the home the place that rightfully belongs to it.

In maintaining the position that the purer the faith and the life of the Church is, the more salutary is the influence that it has on the home we thus do not set aside nor ignore the measure of justice done to domestic claims in other systems. For it would be unnatural for any parent not to seek what he looked upon as the good of his family. Common consent is at one on this matter. But when we take note of the wide range of opinion and sentiment that has to be taken into account we may easily see how the thing that is deemed to be good may differ greatly in the different circles of human society. This divergence of outlook and estimate is due to the havoc that the entrance of sin has wrought on the good order of primitive and unfallen human nature. Those who hold to an evolutionary or naturalistic origin of man and of society are shut out from such an explanation of how the standard of acknowledged good is such a varied one among men. But Christianity as it accepts the witness of Divine revelation to the fact of the Fall and its results, has an explanation ready to its hand of how there is such a marked difference of judgment between man and man, and between land and land. Those who have learned to say, " All we like sheep have gone astray," see how wide a field the straying flock of mankind may cover as they part company in their devious wanderings.

Common Christianity recognises the obligation that lies upon the Church to have regard to the will of the Lord as He has made it known. So the type of ethics that is truly Christian confesses the Lordship of the Saviour and the obligation that is thus laid upon us to honour His authority in doing His will. All that is valid and truly moral in Ethics as taught in the schools of philosophy is taken up and sublimated in the realm of Christian duty ; and the bonds laid upon men by the good order of the original constitution of the race, and of the world, are laid afresh, as it were, on these who are the willing bond-servants of their Redeemer as their Lord. The relations in which men thus stand to one another by reason of their family ties are stamped with the authoritative brand which tells that by coming to be new men in Christ the household of faith have not ceased to be men. All that is incumbent upon them as men in their divers relations to each other is part of the obedience that their Lord who has redeemed them calls upon them to yield to Him as His own right. In the claims that are thus made, those of family life are included, and the household as a unit is held to belong to the Lord who as Creator and King originally gave to it its constitution.

Now the view that is held by the typical and representative thinking in the Reformed Churches as to the Scripture doctrine of what makes up the Church of God is one that lays special stress on the Church in its spiritual reality as it is known to God.   The Church in its real being is constituted of those who have been chosen to eternal life, redeemed by the ransom price paid in the Blood of the sacrificial Lamb of God and called by grace to His fellowship.   At the same time as this entity in its spiritual being and glory is recognised to be the true Church of God, our Reforming fathers confessed the truth of Scripture as to the visible form that the Church assumes in its embodiment on earth.   Thus looked at, it is seen to include all men everywhere who profess the truth of God, who with their children make up its constituents.   This definition of the visible Church as inclusive of the children of believers is a feature of historical Reformed teaching on this subject ; and to it is due the recognition of the household as an integral unit in the Christian commonwealth.   The recognition of the visible Church, in the sense in which the Reformers held it, raises one of the questions on which post-Reformation attempts to improve on their teaching parted company with their thought by taking up narrower ground.   Those attempts achieved the disintegration of the Puritanism of England in the seventeenth century.

The idea of the Church which was entertained by the Independent brethren of the age of the Commonwealth in England was one which recognised the existence of a visible Catholic Church.   But in the Savoy definition they omitted from it any recognition of the children or households of Believers as though these had no place in it.   This we may see when we compare Chapter XXVI. of the Savoy Confession in its second paragraph with the corresponding paragraph of Chapter XXV. of the Westminster Confession.   These paragraphs deal with the Church as visible.   The former reads : " The whole body of men throughout the world professing the faith of the Gospel, and obedient unto God by Christ according unto it, not destroying their own profession by any errors everting the foundation, or unholiness of conversation, are and may be called the visible catholic Church of Christ, although as such it is not entrusted with the administration of any ordinances, or hath any officers to rule or govern in or over the whole body."   The Westminster statement reads : " The visible Church which is also Catholic or Universal under the Gospel (not confined to one nation, as before, under the law) consists of all those throughout the world that profess the true religion ; and of their children ; and is the Kingdom of the Lord Jesus Christ, the house and family of God, out of which, there is no ordinary possibility of salvation."

The Independents look upon the Church as being at bottom a local autonomous unit which is made up of those that have entered into the Church Covenant and have been accepted and acknowledged by the brotherhood into whose covenant and fellowship they have entered.   As a larger unit they regarded it as the aggregate of those who may be at least the potential members of such primitive cells of Church fellowship ; and this might be called the visible catholic Church.   In keeping with this omission of any mention of the household as a unit in the local ecclesia there followed, with a measure of logical consistency, the action that was taken by one wing of the Independent movement.   It was indeed no strange phenomenon that Independents, who, while in other respects they held the common faith of the Reformed Churches, yet stressed the ideal of spiritual individualism which underlay the pure communion which they as Independents sought to secure, should fail to find a place for the household of the believer along with himself in the visible Kingdom of God. And so it came to pass that as the radical wing of Independency they adopted the principles of the Baptists and introduced into the Anabaptist movement the Calvinistic strain of teaching in regard to the doctrines of grace which was by no means a salient feature of the earlier manifestations of a Baptist tendency in the Churches of Britain.   They failed to see that with their definition of the local ecclesia it could have any place in its bosom for more than those who were accepted as candidates for Baptism and were on their own profession and immersion recognised as having the standing of members in the Church to which they were joined.

This wing of the Independent movement cut out any definite acknowledgment of the household as a unit in the Church of God.   By so doing they did not mean to set aside Apostolic teaching in regard to the natural unit of the household or the obligations that the Epistles lay on parents and children alike.   Yet their attitude to the household as such was so far one that was materially different from that which expressed the older Reformed view.   It looked on the children and household of a Church member as being outside the range of the discipline and oversight that are proper to the members of the Churches.   Such a divergence of view had its necessary outcome in the practical working of their Church system in as far as it differed from the standard type as seen in the historical Reformed Churches whose polity they had given up.

The less radical wing of the Independents, by what one

might call a less strict reading of the significance of their departure from the Reformed conception of the constitutive elements of the visible Church, or, as one might express it from the standpoint of those who accept that conception, by a happy inconsistency, still held on to the common practice of Christendom as a whole, which recognised the household of the believer as holy in an outward federal sense and as such entitled to be acknowledged as set apart for God and Christ. They continued the custom of recognising the unity of the household so far as baptized membership of the Church is concerned.   And among the early Independents who took this line there was such a conscience developed in regard to the infants of Church members as kept pace pretty much with the practice of the Reformed Churches.   These Reformed Churches struck no uncertain note in their acknowledgement of the children of believers.

The standing of membership in the visible Church that was thus acknowledged to belong to the children of Christian homes might be treated in two distinct ways in the service of their baptism which was their public recognition as members. One of these ways is taken in the baptismal service of the Anglican Church, a church which in the teaching of its Articles of Religion belongs to the fellowship of the Reformed Churches. This goes on the assumption that the sponsors or sureties for the child pledge in its behalf faith in Christ and obedience to His will.   The service says : " The infant must also promise by you his sureties (until he come of age to take it upon himself) that he will renounce the devil and all his works and constantly believe God's holy Word and obediently keep His commandments."   In charitable anticipation which, it may well be, goes further than the facts of life warrant, the baptized child is spoken of as regenerate.   This service is one that takes for granted that what is professed will be made good and that the child will without fail yield the obedience of faith to the Gospel.   On the understanding that this profession is in due course crowned with fulfilment there is a giving of thanks for the regeneration of the infant.   It is altogether on the basis of such an assumption that the service is constituted.   At the Savoy Conference this was one of the things that Baxter and his fellows who acted for the Puritans sought to have modified. In this endeavour they failed, and, since the Act of Uniformity the Church of England has been in the ambiguous situation of seeming in so many words to teach a Baptismal regeneration to which she is not bound by the teaching of her Articles, while those who adhere to the Reformed reading of her formularies have to stand on the defensive against the attacks of the high Sacramentarians, to maintain the validity of their interpretation of the order for Baptism.

The other way of admitting the children of the faithful to a recognised place among the members of the Visible Church is that which the Westminster Directory takes. Here stress is laid upon the fact that the promise given to the Father of the Faithful that God would be his God and the God of his seed is current still and gives a place to the children of believers among the people of God. It assigns them a place in that holy nation which in respect of calling and privilege God has separated from the world and claims as His own. On them He bestows special advantages and at their hand accordingly He claims that they should yield a return that will respond in love and loyalty to the word of promise and His demands for worship and obedience.

In either of these ways of accounting for the administration of the seal of the Covenant to the children of the Church it is obvious that there is an undertaking given, implied or expressed, that they shall be taught the truth of Law and of Gospel, and that they shall be trained in the ways of the people of God. The fact that in the one case sponsors other than the natural guardians answer on behalf of the child does not free the parents from the burden of responsibility that lies upon them to teach and to train. In the other case the parents are to be expressly exhorted to consider the great mercy of God to themselves and their child ; to bring up the child in the knowledge of the grounds of the Christian religion, and in the nurture and admonition of the Lord. They are to be told of the danger of God's wrath to themselves and their child if they are negligent. And the officiating minister is to require their solemn promise for the performance of their duty. In whichever of these ways we deal with the admission of child members, the Church looks upon the Christian home as a school for imparting the knowledge of the Word of God, and for training the rising generation which is the hope of the future, in the faith and obedience of the Gospel of salvation. The acceptance then of the children as members of the Church lays a special load of responsibility on both the Church which admits them to membership to see to their worthy training, and on their parents who have now the charge in their early years of the acknowledged members of the Church of God, to attend to their tuition.

In contrast with the individualism on which such stress was laid in varying degrees in both wings of the Independent Movement, the attitude of the Reformed Churches in treating the household of the professed believer as having a recognised place among the constituent units of the visible Church was one that called upon the Church and its ministry, as well as on the head of the house, to pay special heed to household consecration, worship and oversight.   There is a close connection between the Reformed emphasis on the family as a unit in the Church, and the view that our Reformed fathers took of the care with which the Lord's Day as the sacred day of rest ought to be observed.   They aimed at teaching the children of the household the habit of waiting regularly on the ordinances of public worship that, having been trained in their youth to do so, they might continue in mature years to practise the assembling of themselves together in the corporate worship of the Church.   They aimed at more ; they called for private exercises for the household of that worship to which they looked upon the day as wholly set apart.   So they gave direction to the household as to its special duty.   In this respect the documents of the unbroken Reformed Church of this country, as they set forth its teaching and practice may be taken as authoritative exponents of the view taken by the Reformed Churches as a whole of the household and its place in the Church.   To this more comprehensive view of the constituency of the professing Church of God, a view that took men at their uncontradicted profession and devoted the fostering interest and care of the Church to the welfare of the household as a unit, and also of those that are not yet in Christ, Rutherford refers in his letter to his friends at Aberdeen, who set themselves to gather out a Church from the general body of professing Christians.   His words on the subject are noteworthy :   "We look upon the visible Church, though black and spotted, as the hospital and guest-house of sick, halt, maimed and withered, over which Christ is Lord, Physician and Master :   and we would wait upon those that are not yet in Christ as our Lord waited on us and on you both."

There are but two of the documents of which we have spoken to which we shall refer.   The one is the Westminster Directory for the Public Worship of God in 1645 ; the other is the Scottish Directory for Family Worship of date 1647. The first of these gives guidance for the sanctification of the Lord's Day, and after indicating what is called for in public in that connection, it speaks of what is to be done at home between or after the solemn meetings of the congregation. Here is what it requires :   " That what time is vacant . . . be spent in reading, meditation, repetition of sermons ; especially by calling their families to an account of what they have heard and catechising them, etc."   Similarly, the Scottish Directory which deals with the Lord's Day says of the head of the household : " And the public worship being finished, after prayer, he should take an account of what they had heard ; and thereafter spend the rest of the time which they may spare in catechising and in spiritual conferences upon the Word of God, etc." This catechising is also treated as part of the daily routine of home worship in the second of the Directories. In those days there were no Sabbath Schools. With regard to them it is obvious that they are fitted to be a priceless asset for the Church in doing aggressive and compassionate work of teaching and evangelisation among the children of those who neither hear nor heed the Word of God. At the same time they should minister confirmation to the parental teaching of children who are taught at home. In this case they second and support the efforts that the parents and guardians put forth to teach their charges the Word of God, and to win their heart to the obedience of faith.

The Reformed Churches by their recognition of the household of the believer as a unit in their fellowship were shut in to what they looked upon as no bondage. Their views on the membership of the Visible Church, as we have seen, found a place in their constituency for the children of those who were saints by profession. These were looked upon as being in virtue of their birth in believing homes entitled to be acknowledged as outwardly sanctified or specially set apart by the Head of the Church to enjoy external privileges in His house, and so laid under a corresponding obligation to take His yoke upon their shoulders. They were regarded as part and parcel of the holy nation of New Testament times ; and therefore it was looked upon as a warranted thing that they should have the seal of the covenant and at the least a probationary place in the ranks of the organised Christian Kingdom. Because they were federally holy they were to be recognised as being so in Baptism.

Such a doctrine as this laid the obligation upon the Church to see to the due training of its infant membership. In this connection the task was looked upon as a two-fold one. It left room for distinct yet concurrent action on the part of the Church and the Home. There was a duty recognised as lying upon parents to teach and to train their children. They were to look upon them as not only their own children, for whose highest good they were naturally bound to labour and to pray, they were also to regard them, since the Church of the Living God had taken them as her own, as the children of the King's daughter, the daughter of the King of Kings. This being so, it was but right and seemly that the children of such a mother should have an upbringing in keeping with their privileged

5

rank. Their parents then, as their natural guardians, were to
bring them up and train them, bearing in mind the need that
their children, owned in Baptism as having a place in the Church
of God, should be taught and guided and moulded by every
means within their reach, so that they shall be shut in to Christ
as their Saviour, and that they may take Him as their own.

The obligation lying upon the Church is the other side of
the task that has to be carried out. The parents are not
relieved of their natural obligation. They have their children
given back to them as their proper guardians in Baptism, and
they are to bring them up as the children of the King's daughter.
She whose adopted and acknowledged children they are has
the task and burden laid upon her of praying, and not only
praying but also labouring for them. She is to see to the due
training of those that she has accepted as her own. In seeking
to carry out the obligation that she thus felt to be laid upon
her, the Church of the Reformation in different lands showed
great diligence in providing manuals of instruction which took
the form of Catechisms. Thus, for example, in the Acts of
the Synod of Dort the obligation to teach the young people
is recognised. " That the Christian youth from their tender
years may be carefully trained in the fundamental truths of
true religion and imbued with true piety this threefold method
of Catechising ought to be taken, at home by their parents,
at school by their teachers, and in Church life by their pastors,
elders and readers or sick-visitors, etc." (p. 48).

Notable among the Reformed Catechisms were Calvin's
Geneva Catechism, the Heidelberg Catechism and the Westminster Shorter Catechism. The aim of the Church in the use
of these was to teach the truth of God's Word to her rising
membership. These handbooks were provided for parents and
teachers as well as for their charges. For one of the things that
the Reformed Church tried to secure was to have a well-
instructed constituency. The Jesuits said that if they had
a child for the first seven years of his life they did not fear
who should have him afterwards. This was a game at which
two could play. And in their palmy days the Reformed
Churches were not behindhand in looking after the young of
the flock. They aimed at raising up within their borders
successors who would range themselves under the banner of
the Gospel and who would seek to perpetuate such a goodly
order. It was looked upon as part of the ordinary work of
the ministry that they should see well to the state of their
flocks in respect of godly nurture and instruction. And the
outcome of such a programme was that—at least in the flourish-
ing times of our Reformed Church in Scotland—in the homes

of the people household worship morning and evening, with the acknowledgment of God at every meal, was the recognised practice of the land. Now worship that called for the reading of the Word of God called for and was fitted to produce an educated community which sought out and sought after the Word of God written, and which strove to bring up its children from the dawn of life in the knowledge of that Word and of the Church's Confession and Catechisms.

Such a catechetical method in pedagogy as found favour among our Reforming fathers was one that cut right across the modern practice in this department which throws the reins loose and lets the horse please itself. Go-as-you-please teachers allow the wishes and the whims of their scholars to map out for them their course. It was the fashion of olden days that the dog should wag its own tail. The modern inversion that the tail should wag the dog hardly looks a natural or a reasonable kind of thing.

When objection is taken to the catechetic mode of instruction by way of question and answer, a mode which calls for the learning by heart of an answer that has been carefully drawn up to convey a maximum of sound knowledge in a memorable form, it is said that this sort of instruction is too one-sidedly intellectual, that it overloads the memory, that it shoots over the head of the scholar, that it does not reach the end of opening up the truth by reason of the very abstruseness and detachment of its matter and method. Those who take such a line of criticism forget a thing or two that it would be well for them to bear in mind.

For one thing, the use of catechetical manuals supplies the parent and the teacher with material that a competent teacher will put to a wise use. He will open up the real content of the answers that the pupil has committed to memory. The instructor may have himself learned these words in his youth and assimilated them only in part. He may now find out that in the endeavour to teach another the thing opens up to himself better than it ever did before, and he may meet with more success in his work than the teachers that he himself had met with in his own case when he was young. Now that he is come to maturity he is better able to grasp the meaning of the words that he learned in his early days. It was good for him to have such words stored up in his memory. It trained and exercised that faculty. And now that he sees their meaning better than he once did, he will seek to bring home to his pupils' understanding what he had himself in his youth failed to grasp.

Then it is a well-known fact that memory is more impressionable and retentive in early years than it is in later life. And while the acquisitive powers of memory are at their best it is possible by exercising them well to strengthen and develop them and furnish the young with what will be a life-time treasure. At the same time the powers of the understanding come to their maturity and strength in later years when the powers of memory have passed their zenith. In the years when memory is at its best the powers of the understanding, though not yet mature, are already at work, so that there should be not only drill in memory work but exposition and explanation to open up the meaning of the lessons taught. One does not need to delay until maturer years to come to an appreciation of truth that is learned by heart.

Then again in so far as the powers of the understanding come later to full functioning, it is well that the millstones of consideration and reflection as they go round should have something to grind. And here comes in a special value that attaches to what has been learned by heart yet has not been quite grasped in younger years. In such a case when the stores of memory give them something to go on with, the millstones do not grind each the other into hard grit. They have choice wheat to work upon. What has been learned at the outset of life is thus fitted to come into its own, and the matured powers of reason and of understanding do not work *in vacuo*. The adult mind has something provided for it which gives food for thought.

In the light of these things we see that there was wisdom and sound psychology in the method adopted by our fathers. They sought to indoctrinate their children in the knowledge and faith of the Gospel ; and, as they did so, they tried to impress upon them the truth that no parrot knowledge of sound words will suffice. It will suffice no more than the parrot repetition of forms of prayer can serve as a substitute for true prayer, for prayer is offered to Him Who is not only its Hearer, but the Searcher of the heart. There is a fault in the method of instruction when it only heaps up in the memory what may be so much dead lumber, or is one-sidedly intellectual. The teacher who seeks to teach indeed will not only store the memory with what is valuable ; he will seek to open up the meaning of the truth that he is trying to teach, so as to make it as clear and as simple as possible. And to make it at once memorable and interesting he will use the method of illustration, call in the legitimate resources of feeling and of fancy, and so enlist the sympathies and rouse an interest in what is taught. The method of learning by rote is one that has been justified by its ultimate results. It bred among us generations who were schooled in the knowledge of Christian doctrine, and who had a keen edge on their discernment. They could tell readily when the teaching that they heard went out of the right way, for their understanding of the truth was disciplined.

The emphasis that our Reformers and their loyal successors laid upon the godly upbringing of the young is registered, not only in the watchful discipline of the Church, which guarded purity of life and the sanctity of the home as the nursery of the Church ; it came out also in the number of helps that saw the light by way not only of Catechisms, but of Commentaries upon them, and the systematic habit of using them. The survival of the old order is within the memory of men yet alive who saw ministerial catechising of the households of the flock as part of the regular routine of the life of old school Presbyterian congregations. Indeed, happily, it is not yet a thing altogether of the past. For such diets of catechising there used to be careful preparation, and when they came they were not shunned but welcomed. Such a devotion to the study of Christian truth could not fail to exercise an influence direct or reflex on the tone of the community. In particular, the homes that were accustomed to the old order of Reformed Scotland, for it is of this country that we speak at present, used to have a fireside Sabbath School, the memory of whose lessons is a bright spot in the record of the years that are gone. When Sabbath Schools were begun it was not meant that they should take the place of home teaching and training. And few would venture to say that the measure in which they have served to oust these and to relieve parents of a sense of duty in regard to the teaching of their households is an index to improved conditions in the life of the Church. The old order produced generations of instructed hearers. And if it might happen that at times there was more knowledge of the letter of Christian truth than there was practical experience and illustration of its power, the blame lay, not with the success of the endeavours to teach, but with the failure of those endeavours. In such instances they did not reach their intended goal. The system did not do everything that it set out to do. But it did much ; and its outcome in the life of the Church and of the commonwealth tells of what good came of it. There is like good that is still to be looked for when the blessing of God crowns loyalty to the claims of household godliness. Such godliness shows itself as of old in the instruction of the children, and in striving to bring home to each of them in turn his personal responsibility and his need of a saving knowledge of the Gospel of our salvation, and of Christ as our Saviour and Lord.

For the fruit borne by the application of the Reformed presentation of Christian truth to the domestic institute we may look to the record of those regions and eras when the application was most faithfully made. If, to the eyes of our Scottish Reformer, Geneva was in Calvin's day the most perfect school of Christ that was to be seen anywhere, one has only to turn to the moral and spiritual elevation of the godly homes of Huguenot France, of the confessing Netherlands, of Protestant and Puritan England and New England, and of this Covenanted country to see what a benign and blessed, what an educative and elevating and evangelising influence this application put forth in the communities that came under its sway. We might take two concrete instances to which we may appeal in illustration, and they are but two out of a countless multitude. Who that has read about the family life of Philip Henry in Puritan England or, as it comes out in Domestic Portraiture of Leigh Richmond, in the hey-day of a reviving Evangel in England over a century ago, can fail to see the beauty of the lives that bore witness to the blessing of God as it crowned the faithful diligence of parents whose resolve was that, as for them and for their house, they would serve the Lord ? Let men but see such homes multiplied, with their influence telling on the commonwealth at large, and it would be evident how beneficent the influence was that was wielded by the household godliness which made the home the happiest place on earth. This experiment has been made on a wide scale already. Let it be made on a wider scale still, and the care that is devoted to the godly upbringing of the young will reflect its working and its power in the life of Church and State both. We have said already, and before we conclude we may repeat it, that we do not make any exclusive claim by way of monopoly. We venture merely to indicate what a close and loyal adherence to the Reformed ideal of the visible Church and its concrete application to the home as a unit in that larger fellowship has done. This is an index to its potency. And the diligence that it calls for in teaching the Word of God, and in showing the beauty of a Christian life lived in the unrestrained freedom of home conditions, is an expenditure of energy that will richly repay itself. The sedulous care that our Reforming fathers called for in the oversight of the young shows how their eye with statesman-like prescience was directed to the future. They were not content with the past whose record was closed, nor with the present with its limited measure of success. They looked forward to the days that were yet to be for the full answer to the prayer that the Lord has taught His disciples to offer that the kingdom of God may come. With its coming the face of the world will be changed ; and a godless and selfish and unbelieving world needs, if it is to be set right, that it should be turned upside down. The natural institution of the family taken up and blessed in the kingdom of God will be a mighty instrument for achieving this end.

RÉSUMÉ DU DISCOURS

Fait par Le Professeur JOHN MACLEOD, D.D.,
sur *La Foi Réformée : Ses conséquences morales dans la Famille*

L'ordre naturel de la vie sociale est basé sur la famille. La qualité de celle-ci influence, pour le bien ou pour le mal, la société, l'état, le monde. Les obligations de l'Église sont exigées d'un homme à l'égard de ses enfants. Les enfants des croyants sont comptés parmi les membres de l'Église visible. Ainsi se lit la Confession de Westminster (le chapitre xxv). Bien que les Indépendants omettent toute allusion aux enfants dans le chapitre xxvi de la Confession " Savoy," toutefois par une " inconséquence heureuse " l'aile moins radicale des indépendants reconnaît effectivement l'unité de la famille des croyants. L'Église d'Angleterre requiert des parrains (articles xxxix) et le directoire de Westminster exige des parents, une promesse au baptême que les enfants seront élevés et instruits dans " la crainte du Seigneur." La conséquence morale c'est que l'on apprend aux enfants à connaître la Bible, à respecter le dimanche, à faire la prière en public comme en particulier et à assister au sanctuaire—tout cela jusqu'à ce que l'habitude de l'enfance devienne la pratique des années adultes.

Le discours examine, avec des détails illustrés, comment cette obligation a été accomplie et avec quels résultats, non seulement dans la famille mais dans la portée plus large du soin de l'Église pour la jeunesse. La méthode catéchistique est discutée avec référence spéciale à sa valeur en Écosse.

L'adhésion loyale à l'idéal réformé et son application concevable à la famille font que la beauté de la vie chrétienne se manifeste dans la liberté sans contrainte des conditions familiales.

Les pères réformés faisaient cas d'une vie familiale sanctifiée, car il se trouve là une promesse de continuité voire même d'une pleine réponse à la supplique inspirée de Dieu : " Ton règne vienne."

Discussion of Principal Macleod's paper was led by Rev.

F. M. Hirst, who claimed that the Baptist Communion, in common with the Presbyterian, sought earnestly to advance Christ's kingdom by family religion.   He illustrated this by a very full account of Baptist activities in this direction.

In reply to a question put by Dr. Rutgers regarding a difference of view that was and is found in the Reformed Churches on the subject of the right observance of the Lord's Day, Principal Macleod said, "After the death of Calvin there was a distinct development of the Sabbatic doctrine, particularly in the British Churches and also, to a less extent, in those of the Netherlands.   The Scottish Reformed Church took the stricter view, even before the controversy awakened by Dr. Bowe in the last decade of the sixteenth century helped to mould the Puritan doctrine in England.   The documents to which I referred in my address represented the mature Puritan view on the subject.   This largely determined the teaching and practice of the evangelical Churches of the English-speaking world on both sides of the ocean.   They aimed at treating the Lord's Day as His in such a sense as that it was altogether devoted to His worship—not, however, to the exclusion of works of necessity and mercy.   These works were looked upon as obedience to the paramount call of duty.   In the golden age of the Reformed Theology in the Netherlands opinion was divided on this matter.   Some men, like Burmann, held the laxer view that came down from the Reformation age, while others took the more strict view that was characteristic of British Christianity.   The practice of the Reformed Churches in the Netherlands, on its Secession side at least, is along the line of this stricter Sabbath-keeping, and the South African Dutch, largely owing to Scottish influence of a century ago, also represent this tradition.   There is an appendix or extended note, in Patrick Fairbairn's typology of Scripture, in which there is a discussion of this question. Calvin's Catechism and the Heidelberg Catechism too, do not go so far as do the Westminster documents."

Thursday, 7th July 1938

AFTERNOON SESSION

Paper No. 4

THE REFORMED FAITH AND ITS ETHICAL CONSEQUENCES IN THE CHURCH

By Rev. Professor G. T. THOMSON, D.D., Edinburgh University

IT would be easy to be academic on this topic, to sketch the doctrine of the Church in the Reformed Confessions generally, and to draw attention to those tenets in it which need re-emphasis to-day. But in a shallow age in which individualism run to seed has produced a crop of ideologies at the other extreme of thought, it is better to stress the need for more depth both in thinking and in personal responsibility, and to indicate the points at which this need appears to be most obvious. Indeed the necessity for a diet of milk and not of strong meat, the necessity for stressing the very elements of Christian conduct, the necessity for bringing a moral searchlight to bear upon the first principles of Christian living, is clamant in the highest degree. Even the Church to-day lays stress upon methods of teaching ; but the methods have gained ground to the detriment of the actual instruction given. False ideas are prevalent as to the liberty inherent in the individual as such to define the content of faith and practice. The unparalleled raids of the Social Gospel upon the substantial doctrines of the Christian Faith give as much cause for justifiable alarm as the unashamed inroads of humanistic modernism. Press publicity for Liberalism in religion is a sore handicap upon the pulpit in these days, for which no one can blame the Press. Pulpit instruction has been rendered futile by irregular church attendance, and so doctrinal preaching has given way largely to topical sermonising. It behoves us, therefore, as teachers of the faithful, to set our minds upon the lost first principles of our theology, in order that by mutual counsel even teachers may learn to lead the way to victory over this double handicap, the way of a return to the true faith. It is scandalous that the Gospel is no longer " news."

The first discord to be removed from the popular mind, both ministerial and lay, is a false universalism. Inevitably this takes several forms to which ministers ought to draw attention.   The type of mind which shudders at election and predestination is ready to stand—though only if asked to ! —for a gospel which includes a salvation for all.   For such the Saviour is clearly not a Saviour ; He saves from nothing. It means nothing to be a Christian.   The presumption must be that the incarnation of God is at best a mere theophany, analogous to the modern organised public demonstrations by which we delude ourselves into thinking that we can get things done.   The doctrine of salvation *sola gratia* is clean forgotten, although it is taught on nearly every page of Scripture.   This sort of " Christianity of good form " may make the world " nicer," but it ignores sin and so does not make man better.

Another shade of this universalism is illustrated by the talk we continually hear about a Christian nation or a Christian world, talk indulged in often by those who scarcely believe in the Christianity of the Church.   The line of separation between the kingdom of God and the kingdoms of this world has become invisible, and many leaders envisage the organised Church as the spiritual home of all the decent-living people in the world.   Anything that is a stumbling-block to anyone who would like to be a Christian must be removed from the content of the faith.   Would it not be more orthodox to prefer genuine publicans and sinners who were forgiven ?   The Church is often, alas ! regarded as a kind of club, the rules of which can be altered or amended to suit the " needs of the times."   Because I teach the fundamentals of the Christian faith as I find them implied in Scripture, and codified credally and confessionally ;   because I have been known to use the dreadful, unkind word " heretic," I cannot be a Christian.   If I say that a Unitarian is not a Christian, I am narrow-minded.   If I object to Anabaptist doctrine, I must learn to live and let live. In the larger Churches of the Reformed Faith there are those whose whole aim is to broaden the basis, so that as many as possible may be allowed to call themselves Christians.   Of course in reality the essential stumbling-block does and must remain. But many are led astray, the blind lead the blind, and all fall into the ditch.   Doctrine, we must make it plain, is based upon facts and not upon opinions.   Unions and re-unions of Churches must be of God and never of men only.   The Church of Christ is one in His eyes, one in reality ; but the rifts in the body visible cannot be closed upon a minimum of doctrinal agreement, or upon some Social or Modernist substitute. Every man has a right to his own opinion, but not every man has a right to call himself a believer because he has self-made rules as to what constitutes a believer. And the Church's answer to unbelief is not to complain that it *is* unbelief and to scold accordingly; it is not to say comfortingly, "Never mind! come in!" It is to preach the Gospel, to state the facts of redemption and not to move from them. Only faith can overcome the offence and the foolishness of what we believe. The victory, our faith, is utterly simple—simple with the simplicity of an act of God. The Protestant Fathers, under God, purged doctrine of false accretions by stringent use of Scripture; used in their works, we are proud to say, great liberty of thought and speech, yet always the liberty of a truly Christian man. Not one father of them all is infallible, and neither are we. Like them in their day, we in ours must canvass the truth of what we preach, compare it under God with the witness of Scripture, and humbly answer to God for our findings and teachings in consequence. We know that not for the rightness of our doctrine shall we be saved but by grace alone. Yet grace itself opens our eyes to the truth and commissions us to utter it. To-day, as every day, the need is urgent. In what we proclaim, if it be indeed the Gospel, there is salvation to the uttermost. This truth we seek to spread abroad is nothing arbitrary; it is as real as the Incarnation, Cross and Resurrection. We do not choose the truth; the Truth chooses us, and His choice is at the same time our bidding. The answer to mere opinion which is heresy is the patient reiteration of the truth, with the prayer as we utter it that God in His mercy and in spite of us will give His Word free course and effect. Our predecessors have shown us that one life is too short to learn and spread the truth. Let us just follow their example in obedience to the imperious call; there is grace behind it.

Without trespassing upon a later paper, I think I may touch upon another aspect of truth which at times vanishes away from our proclamation of the Gospel. Much as I should have liked to do so, I shall not touch upon the relations between faith and knowledge. In the sixteenth century the conflict was only just reaching the popular ear, and the authority of the Church as such was sufficient to keep science in its place. To-day, so far as tyranny is concerned—perhaps I should rather say, so far as the popular ear is susceptible to authoritarianism —science has the upper hand, and certain Church voices in the land are heard calling for an approximation between truth as science knows it and truth as Christians know it. M. de Saussure will, no doubt, prove to your satisfaction that the two realms do not really touch, and never did. That is his task. But my assignment forces me to say this much, that a great deal of the conflict between science and religion so-called was and is due to our failure to preach the Christian facts. Now every Christian fact is a miracle, proceeding from, rendered credible by, authenticated in, the central miracle of the Incarnation.   Deism, roughly speaking, was a philosophy of rationalism, expressed in Christian terminology, and the popular preacher and public letter-writer who urges us to scrap Scripture where science does not like it, is just a Deist or a rationalist, whose sole message is the gospel of being good ; in other words, an ethic falsely called Christian.   Our popular friend would probably be shocked at such terms of abuse. But they describe, if not the results, at least the intentions of his mind.   And he is a Deist and a mere moralist because he has either forgotten or has never known the feel of real miracle known as the forgiveness of sins, or the breaking of the power of cancelled sin.   Awareness of the miracle of God in Christ has many urgent corollaries, which the mere moralist cannot glibly infer without moral outrage.   To say that God just naturally forgives everyone because *c'est son métier*, is a moral outrage, unless the speaker has himself been forgiven for no other reason than that it pleased God to reveal His Son in him. Nor may we venture to assure the believer that God is on constant tap to him ;   that would be a rational conclusion which the most elementary experience of faith would deny. All God's intromissions with us are according to His own good will and pleasure.   No doubt His good will and pleasure are mirrored in the Gospel of His own Son.   But that does not give us power to call up God at our pleasure.   We must learn to be still until we know that God is communing with us. God's providential care of the creature is one thing, extending to the unthankful and evil as well as to His adopted children in Christ ;   His direct communion with us in the Holy Spirit is as and when He wills.   If God begins His dealings with us with the miracle of regeneration, and if we are always miserable sinners nevertheless, our hope—which indeed maketh not ashamed—is that He will do more miracles, keeping us in the faith until by Christ's merits alone He changes faith at last into sight.   As the palsied waited for the stirring of the waters, all sinners must wait for the blowing of the Spirit, who bloweth where He listeth, and not at our whim.   As soon as we take one single item of the Christian revelation for granted, we have lost our way, we are saving ourselves, our last end is worse than our beginning.   It is a constant difficulty with me in teaching doctrine, that men and women glibly accept Christ in the hero sense, but find " difficulties " in many subsidiary truths of faith.   Am I not right in replying that if a

man can accept Christ, he can accept anything scripturally
true ?   That Jesus Christ is the colossal stumbling-block, the
colossal miracle, beside whom everything else is light as the
dust of the balance ?   The term " Christ " and " Son of God "
and " Son of man " are so explained nowadays, that almost
anyone can read almost anything he likes into them.   Luther
calls Him whom we serve " Jesus Christ," the Lord of hosts—
that is His name, there is none other."   That is the only name
in which we can be saved, and it is a miracle upon us that we
know it.   What greater stumbling-block than this, that flesh
and blood cannot reveal it unto us ?   For communion with
God discipline (yoga, if you like) is necessary on our part.   But
communion is not a result of our self-discipline ; it is God's
free act upon us, for which we must wait, for which we must
ask constantly, but which when it comes is new every morning
and fresh every night.   Our yoga is nothing more than our
waiting, our watching, our praying.

   Don't you think the Church as a whole needs this lesson
of waiting upon God alone ?   If the Church is one and the
congregation represents the Church, the congregation is one.
Where is there a congregation ?   How far does it feel any
responsibility to meet as a whole ?   We often express horror
at the Inquisition.   In Scotland horror is often expressed at
the way in which the elders in the early days of the Reformation spied upon their people in their districts.   No doubt there
were elders and elders, elders with nasty minds, with inquisi-
torial analogues.   But—elders also who were true Christians,
helping to rule the flock in love.   Why, John Calvin was an
Inquisition in himself, an indefatigable asserter of the truth,
with a burning conviction underneath his legal make-up that
the Christian business was the only saving business, and that
it was business with Almighty God !   This ruling passion in
our lay-officers, this urgency to work in the spirit of Christ for
the weal of the people, we must pray God to restore.   We
tend to be ashamed of the Gospel of Christ, afraid of pushing
it down people's throats.   Perhaps instead of pushing that
good medicine down their throats, we by our laxness are
pushing their souls down to hell.

   This raises the whole question of the Church's responsibility
to God.   The sinful Church that needs to fast, sitting in sack-
cloth and ashes !   Prayer and almsgiving we know something
of, but fasting—what is that ?   The true spiritual fasting in
secret unto God ?   Here the worldly problem of spiritual
health *v.* physical health raises its head.   We do not want to
say that bodily exercise profiteth nothing.   As little is it right
to take the poet's catchword *mens sana in corpore sano* and

transform it into a plea for outdoor life on Sundays, on the ground that if the body is weak the mind cannot be healthy. All knowledge of real faith in others would brand such an assertion as utterly untrue. Muscular Christianity is not Christian because it is muscular, though it is none the worse of some spare tissue to waste. At the same time, because body and mind live so intimately together in us and affect each other so strongly, there is a real duty upon the most serious Christian to keep physically fit, so far as that consists with Divine guidance from day to day. Just as spiritual weariness is not to make us mope instead of exercising the body, just as on the contrary private communion with God is not to be cut off because we are too tired with exercise or business, so the whole life of the Christian must be a true militia, a life of balanced discipline, in which both mind and body are drilled into subjection for the sole glory of God. The glory of God, however, does not consist in our bodily and mental fitness but, so far as we are concerned, in our readiness to surrender anything, to do anything, instantly at God's command. And it seems to me in accord with the Scriptural meaning of the Church, that we should seek the Divine glory, not as members severally of the body, but as the Body. That is part of the meaning of my earlier rhetorical question : Where is there a real congregation ? We must fast unto the Lord as a Church : in communion with all saints, but visibly in the fellowship of our Church members. A revivalist has the sense to pack his audience into bodily contact. A congregation that is alive is a congregation that meets as a congregation, and so is able to act as a congregation. An individual who does not believe in the missionary call of the Church does not belong to the Body, is not yet a member of the Church or of a congregation of the Church. The individual is a unit, having a private life with God, only in order that he or she may grow up into a fit member of the Body. And so the congregation as the local representative of the Body, as the Body localised, must be meeting constantly together. It is created to do the will of God ; it must therefore wait upon God. And so multifarious are the duties it must perform, that it must have all its members at call, with their special gifts of activity. A body minus some of its members is a weak, often a helpless, body. A limb that does not know that there are other limbs —or members !—is not only a nuisance or a hindrance, but it is doomed to atrophy. How are we to get this vital truth across ? Lack of it, lack of real oneness, is the source of all our inefficiency in a careless world. It makes one think. It suggests a great need in us. It calls us to that very corporate fellowship before God which the Church so sorely needs. Perhaps under Providence the disease may work its own cure.

Possibly the last point I take up is more peripheral than the rest, but it probably ought to be made. It is a commonplace of non-Christian economists in this island that Calvinism and big business are twins, and that the other invariably follows the one. That is half truth and half slander. Certainly the pioneers of the Reform did not make much out of it, although some of the secular powers exploited it, and exploited it because they hoped to, and did sometimes, make by it. But the spiritual leaders of it gained nothing in a this-worldly sense. It is true to say that a Calvinistic sense of the Providence and the Grace of God could lead to the making of fortunes. Christians would be careful to husband the mercies of God, to give the Lord usury upon His many gifts, and that from a sense of duty to the Lord, but also, as a corollary, from a sense of duty to their neighbours, " that there might be plenty for man and beast and sufficient for him that needeth." Frugality lies nearer to virtue than to vice, even in the case of mere self-helpers. But because many good Calvinists have made big business, it does not follow that profiteers and dividend hunters are the product of Christian example. When we think of the utter insecurity of the people prior to the Reform, and the venality of the clergy, the Inquisition and many of the temporal rulers, it is small wonder that business integrity was such a great gain. If God is really our Master to whom we are responsible, and if we are receiving instruction from faithful men as to the implication of having such a Master, there is no doubt that success does come to us generally. Trade follows the flag which follows the missionary. In fact our Lord even promised as much, in more ways than one. But this promise, fulfilled in so many cases, does not abolish the fact that the world is still the world in which the boldly wicked seem to flourish like the green bay tree. This paradox of injustice is due to the fact that the sword is wielded in vain against evil-doers or not at all. It is gratuitous libel to fasten the sins of industrialism as a blot upon the scutcheon of the Reform. That flouting of justice takes place at all in Europe is due to the irresponsibility of the Christian consciousness, not to its responsibility. Faith makes us not of the world, but in this life it still leaves us in the world, with a function to fulfil upon the *massa perditionis* of which we continue to be part until the consummation. We have no right under Christ to cut ourselves off from the world, in the sense of ignoring its wickedness and its perpetration of injustice. We have a duty to secure, with all the force that in us lies, that justice is done and that righteousness is the foundation of the seat of government. Politics may be, and is, a dirty game. But that does not excuse us from resisting unrighteousness, or from doing our duty by the body politic, from seeing to it that the oppressed get at least half a loaf rather than no bread. If all who do not yet abjure the name of Christian were to compel themselves to vote at elections, and were thus driven to secure proper candidates for proper reforms, I venture to say that no European nation to-day would be in a frame of mind to knuckle down to ungodliness, far less to rejoice in it. In the world, yet not of it ; convinced of duty to God from whom nothing so fearful even as war can ever separate us ; certain that He will back us to the uttermost for Christ's sake —do not these Christian commonplaces, even in this present year of grace, still speak to us of something nobler than political compromise and truckling to Cæsarism ? I speak of my own country. Of whom shall we of the Reform be afraid? Of God only !

We believe that we are the Church ; otherwise we have no right to assemble as we do. It must cause us searching of heart to consider the effectiveness of our testimony in our day and generation. The habit of the age is to blame others or to blame " tendencies." It won't do ! We have just forsaken the Lord and His testimonies, we His messengers. Perhaps we have had too much security, have believed in progress, and have taken too much for granted. Perhaps that is not to be wondered at, since the almsgiving, prayer and secret fasting of the true Christian are but pallid replicas of the original ; since the corporate character of congregational life is becoming more and more spasmodically, transparently thin ; since more and more is being left to and expected of the ministry ; less and less (money excepted) expected of the laity. We believe that it is good that the State should supply our revenues ; we do not abjure the temporalities completely, any more than Rome does. Perhaps, though, we need more of the liberty of Christian men, who know whom they have believed, who can give a reason for the faith that is in them, who have heard the call, whose living is henceforth a responsibility to God. The solution, whatever it be, we can learn only from God. We shall never find it by ignoring Him, by substituting for revealed truths the kaleidoscopic nostrums of religious publicity quacks. Back to prayer, back to Scripture, and so back to the one Revealer and Revelation, without whom there is neither Church nor salvation ; *with* whom we are responsible creatures of the Lord, with a mission from the Lord in urgent need of fulfilment, if the world, this dear, desperate, sinful world of men, is to be saved at all.

LE CONGRÈS CALVINISTE

LA FOI RÉFORMÉE ET SES CONSÉQUENCES MORALES DANS L'ÈGLISE

(par le Professeur G. T. THOMSON, D.D.)

RÉSUMÉ

Les deux grands obstacles contre un protestantisme efficace sont l'évangile social et le modernisme humaniste, puisque cela signifie que la vraie doctrine n'est plus prêchée ni même plus désirée ; et les fidèles potentiels sont nourris de sermons remplis de lieux communs, s'ils sont nourris de quoi que se soit du christianisme.

Quelques-unes des conséquences principales de ce manque d'instruction chrétienne il nous incombe de les traiter. La première c'est le christianisme appelé " universalistique " avec son implication qu'il n'y a pas besoin d'un salut ni d'un Sauveur. La seconde c'est l'universalisme qui croit qu'une nation ou un monde est chrétien ou sur le chemin de le devenir. L'antithèse de l'Église avec le monde est dans ce cas minée et l'hérésie devient une impossibilité. Une troisième conséquence est la prévalence d'un nouvel autoritarisme, qui peut rejeter toute religion non-païenne et même mettre les intérêts de l'État au-dessus de toute autre considération. Ceci comprend l'intolérance pontificale du dogmatisme scientifique envers la foi et son infection en diverses façons de la prédication et de l'enseignement de l'Église.

Toute la question est vitalement soulevée du manquement de la responsabilité chrétienne envers Dieu, non seulement individuellement mais collectivement. Quelques déductions qui s'appliquent à la vie chrétienne sont tirées, et, en conclusion, la calomnie qui accolade le calvinisme et le libre trafic ensemble comme cause et effet est réfutée.

Called on by the Chairman to speak at this point, Professor Lecerf said that he had closely followed the argument of Professor Thomson's paper and had been struck by its genuine Christian spirit, by its loyalty to God's Holy Word, and not least by its typically Calvinistic spirit. As Calvin did in his day, Professor Thomson saw the danger for Protestantism—for Christianity—in what is called the " social gospel," in humanistic would-be theology, which is not even a philosophy in the proper sense of the word. Professor Thomson showed a vivid sense of the mystery of Christ, the great stumbling-

6

block to every kind of unbelief, as Calvin had pointed out in his tract, " De Scandalis." His view of the relation of the Christian individual to the visible Church—the sinful Church, but still *The Church* was thoroughly in accord with one of the chief thoughts of Calvin. Thanks were due to Professor Thomson for stating that in quite an original and personal form. The Church must declare its faith again in true Christian love, not in humanistic philanthropy.

Paper No. 5

CALVINISM IN SOCIETY

By Rev. Professor R. J. G. M'Knight, Ph.D., D.D.,
read in his absence by Rev. W. J. M'Knight, D.D.

Calvinism, objectively considered, is a philosophy, a system of thought, a plan of life, a method of proceeding towards a definite goal. On its interior sphere, however, it is more than that ; it is an ineradicable conviction that this metaphysical conception of things has its origin in God, and is therefore embedded in the moral order of the universe. Men, accordingly, when they accept Calvinism intelligently and whole-heartedly in all its expansive scope and grandeur, move through life composedly, steadied in every emergency by a serenity born of a blissful consciousness that they have been chosen in eternity for the precise situation in which their lot is at the moment cast, and that in consequence of this foreordained pre-arrangement they are undefeatable, providentially enveloped for the end in view in the " celestial panoply " of sheer omnipotence. They rest in the calm assurance that to any who would undertake to thwart or interrupt them in the work for which their lives were designed, the Creator and Lord of all will never fail to say, " Thus far, and no farther," and that through the episode, of whatsoever nature it may happen to be, they are to be accounted to have obtained,

" The very crown and proper end of life."

Being in the arc and orbit of the Divine purpose they are immune. Their " soul can no wound receive, ' no more than can the fluid air.' " They are never in the power of their enemies ; they are always in the hand of God, and ever ready submissively to say, " Even so, Father ; for so it seemed good in thy sight."

At bottom, indeed, Calvinism conceives of all mankind as a vast, heterogeneous commonwealth of " labourers together with God " ; not that all who comprise and constitute this conglomerate collection are willing workers, to be sure ; far from it ; yet it nevertheless holds true that even the wickedest of men are so supernaturally overruled that they can do " nothing against the truth," nothing subversive of or fatal to the ultimate reality aimed at, but are obliged, on the contrary, to contribute their assigned allotment toward the rounding out of the Divine ideal—though not on their part " for the sake of " it, but rather, from the Divine side, " because of " it, because of its nature, because it is what it is and was foreordained to be ; because, that is to say, it is not susceptible to effective opposition, and only thrives the more the more it is assailed. Men cannot foil God by working against Him. They cannot even so much as inconvenience Him. He is not so incompetent as to be outwitted by a race of pygmies. Despotic Dictators may succeed in confusing the minds of their supporters for a while, but they are not deceiving the " Sovereign Seer of time." The wrath of God is always able to deflect the rage of men to the " praise " of His wisdom and omniscience and justice and power and immaculate holiness. He that sitteth in the heavens " laughs." Men to-day, as in past ages, are plotting and taking " counsel together against the Lord and against His Anointed," and are still crying, " Let us break their bands asunder, and cast away their cords from us." And now, as then, the Father is quietly reminding this old world of ours that the Most High is " clothed with majesty," and can afford to wait until the Messiah's enemies have done their uttermost and have filled their " cup of iniquity " to the brim—in the meantime merely saying once again, " Yet have I set my King on my holy hill of Zion." Calvinism is the capacity to realise that " the Lord reigneth," that as

> " God's in His heaven
> All 's right with the world."

When we come to think and speak of society we must needs take a plunge into the deep sea of psychology—not indeed of the behaviouristic type, for that to all intents and purposes is dead. In fact, it was stillborn. For when men use their lack of mentality to prove that they lack it, and then grow livid at us who have minds for admitting the deficit, about the only thing left to do is to begin with the rudiments and teach them, if possible, that " a great cause of the night is lack of the sun." The absurdity of behaviourism is simply

irreducible.   Real psychology is different.   It maintains that
each person, each soul, is first of all a product, and then, after
that, a producer.   With its coming into existence the soul
brings into the universe a new potency, a new shaping power,
an illimitably multiplying increment, which lifts it into a
world of its own, far above, light years above, the dictum of
science known as " the conservation of energy."   The first
man, Adam, found himself possessed of a " living soul," a life-
imparting principle or qualification able to set in motion
spiritual influences, unreckonable, indeterminable, unending,
and laden withal with results for good or evil " measureless
to man."   It is not hard, therefore, to see that every ego, every
soul, every person, is launched on the broad ocean of existence
under bond and contract to keep his rudder true.   Where
much is given it is reasonable to conclude that much will be
required.   Where the outcome is infinite the responsibility
will presumably be of the same order.   Professor Pratt of
Williams College, Massachusetts, puts it compactly when he
says : " What we mean by moral action is impossible without
responsibility ; and responsibility in turn is impossible without
some form of spiritual freedom and spiritual efficiency.   And
neither spiritual efficiency nor spiritual freedom is possible for
any philosophy which denies the existence of free and efficient
spirits whose actions are not to be predicted by the laws of
the external cosmos."

Not, however, until we pass from one to two, or from one
to many, do we enter the domain of what is termed " society."
Yet society, it should be noted, is immensely more than the
sum of its units.   It is a union of wholly incalculable pre-
potencies.   Each unit is a contributory source, a creator of
new values.   It both gives and receives.   As Browning's
" Cleon " says :

> " I have not chanted verse like Homer, no—
> Nor swept string like Terpander, no—nor carved
> And painted men like Phidias and his friend :
> I am not great as they are, point by point,
> But I have entered into sympathy
> With these four, running these into one soul."

Even so it always is.   A man not only helps to make
society ;   society helps to make him.   As Emerson says,
" He must be clothed with society ; . . . dressed in arts and
institutions, as well as in body-garments."   Obviously therefore the intricacies and complexities of social life are labyrin-
thine.   Perhaps the common classification is as good as any.
We speak of the individual as the personal unit ; of the family
as the domestic unit ; of the State as the civic unit ; and of the

Church as the ecclesiastical unit. In a manner, it is true, these divisions sweep in the whole horizon. Yet in a sense they are more or less misleading, for when the plummet is dropped a little deeper, everything reverts at last to the individual ego. It is so easy nowadays for speakers and writers who deny the Deity of Christ, and the inspiration of the Scriptures, and the fact and doctrine of the virgin birth and of the resurrection of the Lord Jesus from the grave on the morning of the third day, and who eviscerate the Word of God in unnumbered other vital ways—it is so easy, I say, for men of such a sort to become enthusiastically loquacious over what they fondly call " the social gospel," as though they had discovered something ; whereas what they talk so much about has in reality no separate existence whatsoever. There is but one gospel. It is for the individual, for the particularised unit ; or, as the writer of the eighty-seventh Psalm expresses it, for " this and that man," whether it finds him in Egypt, or Babylon, or Philistia, or Tyre, or Ethiopia. The gospel reaches its destination in the first person singular of the first personal pronoun. Paul in writing to the Galatians crams it all into one short sentence : " I am crucified with Christ : nevertheless I live ; yet not I, but Christ liveth in me : and the life which I now live in the flesh I live by the faith of the Son of God, who loved me, and gave Himself for me." But when the gospel reaches " me " it reaches me in my entirety, in the inner man of the heart ; so that my sanctification, which begins on the instant and in the article of my new birth, " is throughout in the whole man," as the Westminster Confession so aptly words it. Consequently, as a matter of course, the message from on high is bound to make itself felt in me in every conceivable phase of my life, not only in the solitude of my own soul, but in my family, civic and church relationships as well ; and in all these, moreover, irrespective of my calling or occupation, whether I happen to be a carpenter, or a machinist, or an engineer, or an agriculturist, or to be devoted to science, or art, or philosophy, or letters, or anything else one may be able to specify.

Thus it is that Calvinism, since it is but a scientific interpretation of the Word of God, goes to the root of everything. As a life-system it contemplates, and makes adequate provision for, an ideally perfect state of society ; in other words, for an ever-changing terrestrial community of true believers, every one of whom is bent on doing, and absorbed in doing, the will of God " in earth as it is in heaven." To this end it insists that every unit must fill its own place and do its own allotted work, not in cloistered privacy nor on its own account alone, but because of the part it has to play in the design and ultimate outcome of the projected enterprise—that " one far-off Divine event, to which the whole creation moves."

That this is what the Bible teaches is indisputable, for in no end of instances it portrays a radiant future for the human race. It foretells how Christianity is some day to become the universal possession of mankind, thus producing an idealistic society in which the Son of man will be every soul's Sovereign, every soul's Saviour, every soul's Companion, every soul's Counsellor and Guide. In that day " they shall teach no more every man his neighbour, and every man his brother, saying, Know the Lord : for they shall all know me, from the least of them unto the greatest of them, saith the Lord." Think of it—no need for anybody to teach the Christian religion, and for the simple reason that every person on earth will have come, one by one, individually, to know it—to know it, that is to say, experientially, and in such a way as to make it articulate through every avenue of expression of which the regenerate life is capable. And it is owing precisely to this state of affairs that in the golden age to come " the earth shall be filled with the knowledge of the glory of the Lord, as the waters cover the sea."

Let us pause a moment here, if you will, over that expression—" the glory of the Lord," or in briefer form, Jehovah's glory. What can the prophet mean ? Well, after all, what, for example, is the glory of a piece of mechanism, let us say, but just this, and nothing else than this, namely, the efficiency and thoroughness with which it does its work and serves its purpose ? What really red-blooded man ever cares a kopeck whether the watch he carries is encased in gold or silver, or even pewter, so long as he can depend on it to tell him to the fraction of a second what time of day it is ? The glory of a timepiece is that it keeps time. Similarly Jehovah's glory inheres in the exactitude with which His plans eventuate. Pragmatically speaking, they work. They carry through. The immediate thing the prophet Habakkuk was envisaging at the moment, it is true, was the total and utter destruction that was soon to overtake the great world-tyrant of his day, but he was only thinking of this as a step toward that splendid hour which Isaiah, in the use of practically the same words, had already described as the coming era of universal peace. Jehovah, in whom all sovereignty, and all power and wisdom, resides, is efficient ; efficient alike in removing in wrath the foes of righteousness out of the way when the clock strikes the zero hour, and in making all things work together for good in the society of the redeemed, who severally and collectively love

God and take up their daily tasks and burdens, conscious that even the lowliest of their lowly duties have been assigned them according to the eternal purpose of Him who " for His own glory has foreordained whatsoever comes to pass." If we may use the words of Emerson with a somewhat different thought in mind than he had, we may say of every true Christian, or if you prefer it, of every true Calvinist, that " there is one direction in which all space is open to him. He has faculties silently inviting him thither to endless exertion. He is like a ship in a river ; he runs against obstructions on every side but one, on that side all obstruction is taken away and he sweeps serenely over a deepening channel into an infinite sea."

What the world needs to-day to lift it out of darkness into light is just plain Calvinism pure and simple ; Calvinism in its full-orbed completeness ; Calvinism working effectively in each and every unit of the social order ; the Calvinism which originates in the Word of God and hews to the line with tremorless precision down to the last and faintest edict of the human will ; the Calvinism which, by permeating and controlling the " whole man " in all his relationships, is destined in due time to season and flavour society as universally as salt does the sea. Men talk about making the world safe for democracy. The statement needs to be turned end for end. What it rests with men of common sense to do is to make democracy safe for the world. Ethically, an unchristianised demos is just as bad as an unchristianised dictator. A rotten democracy will put rotten men at the head of its affairs. Society's inequalities are not to be laid at the doors of the rulers any more than at the doors of the peoples that tolerate them. Men do not get into high positions by a mere stroke of fortune. There are many links in the chain by which they reach the top.

> " The fault, dear Brutus, is not in our stars,
> But in ourselves "—

and not merely in the fact that " we are underlings " either, but rather in the fact that we are not Christians. One would think that six millenniums of recorded history ought to be enough to teach the world that apart from Christ we can do nothing. By Him all things were made, and in Him all things consist, and the sooner the men in the rank and file come to appreciate this tremendous reality at its face value the sooner they will begin to see earth's present-day Saharas blossoming as the rose. Calvinism is the system that binds men to Christ, and insists that they shall live accordingly. Christ acknowledged the Father in everything, and it was because He kept this connection uninterruptedly intact that He was able to live a spotless life on earth.   When civilization takes the same attitude, then, and not till then, will there be peace on earth and goodwill among men.

Thus when we think of society as an extensive corporeity on the one hand, and on the other survey it in its separate creative units—as innumerable, to use the Bible's own figure, as the sand on the shore plus the stars in the sky—and then allow our minds to dwell on the capacity of each unit to inaugurate new processes of thought and achievement, to produce ever enlarging spheres for the exercise of voluntary choice, and consequently to multiply to infinity the occasions for issuing fresh mandates of the will, all of them certain yet all of them free, we begin to realise what an immense expanse the Calvinistic system englobes.   It discerns as through a telescope the omniscient Sovereign on His white throne, in the morning of eternity, predetermining the unchangeable course of all events ; and pierces and peers as by a microscope into the deepest recesses of the human soul, taking account of everything there, even to the remotest act possible within the realm of free moral agency.   It is a system which allots to both God and man their respective places without marring the perfections of either.   It draws the line as no other system has ever done or can ever do between fate and foreordination. A Calvinist can see how an act may be certain without its being necessary for the doer of it to do it.   He can understand Johannes Agricola, where Browning makes him say :

> " Ere suns and moons could wax and wane,
>   Ere stars were thunder-girt, or piled
>   The heavens, God thought on me His child ;
>   Ordained a life for me, arrayed
>   Its circumstances every one
>   To the minutest ; ay, God said
>   This head this hand should rest upon
>   Thus, ere He fashioned star or sun "—

a Calvinist can understand all this—or if I may resort to the personal pronoun for the sake of the sentence I have in mind —I can understand all this, or at least see it through a glass darkly, and yet at the same time know that I was free to let my hand hang at my side, a moment ago, instead of touching it to my brow as I did.   In Calvinism resides the glorious liberty of the sons of God.

Discussing the subject of Professor M'Knight's paper, Professor Davidson stressed three conceptions in the Social

Philosophy of Calvinism : (1) The theocratic conception which, while compatible with human freedom, excludes modern humanism ; (2) the unitary conception. Mankind is a single society, not ultimately divided into nations or other absolutely independent groups ; (3) the victorious conception—ruling out pessimism. Society is destined for the kingdom of God. He dealt also with two main charges brought against Calvinism, particularly in Scotland. (1) It encourages formalism, or ethical externalism, through its vigorous discipline. (2) It tends to Puritanism and is apt to be a kill-joy. These charges were partly well founded, but they overstressed the vices of the virtues of Calvinistic ethics.

RÉSUMÉ DU DISCOURS NO. 5 SUR LE PROGRAMME DU CONGRES

" LA FOI RÉFORMÉE ET SES CONSÉQUENCES MORALES DANS LA SOCIÉTÉ "

à savoir

" LE CALVINISME DANS LA SOCIÉTÉ "

Par Le Pasteur R. J. G. M'KNIGHT, Ph.D., D.D.

Le calvinisme est un système philosophique où la pensée est dirigée vers un but positif, système dominé par une conviction que comme conception métaphysique il a son origine en Dieu et fait partie de l'ordre moral de l'univers. Les calvinistes de pleine compréhension ont la conscience sereine, puisqu'ils sont assurés d'un plan divin fait pour eux et de l'accomplissement certain d'une intention divine. Le sommaire de leur philosophie c'est : " Cela est ainsi, mon Père, parce que tu l'as trouvé bon."

L'humanité est une république de travailleurs avec Dieu, quoique beaucoup d'entre eux soient mal disposés, même rebelles. Les hommes ne peuvent manquer à Dieu ni même l'incommoder. La colère même de l'homme contribue à la louange de Dieu qui " Dans les cieux s'en rira " (Ps. ii. 4). Le calvinisme c'est la capacité de se rendre compte que " le Seigneur règne."

Penser à et parler de la société c'est plonger dans la psychologie—non du genre du behaviourisme, car cela c'est toujours faire une pétition de principe. La psychologie réelle postule et voit l'individu chargé d'une responsabilité conforme à sa capacité. La société est le multiple de l'individu, et cependent plus que le seul sommaire. Chaque individu ajoute à et soustrait de la totalité ; l'individu doit être " vêtu de la société," comme le dit Emerson. La réflexion claire exige une classification des unités : l'individu étant l'unité personnelle ; la famille l'unité domestique ; l'état l'unité civique ; l'Église l'unité ecclésiastique. La tonique de la psychologie, voire même de la pensée, est l'individu. La révelation est pour et envers lui. Il n'y a guère une chose telle qu'un évangile social. L'évangile fut et reste un message de vie pour chaque homme. Le résultat se fait voir dans tous les rapports que l'homme possède dans la société.

Le calvinisme, comme l'intérpretation scientifique de la parole de Dieu, va à la racine de tout ; il vise un état de société idéalement parfait, dans lequel la volonté de Dieu sera faite comme au ciel. La vraie piété ne se trouve pas dans la solitude du cloître ni ne suffit pour soi-même seul. Dans la société parfaite " tous, depuis le plus petit d'entre eux jusqu'au plus grand, connaîtront le Seigneur : et la terre sera remplie de la connaissance de la gloire de Dieu."

La gloire de Dieu implique l'accomplissement de son intention éternelle par ou, " pour sa propre gloire, il a prédestiné tout ce qui arrive."

" Rendre le mond sauf pour la démocratie " est une expression qui devrait être intervertie. Le Calvinisme rend la " démocratie sauve pour le monde." Le Démos moralement inchrétien ne vaut pas mieux qu'un dictateur antichrétien. La grande masse des hommes doit servir Jésus-Christ, ensuite la société le servira.

La société, le multiple, le sommaire grossi de l'individu, est étonnamment grande, car les capacités individuelles sont étonnamment grandes. Le calvinisme rend compte de cette immensité lorsqu'il affirme que l'homme, individuellement, doit employer sa capacité dans l'hommage et le service de Jésus-Christ ; et néanmoins le calvinisme reconnaît la liberté individuelle, la glorieuse liberté de fils de Dieu.

Thursday, 7th July 1938

In the evening a public meeting was held in the Free Church Assembly Hall, presided over by Dr. Lamont who introduced the four speakers.

1. Rev. Professor G. D. HENDERSON, D.D., D.Litt.,
Aberdeen University

THE SCOTTISH REFORMATION

I am speaking to-night to an audience presumably already well acquainted with the history of the Reformation in this and other lands, and presumably sympathetic towards the theological and ecclesiastical and religious principles of the Reformers. I need only, therefore, in this short address attempt to underline or emphasise a few familiar and, I hope, generally accepted points.

The first is suggested to me by this Calvinistic Congress which is being attended by brethren from France, Switzerland, Holland, Germany, Hungary, United States and elsewhere; even that " auld enemy " England being well represented. And what I have in mind is what we here have in common, and what is the common inheritance of the Reformed everywhere. Our Scottish Reformation was no eccentric and isolated phenomenon. You and we all belong together. We are being reminded of it in our Conference. We should remember it much more and much oftener than we do. We are one family in Christ Jesus. Here in this country we are in some respects on the edge of the map. Movements more or less common to Europe reach us only by and by, after a time. When the stress and excitement and misunderstanding is largely over, we step in quietly and reap any benefits available. The struggle against Communism, for example, to all intents and purposes, if we compare facts here with facts in many continental countries, has scarcely affected us as yet. That does not mean that we shall never have to face it as it has had to be faced elsewhere. But our continental brethren bear the brunt of the conflicts, and often they have saved us, or at least spared us the worst. Sometimes, as in the case of the Reformation, they have fought the thing out and it was ready for us when we were ready for it. The Reformation was in an important sense and to an important degree one throughout Europe. Conventionally, we agree that it began with Luther's Theses at Wittenberg in 1517. It was longer

in coming to a head in Holland and Scotland than in some
other lands.   Its immediate causes were different in different
countries.   The circumstances of Calvin and Beza were not
those of Luther or Zwingli or Henry VIII or Knox.   But
as each of these suggested that a change was needed, his
particular part of the world responded, the reason being that
a change was indeed very much needed.   And almost anything was apparently sufficient to bring it about.   Henry
VIII's intrigues did not cause the Reformation in England,
and it could never have happened had it not been that
similar conditions prevailed in England to those which had
induced Reformation elsewhere.   It was one and the same
movement, though it had not in Scotland precisely the same
immediate causes as it had, say, in France.   After all, human
nature is deeper than national distinctions and is practically
the same everywhere.   It has the same fundamental needs
and it knows when these are being thwarted and are remaining
unsatisfied.   And Europe is not a large affair.   Just as plague
was not at all particular about national boundaries, so good
influences appeared in this country and in that at much the
same period for reasons not very dissimilar.   The conditions
were much the same.   Common to all lands were the same
ignorance and insufficiency of the clergy, the same clerical
oppression, the same papal worldliness and tyranny, the same
superstititons, the same corruptions and accretions, the same
general abuses.   The Scottish Reformation was a constituent
part of the one great movement which we call the Reformation.
It was in some respects unfortunate that the advance of
nationalism carried with it the separation of the national
Churches   one   from   another.   Vernacular   translations   of
Scripture, national confessional documents and much else
tended to allow the Reformed Churches to drift apart, and
to-day they are far too far apart, and have not sufficiently
the mutual support they need in face of great new hostile
world-forces.   The essential unity is worth stressing and such
a conference as ours should bring home to all our consciences
the claim of our brethren to our charity and prayers and
practical help.   The Scot and the Dutch and the Swiss and
the French and the Czech and the Hungarian, the English
Presbyterian, the American Presbyterian—they should know
one another better, remember that they are all alike the sons
of the Reformation, and so contribute as no expenditure on
armaments will ever do to real peace.

I mentioned that somewhat similar conditions prevailed
throughout Europe, or at least northern Europe, at the dawn
of the Reformation.   This leads me to my second point.   It

is a simple one. I want to remind you that the Scottish Reformation, like that in other countries, was a religious movement. This is not such a commonplace as it sounds. We know that similar economic and social changes, the same marvellous Renascence of learning, the same progress in printing, in trade, in exploring enterprise, even the same general weather and health conditions existed, and there is a tendency to-day to explain the Reformation and everything else entirely by such causes. Economic causes in particular are popular nowadays as complete explanations. There are people who can see every possible influence at work except that of religion.

The contributing causes in Scotland were as complicated as elsewhere. There was certainly a strong social, economic, political element, the relation with England, the French policy of Mary of Guise, the unhappy effects of frequent minors on the throne, the developing independence of the prosperous burghs, the poverty of the nobles relative to the wealth of the pre-Reformation Church. And in Scotland, as elsewhere, the Reformers naturally found upon their side all those who were only too eager for any excuse to attack the Church and the clergy. Such people were not interested in the improvement and upbuilding of the Church, in the resurrection and rediscovery of Christianity ; they only wanted to destroy. Admittedly there were many influences at work. But the main influence was that of religion. We must recall that Luther was brought up in a religious home. He had the root of the matter in him. There must have been many similar homes in Scotland, homes where the Spirit of true worship had never died out. There must have been many hungry hearts and thirsty souls waiting for the consolation of Israel. It was the eager response of such that made the Reformation, and made it so complete, in Scotland. Some people when they write of a Reformer like Knox find him everything but a religious leader. This mistake is easy to explain. The irreligious cannot understand the religious. We all judge other people by ourselves. We tend to attribute to them our own motives. Cardinal de Retz in his *Memoirs* quotes a contemporary as saying : " These wretches have represented both you and me such as they would have been themselves if they had been in our posts." And so it seems to many utterly unbelievable that anyone should in a real spirit of devotion, for the sheer Glory of God, sacrifice and slave and suffer. Yet, of course, so it was. John Knox was a religious man—not just a pulpit-thumper and a writer of tirades against the monstrous rule of women, but as he is described by his own servant : " a man of God, the light of Scotland, the comfort of the Church, the mirror of godliness and pattern and example to all true ministers in purity of life, soundness of doctrine, and boldness in reproving of wickedness." Not just the passionate orator, who could sweep the crowd off its feet ; not just the idealist of the First Book of Discipline; not just one who in his life never feared the face of man (as was declared over his grave) ; not just the devoted admirer of John Calvin, but also one who could turn to the seventeenth chapter of the Gospel of St. John in which he had first cast anchor as he said himself, and the fifty-third of Isaiah where he found Christ the Redeemer. Let us insist that first and foremost the Scottish Reformation was a religious movement.

And this points our attention to the place of the Bible in the Scottish Reformation. I have mentioned that Knox was a follower of Calvin and to that I shall presently return. But at the moment I would only ask : Why was Knox a follower of Calvin ? and I would answer the question by saying : Because he believed Calvin to be a follower of Christ. Knox went to the Bible for his inspiration, and it was because he found that Calvin had been there before him that to Knox Calvin was " that singular instrument of God." The Scottish Reformation was guided by the principle " that whatsoever God approved by His eternal word shall be approved and whatsoever He condemned shall be condemned, though all men on earth would hazard the justification of the same." The Scots Confession of 1560 has the famous sentence in its Preface : " If any man note in this our Confession any Article or sentence repugnant to God's Holy Word, that it would please him for his gentleness and for Christian charity's sake to admonish us of the same in writing and we upon our honours and fidelity by God's grace do promise unto him satisfaction from the mouth of God that is from his Holy Scriptures or else reformation of that which he shall prove to be amiss." And the first mark of the true Church for Knox was " the true preaching of the Word of God." The Scottish Reformation was meant to be a return to the Christianity of Christ and of the Bible, and the Bible has always had a special place in the life of the Scottish laity. Knox writes jubilantly of what happened in 1543 when permission was granted to read the Bible in the vernacular. " Then," he says, " might have been seen the Bible lying almost upon every gentleman's table. The New Testament was borne about in many men's hands." Burns's " Cottar's Saturday Night " shows us how real the Bible became to the people, and remained for the people, through the Reformation.

Closely dependent upon this characteristic was the conviction that the Scottish Reformation was a struggle against Antichrist. Knox was no schismatic. He would have accepted the famous utterance of that eminent Scottish divine, James Durham : " Never did men run to quench a fire in a city swifter than men ought to stir themselves to quench this in the church. Never did mariners use more speed to stop a leak in a ship lest all should be drowned than ministers especially and all Christian men should haste to stop this beginning of the breaking in of these waters of strife lest the whole church be overwhelmed." But the Reformation was not a case of some small difference of opinion within the Church. It was not a case of trying to improve this and that. It was a case of change of heart, change of spirit, change of direction. It was a case of rising up against a usurper upon the throne of the universe. Not only Knox and his contemporaries, but the stoutest Scottish Episcopalians of the seventeenth century, believed that Rome was the Antichrist of the Book of Revelation. There was therefore no excuse for compromise. It was a choice between Baal and Jehovah. This explains the thoroughness of the Scottish Reformation. In some respects it was more thorough and radical than reforms elsewhere. It went further than Geneva in certain points, as, for example, with regard to Ordination and with regard to the Festivals of the Christian Year. Its thoroughness is patent in the wording of the Negative Confession of 1581, which has been described by a Romanist as " the most violent condemnation of Papistry that ever issued from a Calvinistic pen." It was thorough. It trembled lest unwittingly by permitting the introduction of anything not strictly Scriptural, it might fall into Idolatry and be worshipping Antichrist. It had its difficulties. Political considerations weighed heavily with Regent Moray and Regent Morton and adequate financial support was at no time available. The establishment of the Reformation Church was slow. Ministers had to be educated to a Protestant standard, and that took time. Some parts of the First Book of Discipline long remained " a devout imagination." But Knox's spirit comes out when he says that one mass is more fearful to him than if 10,000 armed enemies were landed." Some of his own party thought him " too extreme." He had certainly no use for compromise. Perhaps there is need for something more of this assured and determined attitude to-day. Antichrist is always present in some form, and certainly to-day he is openly active. The anti-God movement is growing in power. The Church seems to be afflicted with that modern disease, an inferiority complex. But a half-hearted Church will never meet the situation. We need rather the attitude of Knox. " He that is not for me is against me."

I have alluded to John Knox's admiration for Calvin. This is the only other point I have time to discuss. The Scottish Reformation owes a very special debt to Calvin. In Scotland, as in France and elsewhere, early Reformation tendencies were indiscriminately labelled "Lutheranism." For a time, too, English influence was felt, and the Second Prayer Book of Edward VI was employed by Erskine of Dun and the other Lords of the Congregation. But by 1560, when the Reformation was finally achieved, the principles and practice of Calvin were the main guide alike in doctrine, worship and government. Knox described Geneva as "the most perfect school of Christ that ever was in the earth since the days of the Apostles." The genius of Calvinism seemed to match with the genius of Scotland. There was no one in the Scottish movement of the spiritual massiveness and intellectual clarity and administrative originality of Calvin. Knox was by nature not a pioneer but a disciple. At the same time, the Scottish Reformation was no slavish imitation. It was rather the enlightened application of Geneva principles to Scottish conditions. It ought to be remembered that Knox's wide career had brought him into intimate contact with the Churches of England, of John à Lasco, of Bullinger, of the Rhine, so that what he urged upon Scotland in the end was the result of deliberate comparison and selection. There was in Scotland some independent experimenting, as, for example, with super-intendents. Something about church courts was also learned from France, and ultimately, under the leadership of the bold and erudite Andrew Melville, Scotland developed what is to-day generally admitted to be the most adequate system of government by graded courts and the best example of unity of control combined with local freedom that Presbyterianism anywhere can show. There is no doubt something we could learn from the experience of our Calvinistic continental brethren, something of liturgical wisdom and discretion from Switzerland, of the possibilities of a Presbyterian episcopate from Hungary, and so on. And we must not forget that Scotland has shown herself capable of learning, always in accord-ance with the teaching of Scripture and the spirit of the Reformation. It outgrew its Scots Confession and its Book of Common Order. It was true to the spirit of Calvin, who reminds his followers that God has not prescribed every detail since times and occasions differ.

There can be no question as to the predominantly Calvinistic tone of the Scottish Reformation. The Scots Confession has clear echoes of the Institutes, and Calvin's Catechism was for long the recognised means of general religious instruction and was printed along with Knox's Book of Common Order. Scottish worship was based on Geneva methods, regarding simplicity and genuineness as practically identical, and believing ceremony to belong to the childhood of the Faith and to be absurd now that Christ had been revealed. And as to Discipline, Scotland soon became distinguished for its educated ministry and for its pious and God-fearing and Bible-reading elders sharing the spiritual supervision of the parishes, and setting a high ethical standard and claiming the co-operation of the civil magistrate in their godly rule.

I have mentioned genuineness. Calvin said : " To lift up our hands to heaven is nothing if our hearts remain below." And the Scots Reformers would have agreed. More than anything else, the Scottish Reformation satisfied the demand on the part of the Scottish people for reality, sincerity, genuineness. We shall be true to the spirit of our Reformers if we put aside what is merely of ourselves, and in simplicity and surrender accept the theocentric outlook, recognise the Sovereignty of God, and seek by His Grace to live and walk ever as in His presence, and make His Glory our chief end.

2. Rev. Professor LECERF, of the Faculty of Protestant Theology, Paris

I bring to you the greetings of the members of the Calvinist Society of France, of the Calvinist probationers and students of the Faculty of Paris, where I teach Reformed Dogmatics, and I can say I am speaking in the name of congregations and also of isolated believers who share your faith. I am very deeply thankful to God that I can do that. Some years ago to do so would have been quite impossible. I could have stood here and two or three of my friends also, but then we should have spoken each for his own person. Now I know I have behind me congregations and young ministers, and that is a miracle of God. When I look to the past, the very near past, in France I feel that according to all human expectations that was not to be hoped for. My professor of dogmatics, for instance, believed in a continual drifting of symbolical ideas which were meant to interpret some vague ideas. My professor of Old Testament believed that Abraham and the Patriarchs were simply legendary figures ; and it was the same in the other branches of Theology. Things were perhaps even worse in the so-called Evangelical Faculty of Montauban. The professor of dogmatics was an Arminian,

7

and he cherished hatred against Calvinism. There was one man, an historian, who became vitally interested in Calvin and became a Calvinist—Professor Emile Doumergue. But things were very bad. You had simply to stand in a Synod and remind people that your point of view was that of Calvin and everyone would vote against you.

And now by the Grace of God and by a kind of miracle I am in the Chair of Dogmatics in the Faculty of Paris.

The old liberal theories are dying out, though slowly, and their defenders are conscious of the fact. They fight, but they fight as soldiers who know their cause is lost. They seem to have lost hope.

I had a Graduation just before I came here, and out of seven candidates five took Calvinist subjects and the two others took Lutheran and Modernist subjects, but I know that they also were Calvinists. Seven Calvinists out of seven! I will not say that every student going out from our Faculty goes out as a Calvinist ; some do not, but many of them after some years of the ministry become Calvinists. The phenomenon is very strange. How can I explain it ? There is a mystery, the action of the Spirit who worketh when and how he wills. But the Spirit makes use of external causes and I think that among these causes Calvin himself is still a very active one. In your beautiful version of the New Testament I read these words applied to Abel : " He being dead, yet speaketh." And that is true of Calvin in France. Calvin wrote in Latin, and Latin is no more a vernacular language even among students ; but he wrote also in Old French, and every educated person in France can read Calvin, and I know of more than one who was brought from superstition or unbelief to the Evangel of the Reformation by the *Institutes*. There is a revival of literary interest in Calvin. He being dead, yet speaketh.

There are other causes. The great crises we are going through have brought disillusions—disillusions of the hopes of humanism. In philosophy great changes have taken place, and so it is that students coming to our Faculties are ready to understand the message of the Evangel of the Reformation.

And now what are the prospects ? I was discussing the subject a few days ago with one of my colleagues, a Modernist and a Lutheran but a very candid man. He said to me a prophetic word. He said : " Yes, they need a doctrine and a strong doctrine. I think that God has something in store for His Church and something very dreadful, and as God knows that His Church needs a backbone He brings her back to Calvinism because Calvinism is the backbone of Christianity."

The prospect is a dark one, not for the future of Calvinism, but for the future experiences of the Church. We need friends, and what we need of you is that when you say the Lord's Prayer and when you say " Thy Kingdom come," you will pray the beautiful answer of your Westminster Catechism. I used to know it off by heart but have forgotten the exact words. Read it again. Read the prayer for the Church in the explanation of the Lord's Prayer and when you read that and pray afterwards, then think of your Reformed brethren in France and of the future which perhaps hangs over them.

3. Miss M. P. RAMSAY, Edinburgh, Doc. de l'Univ., Paris

My paper is merely historical. I want to try to show very briefly the interest, other than theological, which Calvinism has for us and its claim on our respect, in so far as we are interested in and respect the ancient traditions of Scotland. It seems to me that the Scots were in the past a people who from earliest times were conscious of their nationhood ; a people who were animated by patriotism, loved liberty, upheld democracy, cherished religion—ideals which are all of them called in question to-day, even repudiated, in one quarter or another. I am not concerned to-night to defend, but simply to state, certain ideas which deeply influenced our evolution as a people. It may be, however, that those of us for whom Calvinism is, for personal reasons, the most satisfying interpretation of the Christian Revelation we have found, may welcome evidence that it has been the system of theology most closely associated with traditions we venerate for other reasons. By the use of quotation as much as possible I shall let you hear our forbears' own words, for I think I can best demonstrate in this way the characteristics I attribute to the Scots.

I must assume a general knowledge of the outlines of our history, only reminding you that it is impossible to draw the line between political and ecclesiastical affairs in dealing with Scotland, especially in the seventeenth century.

Again, with regard to Calvinism I assume that I need not spend time on definitions. We are all familiar with the democratic character and the parity established by the Church organisation we originally derived from Geneva ; and the Bible, accepted as the sole and sufficient guide and rule of conduct, emphasises in both Testaments the essential quality of men whatever their rank and wealth. But I would remind you that Calvin himself was deeply attached to his native land from which he was so long an exile for conscience' sake, and that Providence placed him in prolonged and close co-operation with the heroic little city-state of Geneva whose independence he confirmed and helped to maintain. He found the national conception and ideal asserted and sanctified in the Bible, especially in the Old Testament in the case of the Jewish people.

On the question of civil government the Calvinist position may be summed up briefly by saying that all government is by God's institution ; the power of the king (or magistrate) is limited on the one hand by God's decrees, and on the other by the rights of the subjects, rights which are also decreed by God, and, like the ruler's power and dignity, established and confirmed by Divine mandate

I think I may legitimately take the Declaration of Arbroath as representative of the ideals of our ancestors in pre-Reformation times. That Declaration was signed on the 6th of April 1320, in the fifteenth year of the reign of Robert the Bruce, and took the form of a letter to the Pope, from the " Barons, free-holders and whole community of the kingdom of Scotland." First we have a typical statement of the great antiquity of the Scottish nation, then a reference to the special Grace of God towards the Scottish people in that the first of Christ's apostles, though second or third in order of naming— Andrew, the brother of Peter—became the messenger of Christianity to Scotland and her patron saint. Then there follows a statement of the wrongs the Scots have endured by the efforts of Edward of England to enslave them and their country, and a description of their delivery and continued independence through the leadership of Robert the Bruce, their hereditary king. They then proceed to say :

" To him, as the deliverer of the people by preserving our liberties, we are bound to adhere, and to him we all will adhere. But if King Robert desist from what he has begun, and show any inclination to subject us, or our kingdom, to the kingdom of England or the English, we will use our utmost endeavour to expel him immediately as our enemy and the subverter of his own and our right ; and we will take another king who is able to defend us ; for so long as an hundred Scotsmen remain alive we will never be subjected any manner of way to the dominion of England. It is not for glory, riches and honours we fight, but only for liberty which no good man loseth but with his life.

" Wherefor, Reverend Father and Lord, we with the greatest earnestness and humility beseech you, that . . . considering that with Him whose Vicegerent you are in earth, there is no respect of persons, nor distinction of Jew and Greek, of Scot and English, . . . Your Holiness would be pleased to admonish the King of England (who should be content with what he possesses . . .), that he may not disturb our peace in this small country lying in the uttermost parts of the earth, and desiring nothing but what is our own, since we are willing in order to procure peace, to do most effectually whatever may be consistent with the Constitution of our Government.''

The translation from the original Latin which I have used is one which was published in 1705, in one of the many books and pamphlets which appeared at that time in the endeavour to prevent the Incorporating Union with England, then under discussion. I mention this to show how these heroic words of our ancestors were recalled in times of national danger.

Now although the patriotism of the Scots and their love of liberty were continually demonstrated in the field during the fourteenth and fifteenth centuries, and inspired a great poem, *The Brus*, by Archdeacon Barbour, and a popular epic, Blind Harry's *Wallace*, we have to wait till the Reformation for a revaluation and restatement of the ideals of the Declaration of Arbroath. At the Reformation, the Calvinist theology, and the ecclesiastical and civil conceptions associated with it, were adopted by the mass of the Scottish people. From that time, at least till the age of scientific discoveries and the Industrial Revolution, we are justified in regarding the influence of Calvinism as of decisive importance in the evolution of Scottish history and ideology. And the old ideals, the patriotism, the love of liberty, democracy, and religion, not only survive but become more clearly defined, and more philosophically and more frequently stated, amongst the staunchest Calvinists.

I begin with John Knox. With regard to his patriotism, it is rather the fashion to-day to represent him as not only establishing peaceful contact with the auld enemy England, but as having been a menace to our independence. He himself was at pains to refute any such accusation. In 1559 the Treaty of Berwick was signed between the Reformed party in Scotland and the English, its object being the expulsion from Scotland of the French army which the Queen Regent had brought over ; and the Treaty safeguards at every turn, and most specifically, the integrity and independence of Scotland. Knox in his *History* inserts the agreement to show that this is the case.

" We have faithfully and truly inserted in this our History the said Contract . . . that the memory thereof may abide

to our posterity, to the end that they may judge with in-
differency whether that we have done any thing prejudicial
to our Commonwealth, or yet contrarious unto the dutiful
obedience which true subjects owe to their superiors ; whose
authority ought to defend and maintain the Liberty and
Freedom of the realms committed to their charge, and not to
oppress and betray the same to strangers."

Of Knox's democratic ideas we can judge by the impression
his work made on the Archbishop of Canterbury, Queen
Elizabeth's dear Dr. Parker. The Archbishop was moved to
a very significant and indeed truly English expression of
shocked and scandalised alarm on 6th November 1559. " God
keep us from such visitation as Knox hath attempted in
Scotland ; the people to be orderers of things ! "

Calvinism was not to the taste of Queen Elizabeth ; and
when James VI inherited the English throne from her in
1603, he found Episcopacy much more favourable to absolute
monarchy than Presbyterianism was, and he set about harassing
his Presbyterian Scottish subjects with a view to imposing a
less democratic form of Church government on Scotland. The
divine right of kings as he now saw it did not entail the divine
rights of the people as it did in Calvinistic Scotland. His
Calvinist tutor, George Buchanan, had during the childhood
of James published a Latin dialogue on the Scottish monarchy
to impress on his pupil's mind his obligations as King of Scots.
From it I quote one passage : " The Scottish nation, being
from the beginning always free, hath created kings upon these
conditions, that the government entrusted to them by the
people's suffrages might be also (if the matter required) removed
by the same suffrages."

I have quoted this passage as it was used about the end of
the seventeenth century by the Rev. Alexander Shields in his
defence of the United Societies, or Cameronians as they came
to be called, published under the title *A Hind Let Loose*.

By 1638 the royal claims to absolute power, and also to
the headship of the Kirk, had resulted in a national protest
and the renewal of the Covenant. In 1638 the National
Covenant was promulgated, and accepted by the mass of the
Scottish people. From it I quote only a sentence which bears
specially on the question of the royal prerogative ; the Covenanters declared themselves the loyal supporters of the true
Scottish monarchy.

" In like manner with the same heart we declare before
God and men . . . that we shall to the uttermost of our power,
with our means and lives, stand to the defence of our dread
sovereign the king's majesty, his person and authority, in the

defence and preservation of the foresaid true religion, liberties, and laws of the kingdom."

A few years later, in 1644, the Rev. Samuel Rutherford published a philosophical and judicial statement of the case, entitled *Lex Rex*. In the Preface we read : " All civil power is immediately from God in its root, in that God hath made man a social creature. . . . Kings are elected and made by the people, though the office in the abstract be immediately of God. . . ."

And further : " Pastors are to maintain the rights of the people and the true church, no less than the rights of kings."

From the text itself I quote these phrases :

" Every man is by nature a freeman born " ; and " A free people may not . . . surrender their liberty to a Prince . . . because liberty is a condition of nature, that all men are born with " (Q. XIII. and XIV.).

This book, *Lex Rex*, I need hardly say, was condemned, prohibited and burnt by the hangman at the Restoration of Charles II in 1660, and its author expelled from his parish and otherwise persecuted.

In 1651 we find a very effective statement of the Calvinist position in a sermon preached by the Rev. Robert Douglas before Charles II at his coronation, at Scone, as King of Scots. The text Douglas takes is from 2 Kings xi. 17 : " And Jehoiada made a covenant between the Lord and the king and the people, that they should be the Lord's people ; between the king also and the people."

" Our king is not only to be crowned, but to renew a covenant with God, and his people ; and to make a covenant with the people. . . . As the people are bound to maintain the king's person and authority, in the maintenance of the true religion, and liberties of the kingdom, so the king is bound with them, to maintain the rights and privileges of the parliament and the liberties of the subjects. . . . The King's power is not absolute . . . there is a power above his, even God's power, whom he is obliged to obey. Kings have not only their crowns from God, but they must reign according to his will. . . . In regard of laws, a king is sworn at his coronation to rule according to the standing received laws of the kingdom. . . . The total government is not upon the king ; he hath counsellors as a parliament or estates of the land, who share the burden of government. . . . It is good for our king to learn to be wise in time, and to know that he receiveth this day a power to govern, but a power limited by contract ; and these conditions he is bound by oath to stand to. Kings are deceived who think that the people are ordained

for the king, and not the king for the people ; the Scripture
sheweth the contrary. The king is the minister of God for the
people's good. . . . A king using his power to the overthrow
of religion, laws, and liberties, which are the fundamentals of
this contract and covenant, may be controlled and opposed."

Now against these statements of the constitutional nature
of Scottish kingship, to use a modern term, I have time to
set only one typical statement of the other or anti-Calvinist
point of view.   I take a passage from an Appendix to Archbishop Spottiswood's *History of the Church and State of Scotland* ; the Appendix was added in 1677, a considerable time
after Spottiswood's death, and it is much more extreme in
tone than the work itself.   You will see that all that remains
of the ideals of the Declaration of Arbroath is the old pride
in the antiquity of the Scots.

" The kingdom of Scotland hath been governed by kings
in as long a succession as any nation in the world. The king
is an absolute and unaccountable monarch, and (as the law
calls him) a Free Prince of a sovereign power ; having as great
liberties and prerogatives by the law of this realm . . . as
any other king, prince, or potentate whatsoever. . . . All
jurisdiction stands and consists in the king's person, by reason
of his royal authority and crown, and is competent to no
subject, but flows and proceeds from the king having supreme
jurisdiction, and is given and committed by him to such
subjects as he pleases."

To this is added : " The supremacy in ecclesiastical affairs
was always in the crown since the Reformation."

Among the many notable and noble passages I would like
to quote from the speeches and writings of the Cameronians,
did time permit, there is just one phrase I feel I must give you,
as it shows how closely the words of the Declaration of Arbroath
were echoed by the stricter Calvinists, who laid down their
lives for the faith, and in defence of the liberties of Kirk and
state, in the later seventeenth century, the period known as
" the Killing Time."

The Rev. Donald Cargill, who in 1680 excommunicated
King Charles II, James Duke of York, and the chief officers
of State, and who was executed in 1681, uses the following
words in a document known as the Queensferry Paper :
" Liberty and freedom being a benefit next to life, if not in
some regard above it."

With the Revolution of 1688 and the coronation of William
and Mary, the vexed question of constitutional safeguards
against monarchical tyranny may, roughly speaking, be said
to be settled.   The Calvinist had still ideals to defend.

I can only touch very briefly on the question of the Incorporating Union with England in 1707 ; not only the Cameronians, but also practically all the more zealous of the clergy, as well as the mass of the people, were opposed to the Incorporating Union. It is a mistake to suggest, as is sometimes done, that only the Jacobites were against it. When I remind you that one of the most distinguished of eighteenth-century lawyers, Blackstone, was able later to assert that " Ecclesiastical supremacy is an inherent right of the *British* [1] crown," you will readily understand that not only patriotism, but also religious feeling, was in revolt amongst Presbyterians. From the numerous protests which appeared, I quote a sentence which sums up fairly well both the patriotic and the religious emotion aroused throughout the country :

" The Great Judge and Lawgiver of the world pronounced a curse upon those who removed ancient landmarks ; and if he passed such an heavy sentence upon them, who would by that means invade a private man's property, what must be the fate of such as not only remove but likewise destroy the Boundaries of a Nation's liberty ? " (*Ridpath*).

It was now the business of the Calvinist to bear witness against class distinctions, and to maintain the rights of the people, within the Kirk, against the petty, but dangerous tyranny of Patronage, and the various restrictions imposed on Presbyterian liberty and democracy, as a result of the Incorporating Union with England. Here I quote part of a speech of the Rev. Ebenezer Erskine in the General Assembly, 16th May 1732, the year, that is, before his Secession from the Establishment and the formation of the Associate Presbytery :

" . . . We are charged with the custody and feeding of His lambs, His sheep, His little ones. It is not the world's great ones, or rich ones, that we are intrusted with. No, Moderator ; and yet, by this Act, the privilege of His little ones is conferred upon heritors, and the great ones of the world. I am so far from thinking the Act conferring the power upon heritors beyond other men, to come and choose ministers of the Gospel, to be founded on the Word, that I consider it diametrically contrary to it. What difference does a piece of land make between man and man in the affairs of Christ's kingdom which is not of this world? Are we not commanded to do nothing by partiality ? whereas here is the most manifest partiality in the world. We must have ' the faith of our Lord Jesus Christ,' or the privileges of His Church, ' without respect of persons ' ; whereas by this act we show

[1] *Not English* merely.

respect to this man with the gold ring and gay clothing beyond the man with the vile raiment and poor attire. I conceive, Moderator, that our public managements and acts should run in the channel with God's way, not diverging. We are told that ' God hath chosen the poor of this world rich in faith.' It is not said He hath chosen the heritors of this world, as we have done, but " He hath chosen the poor of this world rich in faith, and heirs of the kingdom." And if they be heirs of the kingdom, I wish to know by what warrant they are stripped of the privileges of the kingdom.

"Moderator, I consider that by this act the Assembly have sunk one of the principal branches of our Reformation inserted in our Books of Discipline ; I mean the right of the Church and members thereof to choose their own pastors—a privilege with the custody of which we are intrusted. Our worthy forefathers handed down this among other branches of the Reformation at the expense of their blood and treasure. And that I may not be accessory to the betraying of a trust which we are obliged to hand down in safety to our posterity and the generation following, I insist that my Dissent may be marked in the Records of this Assembly."

Some fifty to sixty years later the dearest of our poets gave these ideas a universal application, but it was from faithful Calvinists like Erskine that Robert Burns inherited his message. From the passages I have had time to quote, you will see that Calvinism fostered Scots who were still animated by patriotism, loved liberty, upheld democracy, cherished religion. Their cruder civilisation (though not more brutal than the civilisation which to-day is bombing the cities of Spain and China), their frequent intolerance (though not so savage as the inhuman prejudice which to-day has outlawed the noble Jewish race), their often ruder way of interpreting things, could not deform or diminish the essential quality of these ideals.

In conclusion, I want to quote one more passage, from the Acts of the Associate Presbytery in 1742 :

" When the Lord was pleased to bring about the Reformation of this land from Popish darkness, it was by the means of preaching the Gospel-Doctrine of Free Grace, and Justification through the imputed righteousness of the Lord Jesus Christ. This was the foundation and groundwork of the other steps of Reformation, in the Worship, Discipline, and Government of the House of God : the Lord's servants, being animated by Faith's view of Gospel-Grace, were bold and valiant in setting up and defending all the parts of Reformation according to the pattern shown in the Word of God :

And thus a Nation was born at once, and a people brought forth in one day."

4. Rev. DAVID READ, B.D., Coldstream, Scotland

THE REFORMED FAITH AND THE YOUNGER GENERATION

My subject to-night is " Calvinism and the Younger Generation." I can almost hear the exclamation which the juxtaposition of these two phrases must cause. " Is it not your generation that has abandoned the Reformed Faith in your theology ? Is it not your generation that condemns the harshness and rigidity of your Calvinistic fathers ? Is it not your generation that has satirised our tradition so mercilessly in the modern novel ? " To which the answer simply is : No ; not my generation but the one before. It is surprising how many people are a lap behind in their theological thinking. I belong to a generation that has suspended the harsh judgment of its predecessor on our national spiritual heritage ; and to the section of that generation for whom the term " Calvinist " is no longer an opprobrious epithet but a stimulating challenge.

There are, of course, a great number of my contemporaries who are opposed to this movement in which we are taking part. With some the opposition is founded on a sincere conviction that we are heading in the wrong direction ; with others it is founded on what the Roman Church so charmingly calls " Invincible Ignorance." To the latter the most effective answer is always the question : " Tell me, have you read Calvin's *Institutes* ? "

My subject confines me to the realms of theology. I would not have it otherwise. The popular cry, " Not theology but · life," seems to me to be about as sensible as a slogan for the Church as it would be for the National Fitness Campaign to have " Not nourishment but health." It is in the sphere of theology that the Church hammers out the ultimate problems ; hence it is of vital importance to know what way the winds of doctrine are carrying the younger generation in whose hands is the Church of the future.

I don't think it would be an exaggeration to say that during the last six or seven years there has been a distinct change in the direction of theological thought among my contemporaries. It has been a change that has been cheerfully welcomed by some as at least a sign of grace in an unruly generation ; and as loudly deplored by others as a most distressing lapse into orthodoxy. The change has been most notable on the Continent. As it was there that liberal theological thought took its extremest forms, so it is there that the pendulum has swung most violently over. It was while spending a year in France in the Protestant theological faculties that I noticed the strange phenomenon that in every centre the students were very much nearer the historic reformed faith than their professors. But I must hasten to add that there were notable exception among the professors ! I was not many hours in Paris before it was whispered in my ear that I must on no account miss hearing the lectures of Monsieur Lecerf. But while the movement has been most noticeable in France, Switzerland, Germany, Hungary, and Holland, it has been simultaneously happening in Scotland and, to some extent, also in England. Let us have a look at one or two of the strands that go to make up the texture of what is, in actual fact, a coat of many colours.

There are in the first place the young that have been brought up in the sections of the Church which have adhered most rigidly to the Calvinistic tradition. For them I am not qualified to speak, as that was not my own environment ; but it is they who now find themselves in possession of a theological outlook more fitted to provide an answer to the pressing problems of the age than perhaps they had ever imagined. In the second place, there has been a distinct revival of interest in Reformed theology among those whose upbringing was not specifically in that tradition.

During the years I was at College there was a distinct swing of interest towards the dogmatic issues of the Reformed Faith. We discussed the Atonement, the Sacraments, the Fall, Total Depravity, Sovereignty, with an ever-increasing attention to the works of the Reformers themselves. There was a distinct feeling that the works of Calvin and Luther grappled with the problems of to-day more decisively than the theologians of more recent years.

In the third place, there has been the immense stimulus to our generation provided by the dynamic theology of the Word. I hope I may be allowed to mention the name of Karl Barth without being irrevocably labelled a Barthian. He, and, in this country perhaps to an even greater degree, Emil Brunner, has been a mighty formative—or rather reformative—influence on the theology of the new age. For one that will be found to agree whole-heartedly with all the positions taken up by this theology there are a thousand who have been orientated towards the historic Reformed Faith. Time and again I have been asked to explain the peculiar hold that this movement in theology takes upon so many of our generation. Sometimes one feels that there is positive antagonism in the older generation ; but I would hardly go so far as a Canadian friend of mine who once said to me : " Never discuss Karl Barth with any one over thirty-five ; it's a waste of time ! "

In the fourth place, we have to count among the influences making for a revival of the Reformed Faith the movements of modern evangelism. Since the beginning of this century there has been an astonishing increase of movements directed to winning the young to an allegiance to Jesus Christ. The effects of this is now being seen in the theological halls of the country. An increasing number of men have found that their Christian experience could only be adequately interpreted in a dogmatic framework which was nearer to the Reformed Faith than that which was popular at the time. I am not expressing an opinion at the moment as to whether they were right in this judgment or in the way in which they sometimes have reacted to other ways of thought. I am simply stating the bald fact that there has been what might be termed a conservative reaction in theology which is a reflection of the movements of aggressive evangelism of our era.

I have tried briefly to describe the different constituents of the movement that I have in mind. There is no great flowing tide, as the movement might almost be called on the Continent. But the trend is there and is unmistakable. And it is so unmistakable that it has already called forth several kinds of explanation and comment, some welcoming ; some distinctly chilly.

The usual explanation is in terms of what is called Reaction. There are many who hold a cyclic view of theological thought. According to them we are inclining to the Calvinistic interpretation of the faith for the same reason as our fathers inclined away from it—namely, that youth believes that its immediate predecessors were inevitably wrong. That there is a natural tendency for the swing of the pendulum can be readily admitted. We are all liable to excess in the extent of our abhorrence of that which appears to us wrong. But this cyclic view of theology is surely only applicable to the territory which is on the fringe of the Christian faith. Is it not intolerable to imagine that in the sphere of the deep and vital questions on which the destiny of the human soul depends we should be at the mercy of the mere ebb and flow on the surface of men's minds ? When we are dealing with these questions it is truth that matters above all else. And the answer that is given is either true or false. There is surely in Christian theology as in all other sciences a right direction and a wrong direction. And if that is so then those of us who are convinced that the Reformed faith in its general outlines represents the right direction can never rest content with an explanation of our belief which is couched in the purely relative terms of movement and reaction.

There is another explanation of this movement which goes somewhat deeper. It is that which sees in it merely another aspect of the blind groping of modern youth after authority. According to them we are joining in the flight from reason, the flight from relativity, the flight from the pressure of modern upsurging ideas and disquieting problems. The air is full of storms and thunder ; high explosive bombs of dangerous doctrine ; poison gases that threaten the very life of the soul. The movement towards Calvinism then is lined up with the movement towards Rome, the movement towards totalitarianism of any kind, and is condemned as a funk-hole—a kind of spiritual A.R.P. (Air Raid Precautions).

How are we to meet this charge of mere authoritarianism ? In the first place, I think, by frankly admitting that we have sought and do seek an authority in the spiritual realm. We do not believe that the human spirit is by itself capable of finding an answer to the most poignant queries of the soul ; far less of battering its way into the very presence of God. We are dissatisfied with the fruits of the theology which claimed to break loose altogether from authority. We are tired of misty subjectivism. What was once the brilliant sun of liberal theology seems to many of us to be setting in a dull glow of sentiment and irrelevance. Yes, we seek an authority ; but not as a bit of sand into which to stick our heads ostrich-like. There may be some who fly to the new orthodoxy where the weary cease from thinking and the lazy are at rest. But they have come to the wrong port in the storm. For those who have been battered and tossed this way and that by the gusts and storms of modern thought there is always the possibility of hauling down all flags and sailing in surrender into the all-embracing Roman harbour. But for us the Reformed faith can never be a resting-place. A Calvinist, as I see him, is not one who gives a calm acquiescence to every jot and tittle of the master-mind ; but one who believes he has perceived the main current of Christian faith and doctrine and brings to it his own mind and his own soul in a cool determination to seek with all the Church Catholic " the measure of the stature of the fulness of Christ."

What then is the real explanation of the hold that this movement is taking upon the younger generation ? I have only time left to summarise very briefly. It appeals in the first place, because it takes the word " God " seriously.   We are tired of what are called " ideas of God."   We want to hear of God Himself.   Faced with the helpless confusion of modern life, national and international, we want to hear of a God who pursues His own purposes steadily through history and whose Sovereign will of love must inevitably triumph.   And in the second place, it takes Man seriously.   The stern reality of events which are taking place before our very eyes drives out of court all shallow optimistic views of man's nature and relation to this world.   We want a theology that is not afraid to look right into the pit of human sin and tell us the truth. And we want a theology that speaks with no uncertain voice of a Redemption.   And finally, it appeals because it takes Revelation seriously.   Here is no evading of the ultimate issue between God and man ; here is no evaporating of saving revelation in a vague religious syncretism.   The historic Reformed Faith takes these seriously because it is not afraid of doctrine.   This is what my generation sees in the Reformed Faith.   We are not harking back to an imagined Paradise of the past, we look forward ; we have seen a glimmer of Christian realism, and we mean to follow it.

Friday, 8th July 1938

The Congress again assembled at 9.30 in the Martin Hall. Professor Maclean presided and opened the meeting with prayer.   Thereafter Rev. T. Christie Innes, Church of Scotland, gave a devotional address on Isaiah lv. 4 as follows (abbreviated) :

OUR " LEADER " JESUS CHRIST

" I have given Him for a . . . Leader."—Isa. lv. 4.

THE world is ringing to-day with the word Leader.   In no age, surely, have human leaders had such passionate devotion as to-day.   All human beings seem to need some object of devotion, worthy of unlimited sacrifices ; and most complete and amazing sacrifices are being made for objects or ideals or leaders.   For instance, in Germany there is an oath which is worth pondering.   " I swear by God this solemn oath " says every member of the military forces upon enrolment, " that I will render unconditional obedience to the Leader of the German Reich and people, Adolf Hitler, the Commander-in-Chief of the armed forces, and that I will, as a valiant soldier, at all times be ready to stake my life for this oath." It is absolute and final devotion—to a human leader !

It is therefore interesting to turn to the New Testament and find that the word Leader is used four times in describing our Saviour Jesus Christ. The Greek word *Archēgos*, which is translated by a different English word in each case, appears in four verses, and taken together we get an accumulating treasure of truth about our Leader Jesus Christ. Long ago God promised " I have given Him for a Witness to the people, a Leader and a Commander to the people," and when Pentecost arrived Peter stands up to explain to the people in Solomon's Porch that the miracle which had just drawn them together was not performed by mere human power but through the Lord Jesus. And in typical apostolic style he goes to the heart of things in a few words. " The God of Abraham, and of Isaac, and of Jacob, the God of our Fathers, hath glorified His Son Jesus ; Whom ye delivered up, and denied Him in the presence of Pilate, when he was determined to let Him go." But when you did that, Peter goes on, " Ye denied the Holy One and the Just, and desired a murderer to be granted unto you ; and killed the *Author of Life*, Whom God hath raised from the dead ; whereof we are witnesses " (Acts iii. 13–15). So Peter called Christ the " Son," the " Holy One," the " Just " and the " AUTHOR OF LIFE." His claim could not be more radical and absolute.

Second. Soon after Peter had preached in the Temple, and called Christ the Author of Life, he found himself imprisoned for his witness. But the angel of the Lord released him and said, " Go, stand and speak in the Temple to the people all the words of this Life " (Acts v. 20). And when he was taken before the high priest and asked why he had disobeyed the command not to preach in this name, he replied, again in characteristic apostolic fashion, " We ought to obey God rather than men. The God of our fathers raised up Jesus, Whom ye slew and hanged on a tree. Him hath God exalted with His right hand to be a *Prince* and a Saviour " (Acts v. 31). And so we learn the Fundamental Law of the New Life. To many it seems that the Christian life is a complicated set of rules, to be found in a rather jumbled book, and hard to apply to daily living. But the Christian life is Jesus living in the heart, and all that the believer needs to remember is that Obedience covers all the requirements of God. It is the first and the last law of Christ. Not perfection or greatness or even success are asked, but simple and loving obedience to our Leader, our Prince, Jesus Christ.

Third. In the Letter written to proclaim the Finality of

Christ for the human soul, the Spirit of God teaches us that " it became Him, for Whom are all things, and by Whom are all things, in bringing many sons to glory, to make the *Captain* of their salvation perfect through sufferings " (Heb. ii. 10). What a Leader ! He is perfect, but who can fathom the mystery of the love that enabled Him to become perfect *through sufferings* ? The " suffering of death," here again we are reminded, led to His being " crowned with glory and honour " (Heb. ii. 9). The Path of the New Life, which we enter upon when we receive the gift of life from its sole Author, and which we remain in as we obey our Prince and Saviour, involves a long, hard and personal warfare and discipline. But in our sufferings we are not alone. Our Prince is also our Captain. The One Who is enthroned in Majesty is, as it were, also our Captain, with us on the field of battle. He does not say to us " Go ! " He says, " Follow Me, and lo, I am with you always, even to the end."

It was reported in *The Times* recently that the Nationalist authorities in Spain were looking towards future generations, and in a circular these words occur : " The child must learn that life is ' milicia,' meaning sacrifice, struggle, discipline, and austerity." If even the children are to be taught this solemn idea, and for purely human and local ends, how much more ought the Christian to learn it who follows the Lord of Glory, and who is engaged upon overcoming the powers of darkness ? Life is milicia ! " China," writes Madame Chiang Kai-Shek, " is bound to shed her worn-out gown of indifference and laziness—celestially characteristic though they once have been " (*The Spectator*, July 1938). And what a sudden and awful emergency is teaching a great nation, the Christian ought to know and practise from his age-old Scriptures, and from the moment of his own renewal by the Spirit of the Redeemer !

Fourth. After naming some of the representative men and women of faith, who by their faith became more than conquerors, the Secret of the New Life is eagerly given us in these words, " Wherefore, seeing we also are compassed about with so great a cloud of witnesses, . . . let us run with patience the race that is set before us, looking unto Jesus the *Author* and Perfecter of our faith ; Who for the joy that was set before Him endured the cross, despising the shame, and is set down at the right hand of the throne of God " (Heb. xii. 1–2). If you who have been made alive by Christ, and live in His obedience, and enjoy His sympathy day by day as you live for Him, if you would *endure* to the end, and in some ways it is endurance that matters most, learn this secret—you must focus upon Him. To focus is to exclude all other interests,

8

to look off unto, to look away from all other things. It is difficult. Temptations from every conceivable direction will allure us to a " wider view," to a more " liberal" attitude, but only as we Consecrate and Concentrate, as the great D. L. Moody counselled students he once addressed , can we win through. Our life to-day, with its thousand thrilling interests and exacting duties, makes dissipation all too easy, and looking to Jesus all too hard. But it never was more imperative. It is the priceless secret of final and enduring victory.

Paper No. 6

THE REFORMED FAITH AND ITS ETHICAL CONSEQUENCES

THE ETHICAL CONSEQUENCES IN THE STATE

By Professor RUTGERS, Amsterdam

As all other questions put before our Congress, the subject we are dealing with to-day is one of the greatest practical importance.

This practical importance appears in a clear light when we look back to the sixteenth century. At its first appearance as such the Reformed Faith was involved in a sharp conflict, precisely on the duty of the Christian towards the State, with currents which, if they had prevailed, would have proved fatal to the cause of the Reformation. This conflict, deeply rooted in fundamental convictions, dominated at the same time the entire practice of political life. The Anabaptism which formed the centre of the sects living in opposition against existing civil order can certainly not be held entirely responsible for the horrors perpetrated under millenarian inspiration by Thomas Münzer (1524) and Jan van Leyden (1534). But in various forms in sundry countries it rejected existing public institutions. The atrocities of Münster made Europe shudder. Not only did they lead to bloody persecutions of Anabaptists in many countries, but they were also a motive, or a pretext, for persecuting all those who turned away from the Pope and turned to God and His Word. In his famous Epistle to the French King Francis I., to whom he dedicated his "Institution", Calvin complains of the false calumnies by which the true religion is daily defamed in the King's eye. It is represented as crime and sedition ; it tends to ruin reigns and policies, to trouble peace, to abolish laws, to dissipate estates and properties, to subvert everything. The doctrinal exposition in the " Institution " is presented to the King as a defence of the true religion against these accusations. Thirty years later several of the Thirty-nine Articles are directed against the Anabaptists. " The Laws of the Realm may punish Christian men with death for heinous and grievous offences. It is lawful for Christian men at the commandment of the Magistrate to wear weapons and to serve in the wars." Again, " The Riches and Goods of Christians are not common as touching the right title and possession of the same, as certain Anabaptists do falsely boast " ; and so also in regard to a Christian man's oath.

The deeply rooted divergences concerning the authority of kings and magistrates and the appreciation of the existing civic order did not lead subsequently to outbursts as the early years of the Reformation witnessed. The Anabaptists and numerous kindred persuasions turned to a quiet existence, secluded in their communities from national life, objecting to accept public offices and to go into military service, refusing " blood taxes " for the payment of the executioner or for buying off military service, often persecuted and wandering from one country to another ; until they arrived at a compromise between their rigid principles and the obligations ensuing from their belonging to a national community. Once landed there, entering civil service, asserting their rights before tribunals, they had, in fact, abandoned their initial protest against temporal power.

The conflict between Anabaptism and the Reformed Faith, however, is by no means a bygone issue. Does it not sound like an echo of the Anabaptist doctrine of the sixteenth century when the fourth International Congress of Anti-militarist Ministers and Clergymen held in this city a year ago declares : the bearing of arms is from the standpoint of Christianity to be rejected as incompatible with the Gospel of Christ ? In fact, in the propaganda from that quarter, in the contentions of conscientious objectors against military service, the vestige of the Anabaptist doctrine can often be recognised.

It would certainly be unjust to put Brunner's monumental work on ethics on the same level with antimilitarist propaganda. It offers, however, features which recall the sixteenth-century controversies ; Brunner's standpoint shows an affinity to the attitude of Luther, who never came to the clear and scriptural doctrine expounded by Calvin on the relation between nature and grace. So when he writes : " There is nothing real in this world which is not in accordance with the will of

God ; but there is also nothing real in this world which is not in discordance with the will of God. He wills it, in so far it is His creation ; He wills it not, in so far the creational shape in it is perverted and corrupted by sin." And elsewhere : " Coercion in itself is opposed to love, is sinful." As a historical reality the State is the product of collective sin ; it is organised egoism. The State primarily is not a moral institution, but an irrational product of history. Playing the ethical schoolmaster with it is ineffective and can only ruin it. Every State maintains itself by means which in themselves are morally illicit. For the believer a conflict arises : he has to co-operate with a system which is not in harmony with the commandment of love, the only commandment which he can acknowledge as being supreme. In the other-ness of the necessary order as compared with the claims and duties of love, he sees his own evil, and the evil of mankind. Will not the true believer feel keenly the injustice, the brutality, the life-destroying hardness of all those orders at all times ; the believer who weighs them against the law of love ; love that gives to every man what he, just he, is in need of. The believer cannot refrain from co-operating with the existing orders, although they appear to him as a chastisement and a penitence. He does not reject the duties involved by his office as a parent, or a teacher, or a magistrate, or a citizen, but he knows that not faith but the rational nature of man created the orders—from a human point of view ; his co-operation, in conformity to the rational rules drawn from their purpose, is not what is specific for Christian life. Christian policy is an impossible thing. To live in the State as a Christian means before everything to hope for a new world beyond the term of history.

When Brunner at the same time qualifies the co-operation with existing orders as the first service of love which is de-manded from the believer, and states that even proceedings which seem in direct contradiction with every kind of love may be necessary for love's sake with regard to the nation as a whole—he thereby does not withdraw any other assertion but only shows the paradoxical character of his theology. He even goes so far as to admit that the statesman has to ask after the will of God, but this remains his private concern, and Brunner abstains from giving any answer to this question.

On more than one occasion Brunner marks his difference of opinion on these points from Calvin. In fact, the latter purposely refrains from laying stress upon the historical sinful origin of existing governments ; what he takes in view is the Divine institution of authority, the providential guidance of history by God, who put magistrates in their places. He certainly does not overlook the abuses of power, the evils with which politics abound ; but far from inferring from this the incongruity of politics with Christian life, he reminds magistrates and citizens of the Divine commandments for the political sphere of life. As always, the doctrine of Calvin is strictly scriptural.

.   .   .   .

As in the sixteenth century, the Reformed Faith to-day must take a firm stand on the solid rock of Holy Scripture, must unflinchingly assert the unlimited sovereignty of God, not shrinking from any consequence therefrom. The world to its full extent is created by God. The " world of sin " is a world in this world, not equivalent nor comparable with the world as God's creation. Sin does not create anything ; it entered into the world, which remains God's world, expression of His will, led by Him to the destination he assigned to it.

The world being God's creation, it is likewise maintained by Him. Through the innumerable manifestations of His common grace He checks sin, tempers its consequences. He promised the restoration of the world through Jesus Christ, and will completely realise it at the end of days. Meanwhile He makes possible the continuance of human life and its development, the unfolding of the faculties of mankind, the progress of civilisation, the course of history.

The common grace maintains the order of nature, the operation of its laws. The curse which sin brought on creation is held within bounds. It is common grace that since the deluge seed-time and harvest, cold and heat, summer and winter, day and night do not cease. Common grace maintains in man a certain natural knowledge of Divine law. Common grace brought into being magistrates and laws ; maintains science and art.

Common grace, however, has not its ultimate aim in itself. Not the provisional preservation of this world, but its total redemption, is the primary object of God's dealing with this fallen world. God sent forth His Son, when the fullness of time had come, i.e. when His providence had led the world to the condition in which He would realise His plan of salvation ; this condition included the apogee of the Roman empire. And likewise, in the dispensation of the fullness of times God will gather together in one all things in Christ. Then it will appear that the development of this world under the common grace has an eternal purpose : the glory and honour of the nations will be brought into the new Jerusalem.

In the meantime the world is the theatre of the struggle of the forces of evil against the Kingdom of Heaven. What, in this struggle, ought to be the attitude of the believer towards the things of this world ? Must he withdraw from them as far as possible, abandon them as belonging to the kingdom of the flesh ? That would be the opposite of what Scripture teaches us. Our Lord did not pray that those who were given to Him should be taken out of the world, but that they should be kept from the evil. God loved the world and sent His Son not to condemn the world but that the world through Him might be saved. He came, not that He might destroy the works of the Father, but the works of the devil. His disciples must not go out of the world, but abide in the same calling wherein they were called, be subject unto the higher powers, consider all things as theirs, hold every creature of God as good, and nothing to be refused, if it be received with thanksgiving, and to esteem godliness as profitable unto all things, having promise of the life that now is, and of that which is to come. The Gospel never fights nature as such, but fights sin down to its most secret hiding-places, always and everywhere.

The world does not belong to Satan, but to God, its Creator, Who placed man in it. The natural things do not receive their consecration—as Rome teaches—from a clergy, God's representative. Their consecration lies in the word of the Almighty by which they are created to be His property. Christian faith has to realise fully this consecration, which for the believer contains a vocation. Whether therefore ye eat or drink, or whatsoever ye do, do all to the glory of God. Calvinism always recognised the proper value of natural things, and gave it a clear and firm expression. We believe, says the Dutch confession of faith, that the Father through His word, that is through His Son, has created from nothing heaven and earth and all creatures . . . and that He maintains and rules them all even now according to His eternal providence and by His infinite power, to serve man in order that man may serve His God.

The calling of the Christian is in this world. God does not need him, but He uses men as His instruments. It is true that the best of them are unprofitable servants, slaves who bring more loss than profit : and nevertheless Scripture affirms again and again that man will be judged after his acts.

Man will be judged after his acts. Moral judgment certainly cannot abstract from the disposition, cannot limit its scope to external acts. But this may not lead to the conclusion that it is the disposition alone which enters into consideration. It is true that Paul teaches us the redeeming of the believer from the curse and from the bondage of the law. But his freedom is far remote from all arbitrariness ; it is a voluntary submission to the law of God. The end of the commandment is charity ; but not so that the commandment is abolished by love, but so that love is the fulfilling of the law. The law must not be seen as an abstract, natural moral law, but as the expression of the will of the living God. In the concrete decision of every moment the question is not whether any abstract norm is followed up, but always whether God and His living commandment are obeyed. Divine law is not abstract. Throughout the Holy Scripture, again and again, we see the preaching of the law, by the prophets, by Christ Himself, by the apostles, applied to the concrete data of life. But it is done in such a way that the unity, the continuity, of the law is clearly maintained. The commandments are not disparate, now pointing in one direction and then in another. Behind the concrete directives lie principles, which are valid for all time.

We get our knowledge of the Divine law not from the scriptural revelation only. There is an innate knowledge of the law ; an intuitive understanding of duty according to the nature of the relations in which man is placed. Man is created with this understanding ; his nature and faculties are fitting to the world, as the world is created to fit men. This natural knowledge is darkened in many respects by sin ; it is a grace of God that it did not totally disappear, and that men still " show the work of the law written in their hearts, their conscience also bearing witness, and their thoughts the meanwhile accusing or else excusing one another." This natural understanding of the law is defective, and does not acquaint man with God's commandments as such nor to their full extent. Insight as to their source and bearing can only be obtained by the light of the Holy Scripture, when the eyes are opened by the Holy Ghost. Only then we understand what it means that love is the fulfilling of the law.

So there are laws relating to the behaviour of the Christian in this world. Then it is necessary to realise their contents. So we have to form an idea of our moral obligations in relation to the State, and to obtain it we must first investigate the teachings of Holy Scripture on the subject. It is not enough to act according to the dictates of conscience ; our conscience is not the standard of our obligations, it gets its standard from elsewhere ; when this standard is false owing to deficient knowledge, conscience urges us in the wrong way. Conscientious objectors against military service are not to blame on account of their acting according to the dictates of their conscience ; what is wrong with them is their false conception of a Christian's duty, and of the relations in the political sphere.

We must not expect to find in Scripture an elaborate code of our obligations in relation to the State. That would be against the nature of scriptural teaching. What we find are general principles, the application of which varies according to the circumstances of given periods and nations.

The New Testament concerns itself primarily with the position not of the magistrate, but of the subject. The men, to whom Christ and the apostles addressed themselves as a rule, did not belong to government circles. Their admonitions on the duties of subjects, however, imply teachings on the nature of government and the duties of magistrates. The Old Testament speaks more explicitly on the latter subject ; but here it must be observed that much relates to the absolutely exceptional position of the people of Israel and its kings, and is not applicable to other nations.

When we survey the teachings of Scripture on the duties of magistrates and subjects, we find instruction on origin, purpose, nature and fundamental rule of State and law.

(1) The origin of State and law : Divine institution.

(2) Their purpose : preservation of mankind, development of its faculties.

(3) Their nature : magistrates are qualified by their power to exact, and, if necessary, to coerce.

(4) Their fundamental rule : justice.

1. The Divine origin and foundation of government is explicitly affirmed not only in the thirteenth chapter of the Epistle to the Romans, but in a number of other places in Scripture. The State does not belong to the creational order ; it came into existence after the fall. But it is not the sinfulness of man which produced the State ; its institution is an act of God's mercy, who by His inscrutable providence brings magistrates to power and who invests them with authority. As it is said in the Dutch confession of faith : We believe that our God on account of the depravity of mankind has ordained Kings, Princes and magistrates, wishing that the world be governed by laws and policies in order that the dissoluteness of men may be constrained, and that all things be done among them according to a good ordinance.

2. So this is the purpose of the Divine institution of government : a good ordinance : " that we may lead a quiet and

peaceful life, in all godliness and honesty," writes Paul to Timothy. The common grace of the Lord maintains such a condition of life for mankind that in spite of man's apostasy human life may continue, the dominion of man over the works of God's hands may subsist, science and arts may progress This grace is not limited to the elect, but extends over mankind as a whole. Our Father which is in heaven makes His sun to rise on the evil and on the good ; when Paul enlarges on the blessing of government it is the Roman Empire which he has in mind. The Lord bestows His common grace on mankind as a whole ; it is not conditioned by any act of obedience from man's side.

Its immediate blessings are of a temporal character. Common grace does not bring salvation, nor work conversion. The Kingdom of God does not come through the work of common grace. Neither is the State an instrument for executing the plan of salvation. This is done by spiritual means, not by the sword of magistrates.

What, then, is the value of common grace and of the State ? One thing is needful. The world passes away and the lust thereof. Peace and order and civilisation, things of this world, have they any real objective value ? The answer is that God placed us in this world, and wills that we attach value to the things of this life. To despise them is against the nature of man as he is created, an excess of spirituality which is not scriptural. God will be served by man in this life. Let every man abide in the calling wherein he was called.

3. The specific feature of Government and State is the power of the sword. In the word of God to Noah : " Whoso sheds man's blood, by man shall his blood be shed," we have the first proclamation of the institution of government. In a number of other places Scripture mentions the power of coercion of magistrates, and teaches that this power has been granted to them by God Himself. In view of this explicit mandate it cannot be sustained that coercion in itself is sinful. Force and the use of force is not condemnable, as long as force remains subservient to justice.

It is evident that here we touch upon a crucial point from the ethical point of view. By virtue of their office magistrates are entitled, and eventually obliged, to a number of acts which, as a rule, for a private citizen are flatly contrary to the commandment of love. Magistrates deprive men of their liberty, and, in the way of taxation or expropriation or forfeiture, of their goods ; they compel them to military service ; they inflict on them corporal and even capital punishment. Such is the duty of magistrates as ministers of God. This is the way in which the commandment of love operates for them. After all, its main object is not to please the neighbour. " Whom the Lord loves, He corrects," says Solomon, " even as a father the son in whom he delights." For magistrates, love means the maintenance of peace and order, the promotion of prosperity, the administration of justice, though it be not always easy to recognise the working of love in those acts, confused as this world is by sin. On the other hand, it is evident that not every measure rightly taken by magistrates can be said to be in harmony with the commandment of love ; even if a measure is inevitable or necessary, if it cannot be challenged by human justice, its moral appreciation depends on the spirit in which it is taken. " Good works are done in obedience to God's commandments and are fruit and evidence of a true and living faith ; works done by unregenerate men, although for the matter of them they may be things which God commands, and of good use both to themselves and to others, yet because they do not proceed from a heart purified by faith, nor are done in a right manner according to the Word, nor to a right end—the glory of God—they are therefore sinful and cannot please God."

4. The passage just quoted from the Westminster Confession deals with works which are sinful, " although for the matter of them they are things which God commands." External conformation to the law in itself never satisfies the ethical standard. This, however, does not mean that the law does not exist or is not binding. Now in the political sphere the law, the fundamental rule for all activity in the State both of magistrates and citizens, is justice. (I use the word not in its theological but in its juridical sense.)

This is not a truism, but it is of the highest importance to establish the fact emphatically. Throughout the ages this fundamental rule has been opposed by men who judged force, and force only to be the base of State and Government. So the old Sophists considered the right of the strongest as the only natural right ; according to them all other right and morality reposed on arbitrary regulations, established by those in power for their own benefit. Similar conceptions were put forward by Macchiavelli, Spinoza, Hobbes and many others in later times. In all countries and at all times politicians have been found, who have exalted utility or power above justice either in theory or in practice.

It would carry us too far to trace the historical development of the fatal concept of State expedience—what the French call *raison d'état*, or to sketch the contemporaneous

nationalist theories which look upon power as the constitutive element and ultimate aim of the State.   But we try
to answer the question : Is it true that State and law are
nothing but dictates of force, and therefore non-moral, some
say ; therefore sinful, says Brunner ?   Or are they determined
not by force but by an idea ?   From the very first another
conception of justice had been maintained against the theories
I just mentioned, a conception which asserts the ethical
character of the State.   In primitive society religion, ethics
and politics are not yet differentiated, and later on an intimate
connection subsists between them.   With the Greeks, politics
were a part of ethics.   In the various conceptions of the law
of nature the obligatory character of justice is maintained.
Now if this obligatory character is not to be a human imagination, a dream, an illusion, it must be rooted in an objective
reality.   The rule of justice, indeed, is based on the moral
order, which is part of the world order established by the
Creator of all things.   In the sovereign will of God justice finds
its firm foundation.

Justice and ethics are not identical.   The ethical judgment
can never abstract from the religious ground in which only true
morality can thrive.   Justice is the ideal to which all human
law and right and jurisdiction should respond.   Now the
administration of justice in a State shows a number of features
which put in evidence the difference between justice and ethics.
As a rule, human justice occupies itself with the external
behaviour ; it sets rules for the conduct of men, which deal
with another province than the commands of ethics, owing
to their objective and external character.   Besides, the scope
of human justice is necessarily restricted on account of the
limitations of the power of governments.   The magistrate
protects property and gives social legislation, but he cannot
assure good administration by every proprietor.   He prevents
manslaughter and assault, but not unkind treatment.   He
punishes bigamy and adultery, but not all sorts of immoral
conduct.   Moses because of the hardness of heart of the
Israelites suffered them to put away their wives.

The contents of the justice which at a given moment is
to be realised in a nation is in a large measure dependent
on the prevailing moral conceptions and usages.   How will a
Christian government enforce monogamy or Sabbath observance on Mohammedan or heathen populations under its
rule ?   So in many respects human justice widely differs
from the prescripts of ethics, even if it reaches the highest
standard which in given circumstances is attainable.   All the
same there is an intimate connection between them.   The

commandments of the second table of the decalogue form directives by which human justice has to orientate itself, in such a manner that it does not try to constrain men to good works in the ethical, religious sense, but aims at maintaining, to the limits of the possible, the civil justice which is necessary to keep up an orderly human society.

This human justice, by no means coinciding with the general prescripts of ethics, constitutes the fundamental rule in the political sphere ; magistrates and subjects have to conform to it. Now what can be said of its demands ?

The first principle, clearly expressed in Holy Scripture, is the respect due to authority. The duty of obedience towards the higher powers is not only pronounced, but motivated too. Paul argues from the utility of power : it is a minister of God to thee for good ; from the awe-inspiring coercion which it can exercise : if thou do that which is evil, be afraid. These arguments can be found out by natural reason ; in fact, they play a considerable part in the theories of a number of political philosophers. With Paul they are raised to a higher level by his primary argument : The powers that be are ordained of God ; whosoever therefore resists the power, resists the ordinance of God ; you must needs be subject, not only for wrath, but also for conscience' sake.

A number of other passages can be mentioned contributing towards giving a firm scriptural base to the authority of magistrates. This does not mean that Scripture might be invoked in support of the theory of the Divine right of kings propagated by Roman Catholic advocates of absolutism. The rights of the magistrate are not holier than the rights of the people. It is not true that Government is the supreme power with unlimited competence, and that no right exists that is not derived from that power. The State is a remedial scheme, instituted to temper the devastating consequences of the fall, in the first instance, by the administration of justice. Government while fulfilling its own task has to respect the rights of other domains of human life. But it would carry us too far to work this further out now.

One point, however, must be mentioned : the teaching of Holy Scripture concerning the limit of the duty of obedience. " We ought to obey God rather than men," said the apostles to the Jewish council. An unjust law should nevertheless be obeyed ; what human law responds perfectly to the ideal of justice ? But there is a limit : the duty of obedience ceases when to obey men is to disobey God. Here the axe is laid to the root of the theory of the Divine right of kings, which makes the prince an absolute ruler, vicar of God, whom the people have to obey unconditionally, to the root of the all-absorbing State absolutism in its manifold appearances.

We can no more than slightly touch upon some other principles of justice which can be derived from Holy Scripture.

International relations are based upon the mutual recognition by governments of their power and authority, each within its own domain. They all have to recognise justice, not force, as the supreme rule of the community of nations. They have to remember that peace, not war with its unspeakable horrors, is the relationship between nations which must be sought as corresponding to the will of God. The scriptural conception of man, created after God's image, corrupted by sin, is determinative for the government of men and the regulation of their relations ; it brought about the revolution of thought, by which slavery was swept away, and had its influence on social legislation. The Biblical conception of marriage, indissoluble and in monogamy, in the past determined the attitude of governments in their legislation, and will continue to determine it. The duties and rights of parents, again and again accentuated in Scripture, ought to be taken into account in the regulation of instruction and education. Sabbath observance should not be furthered on social motives only, but in view of rendering possible the sanctification of the Lord's day. Criminal law must maintain the fundamental idea of what Blackstone called the vicious will, the juridical reflex of moral guilt, and retribution as the ground for punishment.

So the Holy Scripture teaches us principles of justice. Justice has to dominate the entire political life. Every right, every competence, every office, every power contains a vocation ; no talent may be left unused, or be used at pleasure.

The power of government is not a spoil, but a sacred trust. The magistrate may neither surrender nor abuse it. The franchise is not a spoil, but a sacred trust, not to be used to promote one's own private interests, to protect one's own landed property, or privileges, or dole. Colonies—not a spoil, but a sacred trust. Military power—not a spoil, but a sacred trust. Every statesman, every elector, will have to render account of his stewardship.

There is one point more which I have to mention. How far can justice be realised in the policy of the State ? Magistrates are men, liable to error and to every sin. Human justice never reaches the ideal it ought to have in view. How far then is the service of the State compatible with the service of God ? It is not a sufficient answer to say : politics are a dirty business. What makes the business dirty (and what makes every human occupation, without any exception, dirty) is not the vocation but the sinful way in which the vocation is followed up,—or not followed up. Abstention from politics is not in itself holier ; it may be an act of desertion. The circumstances may be such that co-operation of a Christian man with the Government is manifestly excluded. Such will be the case under the reign of the beast which is spoken of in the Revelation of St. John, when no man will buy or sell save he that has the mark of the beast. History, past and present, shows periods of persecution of the Church by governments, with which it seems impossible for any Christian man to co-operate. On the other hand, the examples of Obadiah, the governor of Ahab's house, and of the prophet Daniel, prove that even under a Godless government a God-fearing man may keep governmental office and serve God with a free conscience.

Justice is the guiding principle of political ethics, but coincides by no means with their complete contents. The standard of justice cannot give the final ethical verdict. In so far as specific principles of justice do not vary the application of the general prescripts of ethics, these remain in force. Nor is it sufficient that the private life of the politician should not show blemishes such as led to the downfall of Mary Queen of Scots and of Parnell ; or that he reaches the highest common standard of truth, disinterestedness, honesty. Each of his acts is judged by the commandments of the Lord in the fullness of their spiritual meaning. Even if for the matter of them they are things which God commands—to use once more the words of the Westminster Confession—but are inspired by or tainted with hate, or envy, or illegitimate ambition, or lust of power, they are sinful and cannot please God.

Within the limits of the time allotted it was not possible to give more than a sketch in outline of the considerations and conclusions to which the study of our subject of to-day has brought me. Resuming, I hope you will all agree with me on these points :

For the believer light is thrown by Holy Scripture on the origin, nature, aim and rule of the State.

By this light, rules of conduct in the political sphere can be ascertained, and must be investigated.

The knowledge of these rules alone is of no use : error and sin threaten at every step ; external legality cannot redeem our acts in the eyes of Him with whom we have to do. Here, as everywhere, love is the fulfilling of the law.

RÉSUMÉ DU DISCOURS

DE M. RUTGERS

Sur les conséquences éthiques du Calvinisme dans le domaine de l'état

L'orateur commence par rappeler l'éminent intérêt pratique du sujet, qui s'est montré au seizième siècle. Le conflit entre la réforme calviniste et les sectes qui se groupaient autour de l'Anabaptisme concernait exactement ce point. Calvin dans son Épître au Roi se plaignait des fausses accusations dont la vraie doctrine était victime et qui avaient leur source dans les menées des Anabaptistes. La confession de Westminster rejette plusieurs de leurs doctrines. Si plus tard les Anabaptistes ont abandonné leur rejet de l'Etat, la controverse par là n'a pas perdu son intérêt. Dans la propagande antimilitariste d'aujourd'hui on voit parfois reprendre des arguments anabaptistes. D'autre part la position de Brunner offre des traits qui l'apparente à celle de Luther ; celui-ci n'est jamais arrivé à la doctrine claire sur la relation entre " nature " et " grâce " que Calvin a tirée de L'Écriture Sainte. Brunner voit l'Etat comme produit du péché. Il n'est pas une institution morale, mais un produit irrationel de l'histoire. Son caractère coercitif s'oppose au commandement d'aimer. Pour le fidèle l'Etat est un châtiment et une pénitence. Vivre dans l'Etat comme Chrétien veut dire avant tout—espérer un nouveau monde au-delà de l'histoire. Le caractère paradoxal de la théologie de Brunner lui permet d'admettre en même temps que l'homme d'état doit s'enquérir de la volonté de Dieu ; Brunner s'abstient de répondre à cette question. Du reste cela ne modifie pas son appréciation de l'état.

Brunner ne cache pas sa divergence des conceptions de Calvin, auxquelles l'orateur donne la préférence, parcequ'elles sont en accord avec l'Ecriture Sainte.

L'orateur donne un bref exposé de la doctrine de la grâce commune. Ce monde, qui a été créé par Dieu, et qui est conservé par lui, continue à lui appartenir et non à Satan. Dieu restreint l'action et les effets du péché et de la malédiction. La grâce commune rend possibles le progrès de la civilisation, le déploiement des facultés dont Dieu a doué l'homme. Elle se distingue du salut par Jésus-Christ ; mais en conservant ce monde elle a servi et elle sert à préparer l'exécution du plan divin de délivrance, jusqu'à la réalisation complète de celui-ci, et elle produit des fruits pour l'éternité.

Vis-à-vis de ce monde, créé et conservé par Dieu, le croyant a une vocation. Il ne doit pas s'y soustraire, l'abandonner. L'Écriture Sainte ne condamne pas la nature ; elle condamne le péché. Le croyant doit servir Dieu dans l'état, où Dieu l'a placé, suivant les commandements de Dieu. Il est libéré de la servitude et de la malédiction de la loi ; cela ne veut pas dire que la loi est abolie ; l'amour est l'accomplissement de la loi. L'homme possède une connaissance naturelle, intuitive, partielle des commandements de Dieu, mais il n'en saisit le sens profond qu'à la lumière de l'Écriture Sainte. Il importe d'étudier et de connaître ces commandements ; s'il y a erreur à leur sujet, la conscience elle-même pousse en fausse direction, comme dans le cas des objections de conscience contre tout service militaire.

L'Écriture Sainte ne contient pas un code de règles de conduite dans le domaine politique. Ce serait contre la nature de son enseignement. Elle contient des principes, dont l'application varie selon les circonstances.

L'Écriture Sainte nous instruit au sujet de l'origine, du but, de la nature, et de la règle fondamentale de l'Etat.

(1) L'origine de l'Etat. Il est institué par Dieu, à cause du péché ; il n'est pas produit du péché, mais don de la grâce divine.

(2) Le but de l'Etat. Il rend possible une vie paisible et tranquille, le progrès de la civilisation, la marche de l'histoire. Il n'y arrive par l'obéissance de l'homme à Dieu, mais malgré sa désobéissance. Quand S. Paul parle des bienfaits qui nous parviennent par l'état, il a en vue l'empire romain.

(3) La nature de l'état. Son trait caractéristique c'est le pouvoir, l'épée. L'Écriture nous enseigne à plusieurs reprises que ce pouvoir de coercition a été confié aux gouvernements par Dieu. On ne peut soutenir que la contrainte soit contraire à l'amour, qu'elle soit un péché. Les magistrats ont le droit, éventuellement le devoir, de porter atteinte aux biens, à la liberté, à la vie. Par là même ils remplissent le commandement d'aimer. L'appréciation éthique de leurs actes évidemment prend en compte d'autres facteurs encore que la justice de ces actes en soi ; elle s'occupe de l'esprit dont ils prennent naissance.

(4) La règle fondamentale de l'état, c'est la justice. En affirmant cela, on rejette le droit du plus fort, qui depuis l'antiquité a fait tant de mal dans la théorie et la pratique de l'état ; qui est accepté par Brunner

comme loi politique et en même temps flétri comme
contraire à l'amour. La justice est basée dans l'ordre
moral, qui fait part de l'ordre cosmique établi par le
Créateur. La justice-prise au sens juridique ou
politique, non pas au sens religieux—n'est pas
identique à la morale ; elle est la norme des actes
extérieurs. Elle s'oriente à la morale et dépend des
circonstances de lieu et de temps.

Le premier principe de justice sur lequel l'Écriture nous
instruit, est l'autorité des magistrats, et le devoir d'obéissance.
L'autorité vient de Dieu ; mais le magistrat n'est pas vicaire
de Dieu, pouvoir suprême de compétence illimitée, de qui tout
droit découlerait. Cette conception fut soutenue par les
partisans de l'absolutisme monarchique. Elle méconnaît le
but de l'État qui est de tempérer les effets dévastateurs du
péché, en premier lieu par l'administration de la justice. Il
y a même une limite à l'obéissance due aux magistrats : il
faut obéir à Dieu plutôt qu'aux hommes. C'est rejeter la déformation du droit divin des princes, rejeter l'absolutisme d'état
sous toutes ses formes.

L'orateur ne peut qu'indiquer d'autres principes de justice,
qui découlent de l'Écriture Sainte, pour les relations inter-
nationales, pour la conception de l'homme—créé après l'image
de Dieu, tombé dans le mal, conception qui exerça son influence
sur l'abolition de l'esclavage, sur la politique sociale—au sujet
du mariage, des droits et des devoirs des parents, du repos
dominical, de la culpabilité et de la rétribution en droit pénal.

La réalisation de la justice dans l'état est imparfaite. Les
magistrats sont des hommes sujets à l'erreur, au péché. Il
peut même arriver que l'état se tourne de propos délibéré
contre Dieu et ses commandements, et qu'il ne reste aucune
place dans l'état pour les fidèles. Le règne de la bête dont
parle l'Apocalypse en est un exemple. D'autre part Obadiah,
chef de la maison d'Achab et le prophète Daniel ont servi
Dieu dans des fonctions qu'ils tenaient d'un gouvernement
impie.

La justice est le principe spécifique de l'éthique politique.
En tant qu'elle ne varie pas l'application des principes éthiques
généraux, ceux-ci restent en force. Non seulement les actes
personnels, mais de même les actes professionels des magistrats
sont soumis à leurs règles.

Résumant :

(1) Pour les fidèles l'Écriture Sainte jette sa lumière sur
l'origine, le but, la nature, et la règle fondamentale
de l'état.

9

(2) A cette lumière ils peuvent trouver et doivent chercher des règles de conduite pour le domaine politique.

(3) La seule connaissance de ces règles ne sert à rien ; et une légalité extérieure ne peut justifier nos actes aux yeux de celui à qui nous devons rendre compte. L'amour est l'accomplissement de la loi.

In opening the discussion on Dr. Rutgers' paper, Rev. Dr. Hector Macpherson, Edinburgh, said :

Dr. Rutgers has tackled a very complex subject in his paper, and has dealt with it in an able and informative fashion.

With Dr. Rutgers' main conclusions, I find myself in general agreement. The Calvinistic theory of the State, in the twentieth century, as in the seventeenth, stands sharply opposed to all absolutist pretensions. The Calvinistic Churches in the sixteenth and seventeenth centuries led the opposition to the policies of absolutist princes, who, on the ruins of the old mediæval Europe, were engaged in making themselves absolute in both senses—out of control of any supra-national power on the one hand, and dominant over all groups, societies or individuals within the State, even in matters of conscience. As Alexander Shields put it in 1687, " The tyrants, alias kings of Europe, . . . are advancing their prerogatives upon the ruins of national and ecclesiastical privileges to a pitch of absoluteness." Such rulers, he said, would have their laws " reach men's thoughts as well as their actions."

These princes, such as Philip II. of Spain in the sixteenth century, Louis XIV. of France, the Stewart kings of Great Britain, as well as many little German and Italian princelings —were apt pupils of Machiavelli, claiming to be beyond the moral law in their policies, and at the same time maintaining that they were responsible solely to God and not to men. Anglican churchmen provided the doctrine of the Divine Rights of Kings, and thus made the principle of brute force appear more or less respectable.

While the Roman Church pursued a zig-zag policy with regard to the absolutist movement, guided then, as now, by motives of expediency—and while Lutheran and Anglican churchmen, on the whole, supported tyranny in Church and State, Calvinism refused to compromise with the evil thing. The Calvinistic Churches, by their heroic stand for the elementary rights of man, in France, in Holland, in England, and in Scotland, saved not only religious but civil liberty as well. Seventeenth century Calvinists went considerably farther than Calvin in their justification of the right of resistance to tyranny, and even of the right of subjects to rebel

against despotic rulers : but after all, they only developed
what was inherent in Calvin's own thought.

I am somewhat disappointed that Dr. Rutgers, in dealing
with the modern world, has not in his paper differentiated
between various forms of State organisation.   There are in
Europe at the present time three great nations whose form
of government is, in modern phrase, " totalitarian."   In one
of them—Italy—the tension between Church and State is
not so acute as in the other two.   For reasons of political
expediency, Mussolini has had to make terms with the head
of the Roman Church, and has had to watch his steps in regard
to matters religious.   Nevertheless, he claims, even as the
German and Russian dictators claim, that the State—which
means in practice, the rulers of the State—is absolute, and
that all other " rights " and " privileges " are relative.   It
is obvious that such claims outrage the very spirit of Calvinism.   Had German Protestantism been predominantly
Calvinistic instead of Lutheran, the Nazi Government might
have been much less secure at the moment, and might even
have collapsed long before now.   The modern Reformed Protestant attitude to the State must be largely determined by
the form of State organisation, and by the character and
policies of the State's rulers.   The Covenanters in their day
proceeded on these very principles, and were driven into
complete and implacable opposition to the Stewart régime
between 1660 and 1688.

Dr. Rutgers makes mention of the International Congress
of Anti-militarist Ministers (the Ministers' International Peace
Union), which met in Edinburgh a year ago, and he finds in
some of the pronouncements of that body an echo of the
Anabaptist doctrines of the sixteenth century.   Here Dr.
Rutgers touches a very vital issue, whether or not the State
—totalitarian or democratic—has the moral right to deprive
its subjects of a certain age of the right of choice as to whether
they will even lay down their lives or take the lives of others,
in pursuance of policies of which their consciences as Christians
may strongly disapprove.   The issue is an extraordinarily
complex one, bound up as it is with the question of national
defence.   But it is evident that if the Christian is compelled
by a totalitarian government to take part in an unjust war,
which by its very nature violates every Christian principle—
and must not war nowadays do this of necessity, as witness
the massacres in China and in Spain—it is his Christian duty
to refuse, even if his refusal should spell martyrdom.

The modern Anti-militarist Movement is by no means a
mere echo of Anabaptism.   It has come into existence because

of the obvious fact that modern warfare — with its aerial bombardment of defenceless civilians—cannot be reconciled with the Christian gospel, and because, as one of Dr. Rutger's own countrymen, Professor Aertnys, says, military conscription in time of peace is " the slavery of our age, which boasts loudly of its freedom."

As a matter of fact, the Anti-militarist Movement began in Dr. Rutger's own country—and it is no accident that the Calvinist Churches of Holland, Switzerland and Scotland have the largest branches of the International Peace Movement within them. These people see clearly that compulsory military service is the one weapon which in the hands of an unscrupulous government may lead to the complete destruction of our civilisation and of all Christian and humanitarian values. I do not think Dr. Rutgers is justified in saying that conscientious objectors to military service—more particularly in a totalitarian state—have really " a false conception of a Christian's duty." It is true that Calvin was not himself anti-militarist in the modern sense, and that he explicitly sanctioned defensive war. But militarism was not the gigantic menace to human personality and Christian living that it is to-day. It is of more than historic interest to note that among the Covenanters—who were militant in their policy but were keener to find religious warrant and scriptural sanction for rebellion than for international war—there were those who denied the right of the authorities to enforce unconditional military service. During the negotiations concerning the enlistment of the Society People in the regiment raised under the command of Lord Angus in support of the Revolution in 1689, a petition was drafted by those who were desirous of serving in the regiment. Among the demands made was one that " our officers be always of our own choice or approbation, and that none be obtruded on us without our consent ; . . . . that as soon as peace is settled and fears of rebellion or invasion cease, such as have a mind to go off, to have liberty."

It appears to me that the Reformed Church can make terms only with the State organised on a Liberal or on a moderate Socialist basis, and must in the nature of things offer uncompromising opposition to totalitarian régimes, whether Communist or Fascist, which deny or dishonour God, which violate human rights and liberties, and whose policies are in sharp opposition to the way of Jesus Christ.

Objection being taken to the introduction of pacifism and certain political judgments, the Chairman said that the discussion must take place on the basis of the confessional documents, which were not pacificist, and that the Congress was one of theologians, not of politicians. Professor Rutgers, on a point of order, denied that it was a Congress of theologians only. He was himself a lawyer. Politics could not be excluded from a discussion of the subject in hand, nor had it been excluded from the Paper. Dr. Kromsigt thanked Dr. Rutgers for his clear exposition of the doctrine of " Common grace." which makes possible the progress of civilisation, but he felt the speaker had drawn too sharp. a distinction between the Old and the New Testaments, leading to a certain dualism in his doctrine of the State. There were many kinds of civilisation made possible by common grace, but Christians must demand a Christian civilisation. Magistrates must maintain not only the moral and civic order but also the religious order. As Calvin said, the Prince or Magistrate must be *judex utriusque legis tabulae*, not of the second table only. Christ is King of the Church but also the King of the kings of the earth.

In reply to Dr. Macpherson, Dr. Rutgers did not see why a distinction should be drawn between Scotsmen who in bygone centuries fought for their liberties as a nation, and those who to-day might be called upon to defend their country. He had always been a pacificist, but not as implying rejection of the duty of national defence against aggression. There was in the sixteenth century a clear divergence between Calvinists and Anabaptists on the question of bearing arms, and to-day the Anabaptist doctrine was being propagated again. The Anti-militarist Movement in Holland did not come from Calvinist quarters, and its leader, Professor Heering, was certainly not a Calvinist. In reply to Dr. Kromsigt, Dr. Rutgers maintained that the magistrate ought to maintain neither of the two Tables of the Law, not even the second, except in an external sense. The magistrate could not read the hearts of men. He did not draw a distinction between the Old and New Testaments in this respect, but based his exposition on the whole Scripture, Old Testament as well as New.

Paper No. 7

CALVINISM AND ECONOMICS

By Rev. Professor JOHN H. S. BURLEIGH, D.D., Edinburgh
University

THERE will doubtless be many who will feel not a little mystified by the inclusion of this topic in the programme of a Calvinistic Congress, for what can Calvinism, as generally understood, have to do with the theory or practice of economics ? Yet members of this Congress will require no apology from the Programme Committee. If Calvinism be a matter of general discussion to-day, it is this aspect of it that causes most widespread interest, far beyond the theological world. Since 1904, when Max Weber published his famous book, *The Protestant Ethic and the Spirit of Capitalism*, the relations of Calvinism and Capitalism have given rise to lively controversy and a voluminous literature ; and the view is frequently expressed as an accepted fact, backed by quotations from Weber, Troeltsch, Tawney and others, that Calvinism is the parent of Capitalism. A few preliminary observations must be made on the terms of the alleged relationship.

A. CALVINISM

1. It is all to the good that we should be reminded that Calvinism includes more than a system of pure theology or of ecclesiastical polity, that it includes a *sozial-lehre* in the widest sense. It was natural and inevitable that it should. Calvin was professedly the interpreter of the will of God (*i.e.* of the Scriptures) to the men of his generation, not only in matters of faith but also in matters of life and conduct, and it was in his day generally accepted that the theologian was, in all such matters, the final court of appeal. In Geneva Calvin was the supreme spiritual authority, an oracle consulted by the city-fathers on a wide variety of municipal problems and treating of them freely in the pulpit and in his letters. Both from France and England his opinion was sought on the hotly debated subject of usury and it was given, not as a mere private opinion but as an authoritative pronouncement, as by one to whose proper sphere belong all questions of faith and morals. The *Institutio* gives but an outline of his social and economic teaching, but elsewhere it is amplified into " a comprehensive scheme of municipal government, covering the whole range of civic administration, from the regulations to be made for markets, crafts, buildings and fairs to the control of prices, interest and rents." Weber, Troeltsch and the others have done well to recall this side of Calvinism, which was apt to be forgotten, and we may regard it as the important thing in Weber's book that he has stressed the significance of the social and economic teaching of theologians and preachers at a time when the materialistic interpretation of history was in the ascendant.

2. Calvinism in the present connection ought to be taken strictly to mean the teaching of Calvin himself and of his

more immediate followers. All is not Calvinism that is taught
" on Calvinistic soil " and some will justly contend that the
Neo-Calvinism of Troeltsch is not Calvinism at all. It may be
that the Roman Church has not moved so far from Thomas
Aquinas as have the Reformed Churches from John Calvin,
but if Calvinism is to be compared with Thomism then both
must be taken in their original forms as historical systems
of teaching. Modifications introduced through changing
conditions, political, social and economic, cannot rightly be
accredited to either. Calvinism influenced those lands which,
since his day, have been in the forefront of what has usually
been regarded as political and economic progress, but that
does not mean that their political or economic theory or
practice has been genuinely Calvinistic. Benjamin Franklin,
whom Weber takes as representative of the Capitalist spirit,
is perhaps not so much the product of Calvinism as of a society
long inured to the hardships of pioneering conditions in New
England.

B. Capitalism

1. Capitalism is to-day almost everywhere a word of ill-
omen. Among its critics are not only Communists and Socialists
but also National Socialists, Fascists and all the paler varieties
of social idealists. Few indeed are found to defend it. That,
no doubt, is the reason why we feel uncomfortably on the
defensive when Calvinism and Capitalism are brought into
relation as parent and child. But, of course, that was not
always so. There was a time when Capitalism was held in
honour and its defects ignored, partly because of the material
advantages to which it gave rise, but also because of the
character which it fostered and exercised and rewarded. An
economically shattered world, or even one in which the limits
of Capitalist expansion have been reached, has made the
defects of Capitalism more obvious. Reinhold Niebuhr can
pour scorn upon the Victorian conception of Captains of
Industry, and the admired figures of that epoch are discovered
to have feet of clay. A critic of the first edition (1926) of
Tawney's *Religion and the Rise of Capitalism* complained of
the use of the word Capitalism in an historical work as a
political catchword betraying a sinister intention on the part
of the author. In reply Tawney claims that it is quite as good
a scientific word as " Feudalism " or " Mercantilism," which
may be true. Nevertheless his hostility to Capitalism is, to
say the least, much less severely academic than Adam Smith's
to " Mercantilism." It is worth observing that few of the

critics of Capitalism, not even Marx, really desire to return to the conditions of life from which Capitalism has raised mankind. So long as we wish to enjoy, and wish all to enjoy equally, the material goods which Capitalism has put within human reach we must, in fairness, acknowledge its contribution to human life and well-being. It was perhaps a bold, certainly an un-fashionable thing, for a recent Swiss author to write of the nineteenth century as " Le Siècle Splendide," but it had its splendours as well as its squalors ; and these not all material. Energy, enterprise, thrift, a high standard of business honour, in short, " Character," are indispensable to any thriving civilisa-tion. Selfish unsocial pursuit of gain, oblivious to all other ideals, is seldom the whole of Capitalism.

2. Many writers of the school of Weber would have us believe that Capitalism, or at any rate the spirit of Capitalism, is a recent thing, whose origins are to be looked for in post-Reformation times. Fanfani justly traces them much further back. " No one," he says, " now denies that the birth of Capitalism took place before the Reformation " in the cities of North Italy, South Germany, the Netherlands and else-where. He also makes an important logical distinction between a Capitalist age and a pre-Capitalist age and describes logically and historically how the former can emerge out of the latter. But he does not point out that such an emergence has occurred twice in Western civilisation and that the reverse process has occurred once. Rostovzeff has no hesitation in describing as Capitalist the industrial and commercial organisation of the later Roman Republic and the Early Empire, on which poets (e.g. Horace) and moralists (e.g. Sallust and Cicero) have scathing judgments to pass, quite modern in tone. The differ-ence between these two Capitalist ages is not one of spirit but of the efficiency of the instruments available. It would be interesting to consider the causes of the return of a pre-Capitalist age in Europe from the fourth century onwards, but that would take us too far from the subject of this paper. It might be generally agreed that the psychological basis of Capitalism is as old as man—who, from the beginning, is a creature of needs and greeds, of economic appetites and of some capacity to seek their satisfaction. We may admit also a certain native inertia which in all ages cleaves to the generality of mankind. In any case " Economic man " is no late emergence in world history, though he had to wait for Adam Smith in the eighteenth century to make his behaviour the object of scientific study and of, perhaps, undue commendation, and for Marx, in the nineteenth century, to identify him with the whole man, unjustifiably.

On the other hand, favourable material conditions are necessary if economic man is to unfold his activities noticeably and continuously and progressively. Order and security are necessary if there is to be any prospect of success in such undertakings. When there is no prospect of success, native inertia will assert itself and a pre-Capitalistic spirit prevail. The conviction that man is incapable of bettering his earthly lot will render him more willing to put his hope entirely in another world. Now these favouring conditions, order and security, have in fact prevailed over very limited areas in space and time, coinciding with the two Capitalist ages in European history. Industry and commerce could hardly thrive in the heaving world of Feudalism. The Mediæval town, an anomaly in a feudal age, chartered out of the society which surrounded it, offered the first opportunity since Roman times for peaceful enterprise ; a widening opportunity, as alliances between towns or the growth of strong central governments extended the area of order and security. In the words of Dr. H. M. Robertson (*Aspects of the Rise of Economic Individualism*), " The spirit of capitalism has arisen rather from the material conditions of civilisation than from some religious impulse."

3. Economic History might conceivably be limited to the statistical account of man's pursuit of material wealth. Many are prepared to reduce economic theories to insignificance, as mere rationalisations of contemporary facts or as epi-phenomena accompanying them. Adam Smith's *Wealth of Nations* would, therefore, be but a symptom of " the shift in importance from the merchant to the actual producer of commodities in the last third of the seventeenth century." His place in economic history would accordingly be but a subordinate one. Calvin, if mentioned at all, might be dismissed in a phrase as the theologian of the bourgeois mind. Nevertheless, the history of economic thought has an interest of its own, whether it be regarded as important or unimportant. The thinkers, whether we hold them to have been influential or not, throw light on the movement of opinion towards the recognition of the autonomy of economic man and his liberation from the restraints of custom, habits of mind, ecclesiastical regulation and, finally, governmental control. Figgis has traced the secularisation of politics between Gerson and Grotius, showing how, from being a department of theology, it became a rational science or even a matter of expediency. Similarly, economics was once a department of theology, was taught by Adam Smith himself as a branch of moral philosophy, before it became an independent science with its own rationally grounded axioms and its own calculus of material wealth. Within this trend of

thought, dominated by, rather than dominating, economic fact, what is Calvin's place ? Or, if we may borrow Walter Lippmann's striking phrase and call economics a lost Province of Religion, what part has John Calvin in the loss of this Province ?

CALVIN AND THE CAPITALIST CLASSES

Obviously the answer to this question is bound up with the answer to another, namely, How far did Calvin take his stand by the classes which had, for some time, been rising in importance and were soon to dominate the economic world ? How far is he the theologian of the bourgeois mind, opening the way to a " Reconciliation between the duties of religion and the calls of business ? "

" The environment," says Tawney, " of the industrial and commercial classes is foremost in the thoughts of Calvin. Calvinism, like early Christianity, was an urban movement. His followers addressed their teaching, not, of course, exclusively, but, none the less, primarily, to the classes engaged in trade and industry." Certainly Calvin had not lived and worked in Strasburg and Geneva for nothing, and his thought was inevitably and properly conditioned by his actual situation. But he believed himself to be simply the interpreter of the Bible or Word of God as the absolute authority for man's life. That his interpretations were coloured by the accidents of time and place and circumstance is to be expected. Indeed, Calvin recognises that, in the Divine Providence, at different times and places, different political and social arrangements will be necessary, but with all such " relativism," which is well known also to Augustine, there can be no question as to the absolute authority of the Word of God over all situations. It is certain also that, though Calvin did address his *Institutio* to Francis I., his doctrines did not appeal to many princes. In some quarters they won aristocratic support, possibly often for economic reasons, which are not those which concern us here. In Scotland the Knoxian Reformation had the steady support of the towns, " rascal multitude" as well as prosperous citizens, but these towns in 1560 were somewhat remote from the main line of commercial and industrial development. Moreover, by 1638, the Scottish peasantry had been reached and formed an important element in the strength of the Calvinist Movement. The fact that it was on Calvinist soil (in Holland, among exiled Huguenots, in Puritan England and, at a much later date, in Scotland) that the immense development of industry and commerce took place with its consequent secularisation of economic thought, is certainly significant. But it is really impossible to determine whether either development was the result of Calvinism or of purely material conditions, geographical or geological.

To return to Calvin himself—in common with all the Reformers he attacked the mediæval conception of a threefold hierarchy of cleric, soldier and mechanic and, in particular, the conception of the two careers, religious and secular, contemplative and active. Whether the abolition of a class formally, if not always actually, " religious " and " otherworldly ", led to an impoverishment of the witness to religion in social life may be a debatable point. At all events, it was Calvin's endeavour to extend the religious conception of life to all ranks and conditions. If it brought with it an enhancement, in value and dignity, of the life in the world, it also brought the life in the world into the religious scheme of things as the Will of God for man.

Moreover, hostility to the mediæval hierarchy does not imply that Calvin abandoned the conception of the social organism. He is no teacher of atomic individualism or of the equality of all men. Social climbing, though not forbidden, is sternly frowned upon. His hierarchy is one of worldly callings, some higher, others more lowly, all of which must fit into the unity of the State or Society and serve it as the members serve the body, in strict subordination to the whole. Luther, too, valued the earthly calling but dwells rather on the pathos of it. It is the burden which must be borne in this world, even by the true Christian, who knows the sweetness and the freedom of the Love of God. Calvin is aware that some callings may be irksome, but his emphasis is on the calling as a noble service to be undertaken and carried on with a positive sense of its worthwhile-ness. It is to be conceived as a call or command from God, to be accepted thoughtfully and reverently and followed devoutly and intently. Such activism does not imply the notion of " work for work's sake," much less that work is to be done for the success or reward it may bring, but rather that a calling is the God-given opportunity to fulfil the Gospel commandment, " Thou shalt love thy neighbour as thyself." " Through love of neighbour the calling receives its true quality and, by the thought that a man in his calling has to do with God, to Whom he must give an account, it receives its special consecration."

It may be claimed that Calvin thus gives to the moral, *i.e.* the active, life a more important place than had been possible for the mediæval moralist. He concedes to it a relative independence in so far as its immediate object is not the earning of salvation but the service of our fellow-men in the earthly community. Here in effect Fanfani (*Catholicism, Protestantism and Capitalism*, pp. 205–6) finds the main contribution of Calvinism and Protestantism generally to the development of Capitalism. " It denied the connection between earthly action and eternal recompense, invalidated any supernatural morality " and " banished Saints." He thinks that the complete secularisation of economic thought was the logical issue of this. We must insist, however, that, if Calvin broke down the special relations between morality and religion, established by the scholastic moralists, he aimed at a more thoroughgoing integration of the two; and that, if within Protestantism there has been a trend towards secularism and utilitarianism, the ethical record of Protestantism, even without saints of the Catholic pattern, has been a high one.

Weber called attention to Calvinist asceticism to which the name " innerweltliche askese " has been given and which hardened somewhat among the English Puritans. So far as Calvin is concerned, what he demands is simply the bringing under of the body in the interests of the community of one's fellow-men, the mortifying of all purely selfish endeavour and ambition. Weber compares it, in its result, with the asceticism of the monasteries which came to be wealthy corporations, and shows that the Calvinist asceticism achieved the same result for the individual. The comparison is instructive, but we must agree with Brodrick (*Economic Morals of the Jesuits*, p. 151, note) that " the basis of Puritan and Catholic asceticism were utterly different. The Catholic conception was and is rooted in supernaturalism, whereas the Puritan conception remained intramundane and non-contemplative." When, however, he continues—" Confined to the relatively narrow spheres of domestic life and business activities " we should prefer to say " applicable to the real moral life."

In Calvin's appraisal of the various callings within the Social hierarchy there is little that is startlingly new, unless it be hostility to beggars, mendicants, official and unofficial. The idle beggar had no place in the Calvinist community. Either he must work or, if unable to work, must be publicly provided for, for which there is Scriptural warrant. It is his treatment of the merchant class which here interests us most, whether or not it was foremost in his thought. This class had long exercised the schoolman who patiently discussed whether trade were allowable at all and what restrictions should be imposed. In spite of them, it had come to stay and to increase in influence as the world situation became more stable. Favoured by princes, to whom it was useful, hated by the feudal nobility, which declined before it, suspected by moralists, the merchant class held steadily on its upward way. Among the Reformation figures its chief enemies were Ulrich von Hutten for social reasons, and Luther on moral grounds. No class perhaps wholly escaped the fury of the Reformer upon occasion, and the merchants, with their frauds and speculations, came in for unmeasured invective. That it found means to justify their transactions was one of the main items in his indictment of the Roman moral theology. "Nicht viel gute Sitten in ein Land gekommen sind durch die Kaufmannschaft." But there the Kaufmannschaft was and would be the despair of the pulpit and the moralist. Luther is fain to hand over commercial regulation to the jurist and the "Obrigkeit.' The preacher must take his stand on the plain Bible text, declare the absolute Law of Christ and close his eyes to the practical problems of its application to real life.

In sharp contrast to this is Calvin's attitude. With the schoolmen he holds that the merchant is not, as such, a rogue and a robber. Admittedly his calling is liable to special temptations—greed, dishonesty, price manipulation, pride, luxury, self-glorification in success. Yet, these vices are not inherent in the calling itself, which is useful to States and Communities, as, for example, Venice and Antwerp, and brings them a fuller and richer life than does cultivation of the soil. "Prosperitas ut Dei donum est, non erit per se damnanda." The economic life, therefore, can be moralised, brought into subservience to moral ideals and into the service of God. On the other hand, Calvin is at one with Luther in his hostility to the subtleties of the scholastic treatment of commercial dealings, which asserted a principle and nullified it or evaded it by casuistry. Both realised that the New Testament contained a mighty protest against just such procedure ; only, while Luther cleaves to the literal text of Scripture in the prohibition of usury, Calvin takes another way and has won notoriety in certain quarters as the first theologian to justify usury. No doubt he did say that usury was not, in all cases, forbidden by God, but that is much too simple a summary of his doctrine.

The mediæval moralists founded on two authorities (1) The Scriptural prohibition of usury, both in the Old Testament and the New, and (2) Aristotle's condemnation of usury as a censurable attempt to make money breed money, a proceeding contrary to nature, for money is (or ought to be) sterile. The sterility of money was a dogma with the schoolmen and one which was not contradicted by experience before the advent of a commercial age. A loan is a sum of money which would lie unused in a coffer unless it were given for a stated period to a neighbour in need as an act of charity. If the neighbour made profit by it, that was due solely to his industry and he was, therefore, entitled to it as his own. All he could be asked to pay back was the original sum. All else was usury and against the Law of God. But, of course, this is too simple a doctrine and requires much explication. (1) If the loan is not paid back at the stated time, the lender is entitled to exact a penalty in the shape of an additional payment. (2) If the loan involves risk something may be exacted by way of insurance. (3) If the lender could state that the loan involved him in loss or prevented him from using his money profitably and that he actually had the intention so to use it, then he could justifiably claim interest. Thus the authority of Aristotle and of Scripture might be upheld and the law of usury made applicable to actual life. Both Luther and Calvin believed that all this was pure sophistry; but, while Luther sticks to the letter of the law, Calvin attacks the problem afresh. So far from being sterile, a sum of money can be as productive as, or even more productive than, a parcel of ground or a house, for which rent was charged without any objection being taken. Here is a clear source of revenue, distinct from the wages of labour or the rent of land. Interest is a share in the profits of capital productively used. At the least, we can say that this insight represents an important step forward in scientific economic analysis. It might also be held to be a simplification and a clarifying of the moral problem by the elimination of the complexities of the later moral theology, however well intentioned they may have been. Is it also a concession on the part of theology of a certain measure of autonomy to the economic life—even a sanctification of that autonomy? This is to raise the problem of the Scriptural prohibitions of usury and Calvin's interpretation of them.

The Old Testament prohibition is limited to transactions of Jew with Jew and is governed by the special position of the Jewish people among its heathen neighbours, while Christianity has abolished all distinctions of race; besides, it was adapted to social and political circumstances, very different from those of modern times. As Augustine says, when pressed by Manichæan objections to the warlike commands of the Old Testament, " Does not this show how, without any inconsistency, precepts, counsels and permissions may be changed as different times require different arrangements ? " The

New Testament prohibitions (Matt. v. 42 and Luke vi. 34) say nothing at all about interest or usury and may well mean that the lender should be prepared to part with his capital too, to help a brother in need. What God is doing is not laying down a law, the application of which to actual circumstances must be the subject of " longae disputationes," but is presenting a norm for all conduct, the law of equity, which is identical with the Gospel command of Love. " Cognoissons en somme que nostre Seigneur sous ces mots a voulu commander que nous usions d'equite et droiture en tous nos actes et surtout quand il est question de prester."

Lending and borrowing are not, therefore, autonomous transactions, free of all moral and Christian considerations, and Calvin proceeds to hedge them with all manner of restrictions. To take interest from one who is able and ought to be willing to pay it is permissible, but extortion and oppression are not permissible. From the poor no interest may be demanded, and the Christian is commanded to be ready to give to him freely, according to his need. That Calvin takes these restrictions seriously is clear from his attack on the banking profession, even though it figured already in the business life of Geneva. The professional banker, who, without working, enriches himself at the cost of others " is not to be endured in the Church of God, and ought to be utterly cast out from the society of men." This somewhat curious opposition to purely financial business maintained itself for a generation in Geneva, France and Holland.

Here, however, we come to what has been regarded as a weakness in the position of Calvin. Granted that all conduct, and especially business conduct, is to be governed by the Law of Love, by the principles of " equite et droiture," who is to say what the Law demands or the principles imply in any given case ? Rome claims to answer all such questions with an unchallengable authority. Luther was apt, in despair, to relegate them to the jurists. Calvin's appeal, in the last resort, is to the individual conscience. " Leur conscience leur en peut assez dire." This, of course, at first sight looks like naïve optimism and a dangerous concession to the individual to constitute himself judge in his own case. It is true that Calvinism has been the nursery of sturdy individualism, and yet his own closely knit system of faith and discipline actually left but little over to the individual. Tawney can even designate it a " collective dictatorship." The conscience here appealed to is not simply private judgment in the modern acceptance of the term. It is a conscience directed by the Word and by the Gospel Law of Love, subject also to ecclesiastical discipline, founded on the Word, but which so accepts these restraints that even in obedience it feels its own autonomy. This is genuinely in line with the Pauline ethic. If Calvinism abdicated its rights to rule the economic life and became content to be a purely theological and ecclesiastical system, if it limited its discipline to matters of personal ethics, it did so, not without a struggle and perhaps only when overcome by the spirit of the Age of Reason. But surely Fanfani surprises when he states : " The Protestant who still envisaged a should-be " state was illogical. " The fundamental principles of Protestantism lead inevitably to the sanctification of the real." This is, at least, as grossly unfair and uncharitable as to say that the fundamental principles of Catholicism inevitably lead to a disingenuous legalism which veils in subtleties its compromises with the actual. A world-dominating Church has proved a delusion and, in any case, is now an impossibility. The mission of Christianity is, perhaps, best regarded as a spiritual force, making for tension in the common life of man. Protestantism and Catholicism has each its own methods of keeping alive that tension. Which has been more effective it is as yet presumptuous to say, but Protestantism has had the harder battle. Both may take courage from the thought that the " lost province " has irredentist elements within it that look back to the Mother country, which is obedience to the Will of God.

One further point before I close. Weber calls attention to the " unprecedented inner loneliness " of the Calvinist believer, for whom eternal salvation depends upon no human merit, on nothing that man can do, on nothing that the Church can do, but upon a Decree of God, irrevocably predestining a few to salvation and the majority to be lost. For the Calvinist, how could there be any assurance of personal salvation ? The Romanist at least had some promise and help through the Sacraments, penitential discipline and prescribed good works of the Church. The Lutheran had assurance in the blissful experience which true faith engendered. The Calvinist, it is suggested, must repress the question and apply himself to his worldly calling, success in which may be taken as a sign of God's favour. It may be that, in theory, the doctrine of predestination rules out any certainty of salvation : and yet, in practice, Calvinism has been notoriously successful in conveying a sense of assurance. Calvin himself had no doubts and the Calvinistic Confessions have elaborate lists of the tokens of salvation, among which is not included success in business or in one's worldly calling. Where this doctrine has been taught it must be regarded as a caricature of Calvinism. Good works are, perhaps, an indispensable sign of election, but that is a different thing from worldly success. Pride in success is, indeed, one of the sins against which Calvin fulminates.

Calvin lived in an age of rapid change in all spheres of life. In particular the economic life, already strongly developed, was challenging old restrictions and old modes of thought. Some economic dogmas were being discovered to be fallacies and the old rules of moral theology were being strained to breaking point in the endeavour to make them cope with increasing complexities. Bellarmine, as well as Luther and Calvin, recognises the difficulty of teaching economic man his Christian duty. Calvin likewise lived in one of the centres of economic life, a second or third rate one it is true, but one offering all the hardest social and economic problems of the time. He does not dismiss them from his mind as alien problems. They belong to the theologian and to the preacher and come under the jurisdiction of the Church, as of old, but he has a new positive vision of the economic life as no mere field of self-seeking and avarice, but as an opportunity of dutiful and impersonal service to one's fellow-men. Man, in his calling, is still subject to the Gospel Law of Love, positively as well as negatively. In it he serves not himself but his community, and, indeed, humanity, assuring to it its sustenance and well-being. So is the economic life everywhere ethically limited. But there is a Higher than the community, a Higher than humanity, even God, Whom it ever is man's chief end to glorify. For the fulfilling of this chief end the calling is the God-given opportunity. So far from being an emancipation of Economic man, the Calvinism of John Calvin might be claimed as the last historic attempt of a theologian to bring the whole life of man into subjection to the Will of God.

RÉSUMÉ D'UN DISCOURS SUR

"LE CALVINISME ET L'ÉCONOMIQUE"

(Fait par le Professeur J. H. S. Burleigh, D.D.)

1. On a récemment reconnu à nouveau l'importance de l'enseignement social et économique du calvinisme et cela n'est pas de refus, quand même il aurait donné cours à l'idée que le calvinisme fut le père du capitalisme.

2. Dans le but de la comparaison (par exemple avec le thomisme) l'on doit prendre le calvinisme pour signifier strictement l'enseignement de Calvin lui-même.

3. Le capitalisme est en ce jour un mot de mauvais augure,

10

mais même ses critiques doivent, avec équité, admettre qu'il a eu une certaine splendeur aussi bien qu'une squaleur matérielle et morale.

4. Le capitalisme n'est pas un phénomène d'après-Réforme, mais se manifeste partout là où la sécurité politique permet à l'homme de poursuivre avec une bonne chance de succès ses intérêts économiques—dans le monde romain, par exemple.

5. L'histoire économique a une dialectique à elle propre et n'est pas principalement guidée par des considérations religieuses ou théologiques. Si l'économique est une " province perdue de la religion " quelle en est la responsabilité de Calvin ?

6. Son monde à lui fut celui du " capitalisme primitif " et il a dû en tenir compte, mais son appel n'est addressé à aucune classe en particulier et la parole de Dieu est considérée comme l'autorité absolue pour toutes les classes et toutes les situations.

7. L'abolition de la conception de deux carrières, l'une contemplative l'autre active, causa un rehaussement de la dignité de la vie dans le monde. L'organisme social est maintenant une hiérarchie de vocations actives chacune desquelles, dans sa mesure, sert la société et glorifie Dieu. Tout cela vise à donner aux vies ordinaires une valeur morale et religieuse plus élevée, à les rendre vraiment et pleinement " religieuses."

8. L'ascétisme intra-mondain de Calvin revient tout simplement à la subordination de l'intérêt de soi-même aux intérêts de ses semblables dans l'amour.

9. En contraste avec les scolastiques et avec Luther, Calvin a une estime relativement haute pour la vocation de commerçant, laquelle avec toutes ses tentations spéciales contribue au bien-être des sociétés. Ce peut donc être une vie vraiment morale.

10. Tout en rejetant avec Luther la casuistique des scolastiques à l'égard des transactions commerciales, Calvin ne suit pas Luther en les assujettissant tout simplement au gouvernement civil. Elles demeurent sujettes au commandement évangélique de l'amour du prochain lequel doit être appliqué par la conscience chrétienne individuelle.

11. Le problème éthique le plus urgent dans une société de plus en plus commerçante fut la question de l'usure. L'Écriture avait interdit l'usure et Aristote l'avait désapprouvée pour la raison que l'argent est stérile. Dans les derniers temps du moyen âge l'intérêt était communément payé sur des emprunts qui rapportaient un profit et les théologiens moraux avaient défini un bon nombre de titres à un tel versement, extrinsique en supposition à l'emprunt comme tel (damnum emergens, lucrum cessans, etc.) Luther, comme Calvin aussi,

considérait cela comme une sophisterie toute pure, mais alors que Luther se rapportait à la défense littérale des Écritures, Calvin attaqua la doctrine de la stérilité de l'argent qu'il montra comme fallacieuse, et il marqua ainsi une avance importante dans l'analyse scientifique économique. La défense scripturale de l'usure ne doit pas être acceptée comme un commandement absolu pour tous les âges et toutes les circonstances, et est, partout, dure à appliquer dans n'importe quel cas donné. mais elle doit être interprétée comme une illustration de la loi de l'équité et de la justice qui est iddentique avec le commandement évangélique de l'amour.

12. Si bien Calvin donna une approbation de l'usure, il l'entoura tout de suite de qualifications et de restrictions au point de vue de la morale chrétienne et il maintient l'aversion traditionnelle pour la profession de banquier. Il ne peut pas y avoir question pour Calvin d'une libération des affaires commerciales et financières du contrôle de la morale et de la religion.

13. Calvin semble constituer la conscience individuelle comme juge suprême en ces affaires-là et dans une certain mesure le calvinisme encourage effectivement l'individualisme, mais c'est un individualisme instruit dans la parole de Dieu, obéissant envers la loi du Christ et sujet à une discipline ecclésiastique rigoureuse. Son autonomie est l'autonomie paulinienne de la conscience subordonnée à Dieu.

14. L'effet de la doctrine calviniste de la prédestination, qui ne donne à l'individu aucune assurance de salut personnel, a été considéré comme ayant poussé Calvin à rechercher l'assurance dans le travail et le succès commercial. Bien que l'on puisse apercevoir cet effet dans le calvinisme populaire plus récent, il n'y en a nulle trace dans les documents calvinistes originaux.

15. Les églises calvinistes ont du supporter la fureur de la bataille contre les empiètements de l'homme économique qui vise une indépendance complète dans toutes ses entreprises ; il se peut que ce soit une bataille où elles perdent, mais elles n'abdiquèrent pas de leur propre vouloir. On peut revendiquer que le calvinisme de Jean Calvin fut le dernier essai historique d'un théologien pour assujettir *toute* la vie humaine à la volonté de Dieu.

In opening the discussion Rev. PROFESSOR W. R. FORRESTER, B.D., St. Andrews University said :
Weber did not, as is often supposed, bluntly assert that capitalism is " the brat of heresy," but only that capitalism was the sociological counterpart of Calvinism, as feudalism

was of Romanism. It was Troeltsch and Tawney, who blindly followed and outdid him, in relating the two together as cause and effect. We cannot deny—and there is no reason why we should—that for the most part it is the countries where Calvinism is strong that led the advance of the modern age both in industry and in politics. We need not be ashamed of this prominence. But much of the plausibility of the Weber thesis, as it has got out into public currency through Tawney and others, is due to a confusion between capitalism and industrialism. Weber distinguishes between the system of capitalism and the spirit of capitalism, a very necessary distinction ; but he does not seem to see the further distinction between capitalism and industrialism. Undoubtedly Calvinism has contributed very largely to the growth of industrialism, for it produced the enterprise, initiative, industry and self-discipline which are needed for industrial and commercial success. We are proud of that contribution and in no way ashamed of it. But Calvinism is no more responsible for the sins and radical weaknesses of capitalism than it is responsible for the phenomenal growth of capitalistic methods in countries like Japan. We cannot blame John Calvin for Japanese imperialism !

Part of the real value of Weber's thesis is its recognition, in opposition to the prevailing trend towards economic materialism and determinism, that spiritual beliefs and ideals do affect economic processes. Weber is a useful antidote to Karl Marx. Any minister in a working-class area will tell you that while the Roman Catholic section of the population remain at the labourers' level from generation to generation, those really laid hold of by our Calvinistic type of religion tend so to grow in character, and therefore in reliability and all sterling qualities, that within a generation, or at most two, a home mission charge will become a suburban congregation, with all the difficulties and dangers that such social advance in self-respect inevitably brings. For Calvinism is morally and socially creative where Rome is largely recreative. Theologically Calvinism has had a doctrine of vocation which was applied powerfully and creatively to all believers, while Rome till lately confined its doctrine of vocation strictly so-called to those under vows. By denying to the laity the sense of vocation which has been such a strong point of Calvinism, Rome has not merely robbed plain folk of a powerful moral creative motive, but has made them unsure of their own souls' salvation, and so absolutely dependent on the priesthood, to whom alone that assurance of vocation is given in its fullness.

A little Calvinism is a dangerous thing. But the possible perversion of a sense of vocation into a mere lust of ambition and greed should not blind us to the inestimable value of this principle of vocation. It is the only possible sublimation or consecration of those elementary things in human nature— the primitive *conatus in suo esse perseverare*—that otherwise would assume perverted and dangerous forms in various kinds of aggression, ambition, and selfishness.

We Calvinists have in our doctrine of vocation, which of itself is only the positive form of the doctrine of election and the personal rendering of predestination, a far better thing than the fatalistic mechanism which governs the world of all who do not believe in God, or the Roman doctrine of two standards of morality, which degrades the vast majority of believers to a second-rate kind of life, inferior to that of " the religious " in the monastery. This doctrine of vocation is, therefore, only another aspect of the priesthood of all believers.

Seen in the light of this, it enables us to claim, as we do, that the future of democracy, of civil and political liberty in any form is bound up with a recognition of the sovereignty of God and the priesthood of all believers. But this is away from my immediate subject, as also is the other conclusion to which we are slowly being driven, that the only way to international peace is by inviting, and surrendering to, the invasion of the supernatural. International peace cannot be attained without supernatural agency any more than human freedom can be gained without the acknowledgment of Divine sovereignty.

Far from admitting that Calvinism is doomed with the passing of capitalism, its alleged sociological counterpart (as both Communists and Neo-thomists assert and expect), we may confidently claim that the whole future of an indus-trialised civilisation lies in a development and application of the Pauline and Calvinistic doctrine of vocation. The Roman Church is becoming more and more irrevocably committed to Fascism, and the ideals and methods of the corporative state. Its doctrine of the two standards, and the resultant gulf between the sacred and the secular, have prevented it from contributing much either to political freedom or to industrial progress. At the other extreme lies Marxian determinism. Between these two, in a position of great danger and great opportunity, on this stage set for one of the greatest dramas of history, stands our Calvinism. Its doctrine of vocation provides us with a principle of social and industrial articulation and integration, and a principle of ecclesiastical integration as well. (Eph. iv.) The Body of Christ consists of many organs and members, all related to one another and to the whole according to this principle of vocation. The kingdom of God is meant to be a cosmos of callings, where each labours to the glory of God, in obedience to His call. We Calvinists can admit no absolute sovereignty in Church or State, of any man or institution whatsoever, for sovereignty is of God alone. " There are twa kings and twa kingdoms in Scotland. . . ."

If this seem blatant individualism, may I recall that here in Scotland in the past any tendency towards individualism was counteracted by the much prized principle of the covenant, a principle which occupies the place in the Old Testament that predestination has in the New, and which in former days enabled our forefathers to stake their all upon the promises of God. Nothing is more obviously responsible for the ills of our day than the lack of a sense of vocation. But vocation as an individual principle must be balanced by the principle of the covenant. With these we may lead the world far towards the kingdom of God.

Friday, 8th July 1938

AFTERNOON SESSION, Dr. MACLEAN Presiding

Paper No. 8

THE CALVINISTIC PHILOSOPHY OF ART

By Dr. LÉON WENCÉLIUS, Strasbourg, Professor in Swarth-more College, U.S.A.

To many people the title of this paper is astonishing. The idea of our study has surprised numerous scholars, Catholic and Protestant alike. Our intellectual sphere is, in fact, encumbered with ready-made notions, as simple and as comfortable as American slogans, and among these there is none whose life has been so persistent as that which holds that the Reformation is hostile to art. It is sufficient on this score to read in one of the most popular manuals of French literature that " that which in Catholicism had exasperated Luther and Calvin was precisely the introduction of an artistic element into the religious life." We know just such a Protestant theologian who, when seeing the notice of our subject, exclaimed, " But, my dear sir, you are contradicting an historical fact ! "

In spite of these ready-made notions, which, like all ideas of this type, bear witness to a mind unconsciously biassed on the part of those who profess them, we have attempted the rehabilitation of the Reformation on esthetic grounds. We have been encouraged to do so after having studied the esthetics of Neo-Scholasticism which deals with the relationships between art and the theology of Saint Thomas ; we have found in the estheticians of this movement condemnations of the Reformation and of Jansenism which by their very virulence inspired us to verify their foundations.

We have tried to examine the case of art against the Reformation in the specific instance of the French Reformation and its chief, John Calvin. It is perhaps in France that the idea of Protestantism, conceived of as a source of ugliness, has the most vivacity, and it is probably Calvin who has been most attacked on this score from the time of Brunetière to that of Henri Massis, to cite only the nineteenth and twentieth centuries. This is perhaps the field where the accusation has seemed to us the most unjust. Calvin is a thinker who, in the sixteenth century, renewed the existing conception of the universe. At the risk of being fragmentary and incomplete, his thought had to treat of the fine arts. Calvin is a writer. He is the creator of French philosophic prose, and everyone, even Bossuet, who hated so much to admit it, recognised the beauty of his style, the harmony of his thought. Forced to improvise a language in the thick of a battle of ideas, is it not likely that Calvin should have his own ideas concerning the beauty of thought and of style ? Finally, Calvin is a man of action, a professor, the head of a church, and as such he is forced to consider the problems raised by art and beauty, be it only to save his faithful from the seductions of evil or to explain the passages in the Bible which treat of the arts. Would such a thinker, such a spiritual leader, not only have neglected but have detested beauty and the arts ? To state the problem is, alone, sufficient to inspire its examination.

The best way for us to treat this subject was to search through the entire work of the Reformer for material evidence. We wanted to find all his thoughts on beauty and the arts in the text itself in order to discover his true opinion. The search for this evidence has seemed to us of the highest importance. It alone could crush for ever those ready-made notions whose vitality is unfortunately too great. After having assembled the ideas of the Reformer, we were struck by their abundance, their coherence and their insistence. Without doing violence to any one of them, we may say that it is they that have oriented us and have revealed to us in Calvin's thought a systematic appreciation of beauty and the arts. All our research has focussed on discovering in these reflections the guiding thread which would permit us to classify them and to bring the attitude of the Reformer on esthetic problems into broad daylight. A deepened knowledge of Calvin's work was necessary, and after a contact of several years with the thought of the theologian, we were capable of finding the order according to which his conception of esthetics is organised.

The idea of beauty accompanies Calvin in nearly all of his commentaries, sermons and theological treatises. He will talk to us of the beauty of the starry sky, of the human soul, of the sacrifice of Christ or of the holy life. To what is this term " beauty " accountable and how is it to be understood ? To answer this we must grasp the thought of the Reformer in its dynamic form. We must search for beauty in the work of God, that is in Creation itself. If we really know how to contemplate Creation, we shall understand the idea of beauty.

Creation is the work of God. Drawn from nothingness, it is constantly under Divine direction which is constantly renewed in order to realise ends known only to Him. It is Creation which, in the first place, is called upon to acquaint us with the Creator ; it reveals to us His attributes and makes us better able to understand His nature. Creation reveals to us the goodness, the justice and the power of God. The heavens sing the glory of God. For Calvin, Divine glory always expresses itself in the form of beauty. Calvin's theology has often been called the theology of the glory of God, but we have discovered now that Divine splendour is the form taken by this glory when it radiates throughout the world.

For Calvin, therefore, beauty is the natural revelation of divinity. To see beauty, to find it in the world, is a way of knowing the Divine, and it is by means of beauty in creation that God allows us to glimpse not only the splendour of His being, but the radiance of His activity. The examples of the beauty of the universe which the Reformer offers us will be numerous ; witness the angels, the soul, the human body, the sky, the stars, the sun, the earth, the ocean, the plants, the precious stones and the most humble animals, are they not the ornaments of the world, the works of art in the palace which is the earth, " in order," says Calvin, " that we may therein contemplate the majesty of God." The universe is beautiful because of the Divine light which radiates from it, the arrangement of its parts, and the excellence of its order. Its beauty provokes our admiration and our joy ; it inspires us to render supreme homage to God.

But, unfortunately, natural revelation was not sufficient :

and evil and the fall intervened, upsetting and darkening the universe which had been radiant with beauty. Original revelation was compromised by original sin. Satan warped the world and sin blinded the sinner. What had once been the mirror of Divine beauty was now broken by sin into many fragments, and man, seizing one of them, could now see only his own reflection in the glass. Evil had so falsified our vision that we became incapable of seeing beyond immediate appearances. Instead of seeing the sign of the Divine presence in perceptible displays of beauty, the sinner accepts the appearance for reality and even makes of it an absolute which he adores. The deep significance of beauty will, therefore, escape the sinner. Evil will do worse ; it will tempt the damned to adorn themselves with a false beauty in order to attract other victims to itself, and the sinner will no longer be able to distinguish between sham and true beauty. Notice that the devil does not substitute for the real world of beauty an illusory world of appearances of his own ; rather he warps our vision and incites sinners to warp it in such a way that we can no longer see beauty as a sensible reality.

God will not abandon the struggle but will restore the universe, upset and blinded by the fall. His general grace will continue to brighten the world with a diffused light. God will even reveal himself in a particular form of beauty to His chosen people, Israel. In order to make Himself comprehensible to His people, God will show Himself in the guise of beauty in the ceremonies of the temple, in the architecture of Zion, the sacred city, and finally in the spiritual beauty of the prophets' message. Christ will reveal this beauty in all its glory. He will make known the new life of the elect whose task will be the restoration of the corrupt world. Election will create a new harmony between the renewed man and God. Our works will become beautiful in the sight of God. Faith will be a masterpiece, and, thanks to the illumination of the spirit, we will be able to see the universe with regenerated eyes which will once more perceive clearly its aspect of true beauty. The soul will recognise spiritual beauty in clarity, order, equilibrium and new-found purity.

What considerations can we draw from all these reflections on beauty ? With its light the beautiful accompanies all manifestations of divine activity. The latter produced the universe, and, wherever it has been marked by the Creator, the universe will be beautiful. The soul touched by this activity will be doubly beautiful, beautiful in its terrestrial destiny as it is distinguished by general grace, beautiful in its celestial destiny as it is distinguished by particular grace.

The beautiful is ultimately the relationship which, since creation, has established itself between the Creator and the created. It is the mark of creation arrived at its goal.

The beautiful will, therefore, be accessible to both the elect and the damned in so far as it is marked by general grace. Whenever an aspect of the universe puts them in the presence of the activity of God, they will see His mark, which is beauty. Often the action of evil will veil their view, will be in danger of warping it; but, if God grants them this communal grace, it will always be possible for them to see the reality of beauty through the deformation of the world. If one is the recipient of this kind of grace, one can perfectly well be an esthete, see the universe according to the laws which presided at its birth and still be damned. Only the elect, on the other hand, will be able to see the spiritual beauty of particular grace and feel its beneficial effects.

Beauty is not then an impersonal principle as it was for the Hellenists. The object of adoration, it is the light of the ever vigilant intelligence of an ever creative will. It is vital and concrete, and wherever God is, there too is beauty. Neither, according to Calvin, is beauty the noble Thomist cathedral, perceived from the height of the skies by a saintly doctor; it is rather the light which shines on this gigantic fresco, on this universe of men and things forever on the march, which God, with the moderation which is His alone, is leading to the perfection known only to His Divine will.

· · · · · · · · ·

God, Creator of the universe, was called by Calvin the miraculous workman. Transposing this into modern terms, we shall say that God is the great artist, maker of this master-piece which is Creation, whose multiple beauty we have just been admiring. God the Creator heaped gifts upon His creatures, and among these innumerable presents of His general grace are the arts. God permits man to cultivate the mechanical as well as the liberal arts, but it is important always to remember that art is a natural gift. This gift of God is made to human intelligence; is is distributed throughout the entire universe without reference to election or damnation. Pagan nations have received a large part of it, and these presents of general grace contributed to the preparation of the world for the spiritual coming Christ.

Like all Divine graces, art was distributed liberally among men. It is a free gift, granted according to the calling of him who has received it. Like the scholar or the statesman, the artisan has received a determined mission, a talent for

production according to the teaching of the evangelical
parable.

Having received a certain measure from God, the artist
should remain within the limits of the gift which has been
granted him ; he should develop the qualities he has received
in harmony with his intelligence, and he should always re-
remember that art is a natural human activity, that he would
not be able to attain the secrets of spiritual life without
particular grace. Art thus understood will be the creator of
joy, and in order to realise it to the full, the artist will be
humble before God and will forever recognise in Him the
dispenser of his talent.

In some measure God, the creator, permits the artist to
carry out his work according to the natural plan. But once
again sin enters upon the scene to spoil everything. Too
often the talent given by God has been turned to ends contrary
to His will. The artist separated from God has believed
himself to be a little divinity to whom everything was subjected, and, blinded by evil, he has attempted to blind other
men in their turn. Thus turning the activity of men to his
profit, the devil gives rise to arts which are false and perverse
because they have been turned from their true goal. Art will
thus become fatally corrupted as the branch of a flowering
tree separated from its trunk. By this deformation of the
activity of the artist, and by the blinding of men's vision,
Satan thinks to triumph.

To restore art to its true direction, it must be remembered
that its only end is the honour of God, that it is for Him
alone ; and God is not the object of mystical contemplation,
but rather the Creator and Governor of a universe constantly
subjected to the dynamic of His will.

The study of various secular arts will show us how the
Reformer interprets the natural mission of art as God has
determined it, and we will cite here just a few examples.

The plastic arts whose exclusive objective is the decoration
of cities and interiors, are far from being condemned by the
Reformer as has often been repeated. The arts of painting
and of sculpture are gifts of God. They should seek their
models in His creative activity, but, like all the arts, they
should remain strictly secular. Painting and sculpture should
ornament human life as it unfolds according to the plan of
general grace. The object of the plastic arts is twofold.
Paintings and statues can, as Calvin says, be a reminder and
teach some message, or they can simply give joy. Contained
in their proper limits, therefore, the arts of painting and
sculpture are perfectly justified.

Calvin does not condemn them except when they attempt to overstep their limits, that is when they try to represent God. Charged with the exaltation of Creation, the plastic arts can represent only the created, and to approach the uncreated is a grave error. God cannot be represented, because he is spiritual and transcendant. Moreover, God does not will this and has formally forbidden it in the Ten Commandments. The result of disobeying such an interdict will not be long in forthcoming. Unfettered idolatry, followed by its usual train of stupidity, vanity and pride, will once again be evident. God will once more be dishonoured. For this reason, painting and sculpture must remember that, in order to approach God, they must not try to represent His transcendant essence, but must attempt to model themselves on His creative activity and in this way continue creation.

We now come to the great problem of the relationship which should be established between the arts and the service of God, otherwise called worship. Are the arts opposed to the Divine service or, on the contrary, should they aid it ? Faithful to the authority of the Scripture, Calvin will base his reply upon it, explaining to us first the rôle of ceremony in the religion of the Old Testament. Israel celebrated the Divine service with a great display of pomp. Its priests made use of every device that could impress human sensibilities, glorifying God in the midst of light shed from seven-branch candelabra and the smoke of incense and of sacrifice. These ceremonies were necessary to people during the dark period of history which preceded the coming of Christ. They had a definite pedagogic mission. God was trying to arouse the sensitivity, the emotions of the elected race, so that it might become prepared to receive an increasingly spiritualised message. With the incarnation of Christ the reign of light succeeded the reign of darkness, and humanity became able to understand another form of adoration, a new aspect of worship which this time will be spiritual.

This is what the Papists did not understand. Rome tried to imitate the splendour of the Temple service and invented a great number of sumptuous ceremonies. Their beauty is illusory. They mean nothing because they are not founded on any Scriptural text. God now desires only those forms of adoration which He Himself has prescribed. All other forms carry with them the sign of damnation, though Calvin does not make the mistake of indicating all the defects and all the vices into which fall those who observe the ceremonies of that which he calls the Papal Synagogue.

To pay God the homage which he deserves, it suffices to

listen to the words of Jesus, who once said to the Samaritan
that God is spirit and that all who adore Him must adore Him
in spirit and in truth. It is God who is the author of true
ceremonies, and to serve Him it will suffice to obey His will
as it manifests itself in the Word and in the sacraments. As
a matter of fact, it is also necessary to avoid the other extreme
from the Papal Synagogue, which consists of honouring God
with one's heart without taking into account the services
which He demands of us in the Bible. True worship should
be a direct, objective contact between the faithful people and
God. It should be simple, unadorned, sober and pure, and its
beauty will consist precisely in this sobriety and purity. The
service should be a harmony and a melody between the soul
and God, an understanding among the separate souls which
compose the Church, and finally a melody sung by the Church
and the angels together before God.

To magnify the glory of God, only two arts, music and
poetry, are admitted within the temple. Conforming to the
Bible, which contains the psalms and prophesies, which are
themselves hymns and poems, sacred poetry may be sung
within the edifice consecrated to God.

Music is born of joy. It is a direct manifestation of the
soul happy to know itself united with God. Men delighting
in the goodness of God direct hymns of thanks to Him. Do
not the angels sing of His glory and of His sovereign goodness
in their celestial choirs, and did not Jesus Himself like to sing
the hymns of the soul, which are the psalms, with His disciples ?
Music is the art most capable of rendering glory to God. It
is the most dynamic of all, capable of moving all the senses
profoundly ; it can inflame the soul, and when it attains its
end it reaches bliss in the most perfect serenity. Music can
have for its object either the praises of God or the joy of man
who lives in the universe. Secular music in the domain of
general grace has a rôle analogous to that of painting and of
sculpture. It rejoices the soul and represents its emotions,
but, like the plastic arts, it, too, can be marred. It, too, can
swell the heart with vanity, flatter the singer while nursing
his pride, and develop in him hypocrisy, the taste for immodera-
tion, and can thus corrupt him. In just such a way the Tyrians
mollified their ears with voluptuous and perverse songs.

God should be the centre of our songs ; it is to Him that
honour must be rendered, and it is His creation which must
be glorified. When we sing we must do so with moderation,
moderate the intensity and frequency of our songs, respect
the harmony of the whole and insist upon the greatest technical

purity. But that is not enough for the Reformer. Not only should the sacred song be moderate and pure in its expression : it would be only the song of Linotte or of Papegai if the heart's fervour should not correspond to the lips' service.

The singer should have an interior disposition which corresponds to the spiritual reality of the canticle as it is expressed in music. Also when we sing in our temples, we must do it with appropriate weight and majesty and with the interior gravity of soul which corresponds to the depth of the song.

Song thus conceived augments fervour; it unites the soul with God ; it creates a spiritual fraternity among the faithful ; it unites the churches and establishes between God and men the spiritual harmony necessary to those who wish to do Him honour.

The ideas of the Reformer on song had the most profound effects upon the evolution of music in the sixteenth century. From the time of his arrival in Geneva, Calvin recommended the singing of psalms ; he looked for translators and composers, and set himself to work upon them ; but when chance presented him with the psalms of Marot, he gave up his own translation in favour of that of the poet. Calvin discovered the most appropriate melodies for the expression of the psalms' spiritual truth, and these were first the noble airs of Bourgeois and then those of Goudimel. We are, in fact, in the presence of a real renaissance of sacred song. The people of the sixteenth century enthusiastically adopted the psalms, which were to be sung along the " Pré aux Clercs " by all the fervent youth of Paris.

Faithful to Calvinistic sobriety, the composers of the psalter searched for the simplest possible melodies ; they discovered that which Haein calls the immemorial nomes, predestined forms in which the religious fervour and thought contained in the psalms flows with the greatest possible harmony. Once the theme was found, the composers were to treat it in the most simple manner, note against note. Music became simple and its notation underwent a complete transformation. The principal melody changed from the tenor to the soprano voice. The rule of moderation imposed on sacred song by the Reformer was now realised to perfection. All musical critics, including J. J. Rousseau pay homage to the weight and the majesty of the Huguenot cantilena, and Michelet, together with other historians, insists upon the spiritual fraternity uniting for ever those in the same faith who knew how to sing the psalms. So, even during the lifetime of Calvin, the fundamental propositions of his esthetics were realised in music.

All music was to profit by these reforms introduced by the Calvinistic composers into the Huguenot cantilena. The expression which established harmony between song and words was discovered and was to lead to the oratorio. Music, heretofore reserved for the clergy, was to become a universal art, thanks to the Reformation. The psalter, the true siren of Calvinism, conquered many souls for it, and its harmonies soon spread all over the world. The history of the psalter was to parallel that of Calvinism itself, and it is interesting to note that at the present moment, together with a theological renaissance of Calvinism, there is a more pronounced taste on the part of modern Calvinists for the old psalms of the sixteenth century.

LITERATURE

In addition to the music of the psalms, we have the example of another inspiring art, that which manifests itself in the very text of the Scriptures. For Calvin, who created our philosophical prose, there is an art of thinking and of writing to which every writer and every thinker should subject himself. The Bible, the revealed word of God, will give us at once a model of thought and of style, together with the laws which he who wishes to think and to write will obey.

What is the Reformer's art of thought ? To know the value of all thought, it will suffice to know what it is worth in the function of God and His radiation in the universe. The closer it is to the centre, the more dense and profound it will be. Thus every literary text will have its ordered value according to the subject which it is attempting to interpret. Calvin was too much a humanist not to appreciate the value of secular literature. He even believed that there was not sufficient interest in literature, and judged the epoch of Daniel to be more cultivated than his own.

How should our intelligence bring to fruition the gifts which it has received from God ? It should, in the first place, maintain an " attitude of reserve " ; before entering into a discussion, we must be well assured of the truth. The law which thought ought to obey is that of simplicity. Everything ought to be considered in the simplest manner, as it is thus that thought will discover its essential core.

Thought should be conducted in an orderly manner, " so that there may be no confusion," said the Reformer, and Calvin insists on the fact that he always tries to write intelligently and clearly. Order will exclude all hurry. It should be fluid and consistent and, as Calvin says in his vigorous

language, it should not resemble " goat's turds." Deep thought
will repudiate vain ornamentation and will propose the purity
of the Gospel as its model. Calvin recommends that professors
impart their teaching faithfully and discreetly lest they should
serve up a dish that has neither savour nor taste.

Thought should be clear. Every object of thought should
radiate with its own light, that which God has given it.
Thought, by its conformity, its simplicity and its purity, should
be such that its object will traverse it without being either
warped or discoloured. This clarity should be spiritual rather
than logical or psychological. The parables of the Gospel
illustrate this fact, and they have more strength, more efficacy
and more light in their metaphorical form than if they took
the shape of precepts.

Thought, according to Calvin, is like a wild flower. Born
of a seed, it has developed according to the laws which are
appropriate to it ; it has a particular beauty which will suffer
no mixture ; it is adorned with natural colours which the
light sets off to advantage ; it shines with a clarity which
obtrudes itself upon the notice of our intelligence.

Calvin might have been able to appreciate a thought which
was simple, balanced, pure and clear without being capable
of so expressing it in his works. But for so vigorous a spirit,
such an inconsistency could not exist. Style should be in
harmony with thought, and a concise style should correspond
to a compact thought. " Language is created by God to express
cogitation," says he, " and it is perverting the order of God
to beat around the bush, so making the listeners dream and
leave them dreaming."

The Bible, model of thought, will also be the model of style ;
and Calvin celebrates the simple rugged style of the Scriptures
whose rustic characteristics are more moving than the fine
language of rhetoricians. Calvin finds that the style of the
Bible is temperate. For him temperance is translatable in
phrases which are in profound harmony with thought. When
the thought is overflowing with power, the style will itself be
as vehement.

The rugged, temperate style of the Scriptures is sober.
Quite naturally Calvin recommends that the richest possible
thought be expressed by the simplest possible sentences.
Calvin himself takes his place among the more succinct
authors.

Ruggedness, temperance and sobriety then, are characteristic of Scriptural style. Should secular literature observe
these rules to the letter ? The latter has a thought of lesser
density to express, and if it be translated according to the

rules which guided the inspired authors of the Scriptures, the style will evince an earthly beauty. Ruggedness will become simplicity; temperance, harmony; and severity, purity. Calvin is sensitive to the delicacy of its formation. He never ceases to eulogise those authors of the Bible who knew how to write delicately. In the same way, he admires Demosthenes and Cicero; and, as appropriately, knows how to appreciate Seneca.

It is not enough to know the rules of literary art; we must in addition compare Calvin's literary advice with his literary judgments. Before he attempts to criticise, however, the reader should always maintain a certain modesty; and, as Calvin says, he should search for instruction rather than for faults in the work under consideration.

Once this principle is established, against what kind of thought will the Reformer's own criticism inveigh?

In the first place, Calvin objects to thought which is no longer focussed upon its object—to writers who, instead of saying what they have to say, try to please the public. Such people are worldlings, " swollen with the pride of toads."

Thought which dares not express its object for fear of the authorities is forcefully denounced. In fact, a large part of Calvin's *De Scandalis* is directed against authors who let themselves be taken in by appearances and who, without any object in view, write works which are then illusory and dangerous because of the corrupting fermentation they contain. Rabelais is condemned because, having tasted of the Gospel, he was struck blind and the audacity of his laugh profaned the spiritual life.

In the same way Calvin criticises superficiality and truculence of style which too often degenerate into buffoonery. In short, no one stigmatises excessive verbiage more than he does. To say little in a great many words seems to him a grave mistake, and he even brings this charge against some revered authors. In spite of his admiration for Saint Augustine, Calvin does not hide from his friend Farel the fact that the prolixity of the Bishop of Hippo bores him. In a letter to Coligny he declares that the famous *Confession of Augsburg* is " slightly built, feeble and obscure." The Reformer does not spare his friends. He likes Melanchthon, but the great German " digs too far in the same direction." The great Bucer of Strasbourg is " too complicated "; he writes too much for his equals and is too sublime to be understood by the more humble. Farel's style is too confused and too verbose. All these mistakes lead to obscurity, often a direct result of verbosity.

All of Calvin's ideas on thought and style can be found in

II

162 REFORMED FAITH AND ITS ETHICAL CONSEQUENCES

the analysis which the Reformer makes of poetry. He may be said to have used poetry to illustrate them. Each time that an ancient poet has been able to seize a dynamic idea and to condense it in a harmoniously rhythmical line, Calvin will not fail to quote him. Thanks to the poetic form in which it is clothed, truth will see its power of expansion growing, and is it not the duty of everyone to contribute to its spread ? We have looked up the lines which were dear to the Reformer, and we have discovered that for him the message of the poets often confirmed the most important propositions of theology. Poetry is capable of expressing most of the truths revealed by general Grace. It knows how to ridicule human vices and pity human sufferings. It can also sing the beauty of the universe. Finally, when it becomes the revealed word in the prophecies or in the psalms, it is the perfect form which makes it possible for the soul to sing the glory of the Creator. It is true that Calvin lays down for us no poetics in the proper sense of the word, but we cannot help being struck by the breadth of his remarks and the excellence of his taste. The mind and heart of this Reformer are assuredly open to poetry.

Calvin, thus inclined toward poetry, bowed before the genius of Marot and distributed the latter's version of the Psalms. He encouraged Theodore de Bèze to finish the translation, and the most conservative critics are forced to recognise the beauty of Marot's psalms, their fidelity to the text, their grave simplicity. So Calvin not only gave poetry the place which it deserves, but he guided Marot in his translation and with all his authority supported a great lyrical movement— that of the Calvinist poets of the sixteenth century, which was to reach its culmination in Agrippa d'Aubigné.

CONCLUSION

I. To conclude, let us ask one last question : Are there in Calvinist thought the fundamental elements of an esthetic system ? If by this word we mean the place of the vision of beauty and of the creation of the beautiful in a general system of thought, then we will answer in the affirmative. Certainly Calvin was not an esthetician ; he did not deliberately search for the nature of the beautiful by the pursuit of a determined analytical method. Neither is he the kind of esthete who admires an exclusive sort of beauty ; but we find in his work, first a vision of the beautiful integrated in his general vision of the world ; then, a conception of art incorporated in its place in the midst of the other so-called earthly activities ; and finally, a conception of the ugly which serves to intensify his belief in sin. We believe that we are not expanding its sense too much when we apply the term esthetics to such a conception of beauty and of art.

II. We believe that we have discovered in Calvin an element which seemed most original to us: that is, his comprehension of artistic creation. According to Calvin, the artist should commune with the very springs of creation, and in his work continue the work of the Creator Himself. Instead of seeing God in a mystical vision, he should, on the contrary, by means of a great effort, identify himself with his object in order to re-create it. Is not this understanding of the work of art as related to creation something new in the sixteenth century, and do not the following centuries enrich it by their successive contributions?

III. We then noticed a great balance in the whole of the Reformer's conception of beauty and the arts. Beauty is neither exalted nor scorned, but retains its value as a sign of the revelation of the creative activity of God. Calvin insists at once on the importance of the object of art and the qualities required of the artist. Moreover, the Reformer attempts to establish an equilibrium between the moral and the artistic life of the creator of the work of art. Finally, by his tastes, by his enthusiasm for the beautiful and his censure of the ugly, the unwieldy and the obscure, Calvin exhibits the true artistic temperament. That he was an artist can hardly be disputed—he who was able to create our French prose in the midst of a struggle of ideas, he who was the precursor of French classicism.

IV. If in closing we compare the esthetic ideas of the Reformer with trends which are manifesting themselves to-day, especially in literature, we find in the conceptions of Calvin a decidedly contemporary spirit. Are not his ideas on art and beauty timely in that they manifest the same taste for the objective, the same desire to let the purpose of art give its laws to the subject, the same taste for the characteristic, for the essential, for the sober and unadorned lines, and for arts free from all which is not properly within their province? Was not Calvin himself, in the sixteenth century, possessed of just this desire for a clear vision? and was he not also animated by this same aspiration for a renewed fervour—two of the spiritual signs of our era? But to these tastes and these desires Calvin gives a true purpose, which is the unceasingly creative activity of a spiritual truth of which we are, and should be, the inspired recipients.

RÉSUMÉ DU DISCOURS

Fait par le Pasteur Léon Wencelius

Sur *La Foi Réformée dans ses Conséquences Éthiques sur L'art*

Lé titre qu'a choisi l'auteur c'est " La philosophie cal-viniste de l'art." L'objet de l'auteur est de réhabiliter la Réforme sur des fondements esthétiques, en faisant ainsi pour réfuter, comme un Français, une idée française que le pro-testantisme est une source de laideur.

Calvin créa la prose philosophique française, perfectionnant dans ce but une langue déjà remarquable pour sa beauté de pensée et de style. Pour lui était beau l'ordre comme il se fait voir dans la nature, dans l'âme humaine et dans le sacrifice de rachat fait par le Christ.

La création et la perpétuation du monde créé proclament la beauté de Dieu laquelle est un élément dans sa gloire. Le péché n'est pas une simple illusion de la beauté mais sa laide négation. L'Évangile qui opère la restauration des pécheurs est la perfection de la beauté. Il y a en effet une beauté commune qui est appréciée de tous ; les seuls élus voient la spirituelle beauté de la grâce particulière et en ressentent les effets salutaires.

Dieu permet à l'homme de cultiver les arts mécaniques ainsi que les arts libéraux, parce que l'art est, dans son origine, un don naturel—partie de l'intelligence humaine non con-ditionnée par l'élection, mais l'artiste doit, dans l'exercice de ce don, être soumis à la règle divine dont le réformateur était un interprète fidèle.

L'unique objet de l'art plastique est séculaire, pour ce qui concerne la décoration de bâtiments et d'intérieurs, la sculpture et la peinture peuvent donner de l'instruction et causer du plaisir ; c'est-à-dire que l'art peut décemment présenter des choses créées. Il se fourvoie du moment qu'il essaie de représenter Dieu qui est spirituel et transcendant. Le décalogue défend à l'art de devenir le serviteur de l'idolâtrie.

Calvin reconnut la beauté émouvante du symbolisme dans le culte de l'Ancien Testament comme appropriée à cet âge moins éclairé avant que la lumière spirituelle fût révélée en Jésus-Christ. Maintenant il est exigé du culte qu'il soit simple ; sans ornement, sobre et pur en esprit et en vérité, marqué par une harmonie entre l'âme et Dieu.

La musique et la poésie sont les seuls arts permis dans le culte. La musique est la joie de l'âme, un organe convenable de louanges adoratrices lorsqu'elle est exprimée en chansons, modérée et pure, la réponse ardente du cœur au service des lèvres.

Calvin, engageant les psaumes dans la version de Marot et mises en musique par Bourgeois et d'autres, apprit aux gens communs qui jusque-là avaient été muets à être joyeux de la voix.

En littérature également Calvin enseigna et démontra par exemple que la beauté est l'art qui permet que la pensée puisse être mise en ordre avec précision et clarté.

Calvin reconnut la valeur, quant à la force et la faculté de toucher, de la poésie soumise à la vérité spirituelle ; les Psaumes il les considérait comme la poésie principale.

Paper No. 9

LES CALVINISTES DANS L'HISTOIRE DES ARTS

Par M. le Pasteur P. R. Musculus, France

AVANT PROPOS

Avant de vous lire le papier que j'avais préparé, je voudrais dire quelques mots : Il y a peut-être des personnes qui pensent que le meilleur des mondes est une sorte de monde calviniste qui aurait, à cause de son calvinisme, le privilege d'être créateur de toute civilisation excellente, qu'il s'agisse de pédagogie, de droit, de science, de politique, voire même de l'art militaire, de diplomatie ou de finances. Et ces mêmes personnes seraient heureuses de ce que l'on puisse encore compléter le catalogue par de grands artistes, ces grands artistes que Rome s'acharne si souvent à refuser au calvinisme.

Certes, la calvinisme (je le dirai tout à l'heure) a suscité de très grands artistes, et nous avous le droit d'être joyeux de ce que, dans notre Église, le Seigneur ait ainsi appelé de tels hommes à cette vocation. Mais prenons bien garde à ne pas préférer le calvinisme à d'autres théologies parce que, par lui, se seraient épanouies à un rare degré toutes sortes d'arts brillants ou de savantes disciplines. Ces choses nous interessent, nous les constatons avec reconnaissance. C'est un devoir pour nous de les connaître et de les étudier, mais elles ne doivent jamais être présentées comme des garantees qui justifieraient notre doctrine. Méfions nous d'une telle apologétique.

Entre Pentecôte et Son retour le Seigneur appelle par Son

Esprit Saint toutes sortes d'hommes au service de Son Église. Parmi le peuple qu'Il s'est acquis dans Sa grâce, Il suscite des éducateurs et des légistes, des savants et des artistes, voire même des capitaines, des parlementaires ou des banquiers. Mais dans leur vocation particulière et leur obéissance, tous ces hommes n'existent en tant que membres de l'Église de Dieu, membres du corps de Christ, que comme des *pécheurs pardonnés par grâce*, baptisés au nom du Père, du Fils et du Saint-Esprit.

Il ne s'agit donc pas d'échafauder de beaux systèmes ornés d'une garniture de grands hommes et de se féliciter d'une culture calviniste que nous prendrions pour un petit royaume de Dieu sur la terre ; il s'agit simplement, *en toute vocation*, de nous souvenir avec crainte et tremblement de notre vraie condition devant Dieu, notre vie sous la croix, d'être soumis à Sa seule Parole entendue dans la foi, d'être joyeux dans l'espérance de Son triomphe au moment éternel du retour de Christ et de la résurrection des corps. Si nous nous disons calvinistes, que ce soit seulement parce que Jean Calvin nous a appris, comme nul autre docteur avant ou après lui, à écouter vraiment comment Dieu parle à Son Église par toute l'Écriture Sainte et par la seule Écriture Sainte. Notre calvinisme, c'est notre attentive obèissance à cette Écriture Sainte qui nous montre Christ.

Paul Romane Musculus.

Introduction

Cette étude a pour but de rappeler quelle fut la place des calvinistes dans l'histoire générale des arts plastiques : peinture, sculpture, architecture et arts mineurs. Il s'agit donc d'une rapide étude d'ensemble et non d'un travail sur les seuls peintres de scènes bibliques ou les seuls architectes d'églises. Nous montrerons comment des calvinistes ont rempli leur vocation de peintre, sculpteur, architecte, graveur, émailleur, verrier, tapissier. Nous ne nous étendrons pas sur ce que ces artistes exécutèrent officiellement pour les Églises Réformées, ce qui demanderait une étude tout à fait spéciale où les questions liturgiques formeraient une longue introduction.

Depuis le XVI siècle les artistes calvinistes tiennent une place considérable dans l'histoire de l'art occidental. Leur rôle a été capital non seulement dans des pays en majorité réformés comme la Hollande, la Suisse ou l'Écosse, mais dans des pays comme la France où, jusqu'à la Révocation de l'Édit de Nantes, la minorité réformée a compté de grands et très nombreux artistes.

L'histoire des artistes calvinistes est conditionnée par l'histoire générale et par l'histoire de l'Église. Il y a eu des persécutions qui n'ont pas toujours été, au XVIe siècle, aussi défavorables à l'art réformé qu'on pouvait le croire, mais qui, lorsqu'elles se sont tenacement prolongées comme en France après la Révocation, ont amené la disparition presque compléte d'artistes réformés. Il y a aussi eu dans l'Église des périodes de divisions et des infiltrations hérétiques, généralement très néfastes à l'art : si l'on rencontre toujours beaucoup *d'artistes réformés* de naissance ou d'éducation, ou ne peut souvent plus parler *d'art réformé*.

Malgré le caractère très général de cet aperçu, nous insisterons surtout sur l'apport des français qui nous est le mieux connu. Si célèbres soient ils, nous ne mentionnerons pas les artistes dont le calvinisme demeure incertain : les deux Jean Cousin, Jean Clouet, les trois frères Le Nain, l'émailleur Lèonard Limousin, l'architecte Philibert Delorme, le flamand Pieter Breughel.

I. LE XVIe SIÈCLE

A. *Ligier Richier, Jean Goujon et les sculpteurs français*

Si la Suisse Zwinglienne a donné deux célèbres peintres : Hans Holbein et Nicolas Manuel Deutsch, le XVIe siècle français, lui, eut des grands sculpteurs calvinistes plutôt que des grands peintres ;[1] deux d'entre eux, Ligier Richier et Jean Goujon, sont même les meilleurs sculpteurs de leur temps. Tous ont plus ou moins été victimes des persécutions religieuses.

Ligier Richier est lorrain. Pour le mausolée de René de Châlon, prince d'Orange, il a exécuté la célèbre statue funéraire appelée " la mort " ou " le squelette," atteignant un effrayant degré d'audace qu'aucun naturalisme ne saurait dépasser. Mais, dans ce cadavre dressé, aussi bien que dans l'émouvante et si apaisée mise au tombeau de l'Église Saint Étienne à Saint-Mihiel, quelle ferme foi en la résurrection. Persécuté en Lorraine, Ligier Richier dut s'exiler et mourut à Genève. Son art rappelait encore la sculpture du Moyen-Age, celui de *Jean Goujon* appartient tout à fait à la Renaissance. Il sculpte

---

[1] Le peintre le plus connu, *Corneille de Lyon*, portraitiste qui fut presque l'égal des Clouet, à abjuré en 1569 avec sa famille. La famille de *François I*. *Quesnel* (né près d'Edimbourg) a abjuré également.

Jean de Hoey, venu de Leyde et apparenté au célèbre Lucas de Leyde, dirigea d'importants chautiers de peinture décorative à Fontainebleau. *François du Bois* dut s'exiler et mourut à Genève. L'attentif miniaturiste *Isaac Olivier*, né en Normandie, émigra à Londres avec ses parents des 1568.

sur bois de magnifiques panneaux ornant les portes de l'Église
Saint Maclou à Rouen ; l'un d'eux est une illustration fidèle
et détaillée du Bon Berger selon Jean x en même temps qu'une
satire contre le clergé romain. Jusqu'au jour où il dut fuir
les pérsécutions, Goujon a orné Paris et l'Ile de France de ses
œuvres ; il a exécuté le beau jubé de Saint Germain l'Auxerrois,
il a travaillé au château d'Écouen, au Palais du Louvre, au
bel hôtel du président de Ligueris (aujourd'hui Musée Carnavalet). Dans ses écrits, toutes les fois qu'il parle de l'art,
d'architecture ou de sculpture et de l'habileté qu'on lui re-
connait dans l'un et l'autre, il en rapporte toujours le mérite
à Son Dieu : " La cognoissance que Dieu m'en a donné,"
aime-t-il à répéter.[1]

Son contemporain *Pierre Bontemps* apparait en mai 1536
à Fontainebleau où il travaille sous la direction du Primatice.
On lui doit plusieurs figures agenouillées et les gisants de
François I. et de Claude de France dans l'abbaye de Saint
Denis, et deux beaux monuments aujourd'hui au Louvre.
Le Louvre possède également d'importants fragments d'œuvres
de *Barthélemy Prieur* qui suceéda à Germain Pilon comme
" sculpteur ordinaire du Roy."

Maximilien Poultrain, surnommé Colt, s'établit à Londres ;
il est l'auteur du tombeau de la reine Elisabeth et des monuments en forme de berceau des filles de Jacques I., Sophie et
Anne, dans le chœur de l'abbaye de Westminster. On notera
le rôle que des réformés : Ligier Richier, Pierre Bontemps,
Barthélemy Prieur, Maximilieu Poultrain, out joué dans la
sculpture funéraire monumentale de leur époque.

B. Les arts mineurs en France

Tous les arts mineurs : peinture sur émail, orfévrerie,
verrerie, reliure, imprimerie, gravure, brillèrent au XVI. siècle
d'un vif éclat, et ce soit surtout des calvinistes qui perfec-
tionnèrent toutes ces techniques. Ces artistes et artisans nous
ont laissé de bien belles œuvres malgre les effrayables persécutions qu'ils endurèrent : un grand nombre d'entre eux furent
massacrés, d'autres durent s'exiler.

Les émailleurs travaillent surtout à Limoges. *Colin
Noailher* peint en camaïeu de petites plaques avec des scènes
illustrant des versets bibliques ; *Pierre* et *Jean Courteys*,
Pierre Reymond, exécutent des coupes, des assiettes et des
plats émaillés ornés de personnages de l'Ecriture Sainte :
Joseph et Pharaon, Moïse, Salomon, Josias. Cet art, ainsi
que celui des peintres et graveurs calvinistes, se distingue
généralement par son caractère très " Ancien Testament " ;

[1] Voir article d'André Michel, *Foi et Vie*, 1898, p. 69.

il est théocentrique et narratif, alors que l'art religieux luthérien est plutot christocentrique et expressif. On doit aussi noter que la Renaissance et l'humanisme eurent sur l'art des calvinistes français une influence qui ne s'exerça pas aussi fortement sur l'art luthérien.

Bernard Palissy, le célèbre potier et émailleur, était passionné pour le monde des plantes et des petits animaux en qui il admirait la création de Dieu. Il en ornait des vases et des plats un peu trop sculptés et surchargés, et dont la technique est plus admirable que le gout.[1] Les verriers calvinistes sont trés nombreux, surtout à Gabre et au Mas d'Azil.

Les plus célèbres médailleurs (*Nicolas et Isaac Briot, Guillaume et Abraham Dupré*) vivront au début du XVII. siècle ; cependant sous les règnes de Henri III. et de Henri IV. le graveur *Philippe Danfrie* est déjà tailleur général des effigies du roi pour les monnaies de France.

L'universel titre de gloire des calvinistes du XVI. siècle est le développement immense qu'ils apportèrent aux arts du livre : reliure, imprimerie, gravure sur bois et sur cuivre. Les grands imprimeurs se distinguèrent par la beaute et l'extrème correction des ouvrages sortis de leurs presses ; ce furent des hommes très savants et attachés à leur Eglise, de remarquables techniciens qui imprimèrent sans relâche Bibles, recueils de Psaumes, ouvrages de théologie, livres d'édification. Les plus fameux furent *Robert l'Estienne*, ami intime de Calvin et de Théodore de Bèze ; *Geofroy Tory*, maître du graveur de lettres Claude Garamond ; les lyonnais *Sébastien Gryphe* et *Jean I. de Tournes*. Les meilleurs graveurs calvinistes apportèrent leur concours à leurs amis imprimeurs ; suivant le genre, leur œuvre peut être divisé en trois groupes : les portraits de Réformateurs, les scénes bibliques et historiques, les caricatures anticatholiques. Les " Icones " de Théodore de Bèze, expressives gravures sur bois attribuées à *Pierre Eskrich* (dit Cruche), sont l'un des premiers recueils de portraits gravés des Réformateurs. Peu aprés *Théodore de Bry* [2] grave sur cuivre les " Icones " de l'important recueil de Jean Jacques Boissard. Ces ouvrages, souvent réédités, out joui à l'époque d'une très grande vogue.

Guillaume le Testu a composé un magnifique atlas dédié à Gaspard de Coligny et renfermant cinquante-six cartes illustrées et ornées. *Thomas de Leu*, d'origine hollandaise, a

---

[1] *Voir Foi et Vie*, 1935, p. 609 à 612.

[2] Théodore de Bry a gravé les dessins de *Jacques le Moine*, dit de Morgues, attaché à l'expédition de Laudonnière en 1564 et qui avait pu échapper au massacre du Fort Caroline. Ce sont des scénes de la vie indienne, des combats, des ruses de guerre ou de chasse.

gravé les planches de " Architecture et perspective " par Jacques Perret ; ce recueil contient plusieurs projets d'églises réformées. *Jean Duvet* est l'auteur d'une suite sur l'Apocalypse. L'orléanais *Etienne Delaulne* a gravé de scénes de l'Ancien Testament. Les gravures les plus connues, celles qui ont été vulgarisées par de nombreuses reproductions, sont les scènes des guerres de religion par *Jacques Tortorel* et *Jean Perrissin* ; ces saisissantes estampes existent sur cuivre et sur bois, celles sur bois ont peut-être été exécutées par *Jacques Le Challeux*. La caricature eut également une vogue inouïe, elle trouvait un adversaire considérable en l'Eglise romaine. Les deux partis se lancèrent des poquets de sottises et même des plaisanteries immondes, mais beaucoup de ces caricatures sont de belles gravures d'une gaillarde saveur.

Au début du XVII. siècle les calvinistes vont s'illustrer comme remarquables techniciens de la tapisserie. Les *Carraye*, ainsi que plusieurs autres familles réformées, ont droit par leurs travaux et leurs alliances à une part de l'honneur qui reste attaché au nom des *gobelins*, les plus illustres teinturiers et tapissiers. La manufacture des *La Planche*, parents des gobelins, a éxécute les " tapisseries de Coriolan " tissées entre 1600 et 1610.

II. Les Architectes Réformés en France au XVIᵉ et au XVII. Siècle

A. L'Architecture civile réformée

Les architectes calvinistes eurent à la fin du XVI. siècle et au début du XVII. siècle une très profonde influence sur tout ce qui s'est construit en France vers cette èpoque ; c'est d'eux que viennent les grands toits et les nobles façades un peu graves. Ils travaillèrent dans de nombreuses villes : Caen, Montauban, la Rochelle, Orthey, Pau, et surtout dans la capitale du royaume.[1]

A Caen, *Abel le Prestre* bâtit la maison de Jacques de Cahaignes, puis probablement le bel hôtel d'Ecoville avec ses statues de David et de Judith sur l'une des façades, l'hôtel de Mondrainville, et le beau château de Fontaine-Henri.

A Genève, un architecte de Langres, *Nicolas Bogueret*, construit la rampe à arcades de l'Hôtel de Ville. Les arcades

---

[1] Strasbourg, ville libre et bucérienne, connut aussi à ce moment un extra-ordinaire essort architectural. Thomas Ulberger embellit la somptueuse demeure dite de " l'Œuvre Notre-Dame " destinée aux architectes qui dirigent les travaux de la cathédrale devenue réformée. Jean Schoch dirige les travaux du plus grand monument strasbourgeois de la Renaissance, l'hôtel du Commerce. Le Magistrat fait édifier la Grande Boucherie, aujourd'hui Musée Historique.

sont un signe très particulier de l'architecture réformée de l'époque ; on en a de nombreux exemples à Montauban, à la Rochelle, en Béarn, à Paris.

Ce fut surtout Paris qui bénéficia des embellissements qu'exécutèrent les architectes calvinistes sous la direction de Sully. Sur la Place Royale, toute en arcades, la noblesse réformée occupait quelques unes des plus magnifiques demeures. Plus important et plus original que le plan de la Place Royale aurait été le projet de la " Place et porte de France " soumis à Henri IV par l'ingénieur calviniste *Jacques Aleaume* et par Claude Chastillon ; mais la mort du roi en empêcha brusquement l'exécution.

Pour réaliser ses vastes plans Sully a trouvé parmi les membres de l'Église Réformée de Paris ses plus excellents collaborateurs. L'œuvre des architectes réformés de cette époque est d'une importance exceptionnelle.

B. Les Androuet du Cerceau et Salomon de Brosse

Une seule famille, véritable pépinière de grands architectes, jouit d'un prestige considèrable sous Henri III., Henri IV., Marie de Médicis et Louis XIII. dont elle reçoit de génération en génération les plus hautes fonctions.

Baptiste Androuet du Cerceau commence le Pont Neuf, travaille au nouveau château de Saint Germain en Laye, à la chapelle des Valois à Saint Denis, au Palais du Louvre. *Jacques II. Androuet du Cerceau* travaille surtout au Louvre et aux Tuileries ; c'est à lui que l'on doit le projet de réunir le Louvre aux Tuileries. Le neveu, *Jean Androuet du Cerceau,* remanie l'ancien hôtel de Ligueris (Musée Carnavalet), construit le magnifique hôtel de Sully et l'hôtel de M. de Bretonvilliers. C'est par lui que fut édifie à Fontainebleau le grand escalier en fer à cheval déployant avec opulence ses somptueuses balustrades de piene ; tout y demeure noble, luxueux avec mesure : c'est un des chefs-d'œuvre les plus parfaits de l'architecture française sous Louis XIII.

Salomon de Brosse[1] est de la même famille. Il exécute le Palais du Luxembourg qui fit l'enchantement de la reine Marie de Médicis et qui présente une unité de composition que bien peu de monuments possèdent au même degré. On lui doit encore la reconstruction de la grande salle du Palais de Justice (dite de Pas Perdus), le magnifique palais du Parlement de Bretagne à Rennes, plusieurs châteaux, et enfin le célèbre Temple de Charenton construit pour l'Église Réformée de Paris.

[1] Voir *L'Ouvrage de Jacques Pannier*, Paris 1911.

Jean Marot, architecte et graveur du Roy, a réuni de nombreux sujets d'architecture dans ce qu'on appelle " le Grand Marot " et " le Petit Marot." Au milieu de projets présentés pour l'achèvement du Louvre, celui de Marot se distingue par ses caractères français et par son élégance ; c'est une protestation du goût et du génie national contre les projets baroques et italianisants du Bernin et de Rainaldi.

C. L'urbanisme et l'art des jardins

En 1620, un célèbre ingénieur et urbaniste né en Normandie, *Salomon de Caus,* était venu à Paris. Il venait de dessiner des jardins pour le roi d'Angleterre et le duc de Brabant, et le parc du château de Heidelberg pour le Prince Palatin. Nommé ingénieur du Roy il fait les premiers grands projets de voirie de la capitale.

Les grands architectes des jardins royaux sont des calvin- istes. *Jacques Boiceau de la Barauderie* organise les jardins, les allées, les terrasses, les charmilles, les fontaines, les bassins, les grottes, les volières du Luxembourg ; il aménage les jardins du Louvre et des Tuileries, s'occupe du parc de Saint Germain ; il crée les jardins et le premier parc de Versailles où lui succédera comme intendant des jardins du Roy son neveu *Jacques de Nemours.*

Beaucoup plus tard le Notre enverra le réformé *Siméon Godeau* à Berlin pour exécuter d'après ses plans les beaux jardins du château de Lietzenbourg (aujourd'hui Charlotten- bourg).

En résumé, depuis l'Édit de Nantes, les réformés dirigeaient les constructions et les jardins royaux, l'illustre famille des du Cerceau et des de Brosse bâtissait des châteaux et des palais dont la parfaite clarté de plan, l'allure majestueuse, annoncent le grand style de Perrault et Hardouin Mansart.

III. LES PEINTRES DU XVIIᵉ. SIÈCLE

A. Les calvinistes et l'Académie Royale

Sous le règne de Henri IV. il y avait eu à Paris un peintre estimé : *Jacob Bunel* ; il passait à son époque pour le premier de l'Europe mais il ne reste malheureusement plus rien des grandes compositions décoratives qu'il avait exécutées pour le Louvre et diverses églises.

Un très grand nombre de calvinistes furent membres de l'Académie Royale de peinture et de sculpture, mais beaucoup n'eurent quelque gloire que grâce à leur titre ; pour les autres la

dignité d'académicien n'a pas ajouté grand chose à un talent
qui se passait fort bien de cette ratification officielle.[1]

En 1648 Lebrun fonde l'Académie et tout de suite sa
dictature commence à contaminer les meilleurs artistes ; sa
doctrine trompe le peintre calviniste Sébastien Bourdon sur
sa vraie vocation et ce bon peintre s'égare en se voyant propre
à composer de grandes œuvres. L'académisme c'est le triomphe
de la platitude et de la tiédeur, le nivellement de toutes les
personnalités ; que l'on preuve les grands peintres catholiques
officiels ou les académiciens réformés comme Louis Testelin,
toute cette peinture sans caractère est bonne à mettre " dans
le même sac." S'il y eut parmi les académiciens quelques
grands artistes, ce fut malgré l'Académie, on pourrait presque
dire contre l'Académie. *Abraham Bosse* qui y fut professeur
de géométrie et de perspective eut de telles querelles qu'il finit
par en être exclu. Ses belles estampes nous donnent l'image
la plus vraie et la plus minutieuse de la vie de son époque. Il
est avant tout le peintre des vertus bourgeoises, des interviews
honnêtes ; une de ses plus belles gravures représente un père
de famille, au centre d'une grande table, assis sous les Tables
de la Loi disant le Benedicite.[2]

Les autres calvinistes de l'Académie vivent en bons termes
avec cette digne institution. Si l'on excepte les le Main, il y
a déjà sept réformés lors de la fondation en 1648. Le plus
connu est le Montpelliérain *Sébastien Bourdon* qui a décoré
plusieurs églises de Paris et a peint l'histoire de Phaeton pour
la grande galerie de l'hôtel de Bretonvilliers. Le Louvre
conserve plusieurs de ses toiles. Dans ses baltes de bohémiens,
ses peintures de mendiants, il se montre l'émule des le Nain ;
quelques uns de ses portraits et études sont excellents, le reste
de son œuvre est froid, " académique."

Parmi de nombreux autres académiciens calvinistes il faut
citer *Jacob Van Loo, Jean Michelin, Jacques Rousseau* (décorateur
paysagiste qui travailla à Versailles), *Jean Baptiste Forest* et
Jacob d'Agard.

B. *Rembrandt et la Hollande réformée*

Rembrandt van Rhyn est le plus grand peintre chrétien
qu'il y ait eu depuis le Concile de Trente. Après les hésita-
tions de l'adolescence on peut voir deux parties dans son œuvre.
D'abord une période triomphante : il vit avec sa jeune femme

[1] Voir " les protestants de l'Académie Royale de peinture et de sculptire,"
par P. R. M. (la Quinzaine Protestante—2 mai à 16 juillet 1937).
[2] Voir " Abraham Bosse et la société française au XVII siecle," par André
Blum, et compte-rendu dans *Foi et Vie* (février-mars 1934).

Laskia, sa gloire et sa richesse vont croissant, il travaille pour le Prince d'Orange, il réve de devenir le Reubens hollandais ; il exprime alors l'élément dynamique et réthorique du baroque : il aime la gesticulation, choisit des sujets comme les scènes tourmentées de la vie de Samson, Jésus chassant les marchands du Temple, la Résurrection, l'Ascension. Puis, vers 1648, au moment où Lebrun fonde à Paris l'Académie Royale, la gloire et le succès de Rembrandt sont passés, le foyer du peintre a été assombri par les deuils, il est veuf, depuis plusieurs années, il souffre ; les succès mondains sont finis, mais c'est alors que commence la plus saisissante période de création du peintre et du graveur ; Rembrandt se détourne du baroque, il va lire sa Bible comme Parole de Dieu.

Le Christ, dans l'œuvre de Rembrandt, nous est continuellement révélé dans le miracle de sa double nature divine et humaine. Il est le Fils unique de Dieu ayant revêtu notre chair et acceptant de souffrir au milieu des pécheurs, de se solidariser avec des coupables, de pleurer avec eux, d'être puni pour eux. Rembrandt est le peintre de la souffrance car il y a chez lui le sentiment tragique de notre péché, de notre incapacité totale à faire le bien. Chaque misère peinte par lui nous touche comme un reproche personnel, nous devient intolérable, que ce soit l'homme brisé par la douleur que le Bon Samaritain recueille, ou le Fils Prodigue pitoyable et tremblant de repentance, à genoux contre son père aveugle. Aucun peintre ne nous a parlé de l'amour chrétien comme Rembrandt qui fut un peintre de la pauvreté, un homme qui peint les pauvres parce qu'il les aime comme ses frères en Christ et parce que, devant Dieu, il est pauvre et humble comme eux. Toute la véritable grandeur de l'art de Rembrandt réside dans sa pauvreté, sa foi en un Dieu qui s'est abaissé jusqu'au fond de la souffrance humaine. A la profondeur où il nous a placés et où le Crucifié nous trouve, Rembrandt nous dit qu'il n'y a pas avec Dieu de communion plus vraie, plus belle et meilleure que cette pauvreté.

Mais le calvinisme de Rembrandt n'est pas que dans ses toiles ou graveurs à sujets bibliques. Chaque homme reçoit sur terre une " vocation " déterminée qu'il accomplira (qu'il soit dans l'Église ou qu'il n'y soit pas) parce que telle est la volonté de Dieu qui gouverne tout Son univers. Cette doctrine calviniste du don des vocations selon " la grâce commune," beaucoup de tableaux de Rembrandt l'expriment. " Les médicins de la Leçon d'anatomie," écrit Léon Wencélius, " les arquebusiers, les drapiers reflètent tous une vocation spécifique qui doit s'accomplir dans une forme donnée. Tous ces bourgeois ont une vie que déjà leur profession incline dans un sens déterminé, et elle servira à illustrer à sa manière la science, l'industrie, ou le service de l'Etat, qui tous, nous le savons, doivent pour Calvin faire briller la gloire du Créateur." [1]

Autour de la figure unique de Rembrandt les autres grands peintres de la Hollande réformée semblent n'avoir que peu d'importance. Cependant quelle remarquable pléiade de bons peintres que l'école hollandaise du XVII⁰ siècle ! Les portraits, les paysages, les animaux, l'intimité du foyer, voilà ce qui la caractérise et ce que l'on a souvent présenté comme " peinture réformée," quoique cette appellation amène bien des réserves et risque d'enfermer la notion de peinture réformée dans le cadre précis de l'honnêteté et de la morale ; ce qui nous est décerné comme un compliment deviendrait alors un jugement.

Le portrait jouit d'une faveur particulière dans la Hollande du XVII⁰ siècle ; portraits sur commande de riches bourgeois portant la fraise aussi bien que portraits corporatifs composés sur de grandes toiles en longueur. Là, *Frans Hals* est un portraitiste étonnant, parfois un peu débraillé, coptant le rire et le mouvement.

Un autre genre très goûté c'est la minutieuse peinture célébrant les vertus bourgeoises, la vie familiale dans les grandes chambres dallées de noir et blanc ou dans les petites cours aux murs de briques. *Pieter de Hooch* et *Vermeer de Delft* sont les peintres affectueux et attentifs des interieurs hollandais bien corrects et bien sages. *Nicolas Maës* peint de bonnes vieilles méditant, paupières baissées et mains jointes, dans la solitude d'humbles cuisines. *Emmanuel de Witte* se spécialise dans les interieurs d'églises.

Le goût des Hollandais pour les paysages est encore plus marqué. Avant eux on ne peignait guère de paysages que pour y placer de petits épisodes, ou encore comme fond à une scène ou à un portrait. Dans le paysage hollandais, par exemple chez *Jacob van Ruysdaël*, peintre de la mer et de la forêt, quand il y a des personnages ils n'ont généralement aucune importance, la création est magnifiée indépendamment des gestes des créatures. Les paysagistes hollandais expriment une cosmologie.

Un événement se passe à quelques kilomètres de la Hollande, c'est la conversion au calvinisme du grand peintre anversois *Jacob Jordaens*. Il avait grandi sous l'influence de Rubens et, dans son œuvre d'artiste, l'empreinte de sa conversion est peu marquée. Cependant il traite de préférence des sujets empruntés à l'Écriture et il commente ses tableaux au moyen

[1] *Calvin et Rembrandt*, par L. Wencélius, Paris 1937, p. 230.
Voir " Remarques sur Rembrandt, le calvinisme et les Mennonites " (*Bulletin de la Société calviniste de France*, mai 1933).

de versets bibliques, soit en inscrivant le texte même sur la toile, soit en se bornant à renvoyer au verset en question. Avec son épouse il voulut être inhumé près de la frontière hollandaise, dans le cimetière de la petite ville calviniste de Putte ; sur sa tombe, il voulut cette epitaphe : " Christ est l'espoir de notre résurrection."

C. *Calvinisme et Contre-Réforme*

L'art réformé hollandais eut au XVIIe siècle une force d'expansion telle qu'il a pu disputer victorieusement au baroque italien toute l'Europe du Nord, depuis l'Angleterre jusqu'à la Russie, et que le bassin de la Baltique devint à cet égard une sorte de grand lac hollandais.[1] Les grands centres de résistance au baroque (création de la Contre-Réforme, œuvre du Concile de Trent et de l'ordre des Jésuites) furent : d'une part tous les pays conquis par la Réforme, d'autre part la France où la minorité calviniste a joué un rôle important, empêchant le baroque de déferler sur les monuments avec le déchaînement, la fantaisie et le luxueux désordre qui se sont déployés en Italie, en Espagne, dans les Flandres. Ajoutons que l'influence janséniste, elle aussi, a été grande sur l'art français de l'époque. Le roi a fait venir à Paris le Bernin, l'homme du baroque et de la Contre-Réforme, mais pour la grande colonnade du Louvre ou lui préféra un autre architecte, un français, le sévère Claude Perrault dont la famille était internement liée aux Arnauld.

IV. DEPUIS LA RÉVOCATION

A. *L'expansion de l'art français par " le Refuge "*

La Révocation de l'Édit de Nantes fut un désastre pour la France mais un immense enrichissement pour les pays qui accueillirent les réfugiés. Des centaines d'artistes, d'artisans et d'industriels calvinistes émigrèrent ; là où ils s'établirent leur influence fut très grande car ils apportaient avec eux non seulement leur art, leur métier ou leur industrie, mais le goût français. En cinquante ans ce goût français aura conquis l'Europe septentionale et centrale. Ce sont les calvinistes exilés que l'on rencontre à Amsterdam ou à Copenhague, à Londres ou dans le Brandebourg, construisant des places et des palais, traçant des avenues, des parcs et des jardins, créant des manufactures et des ateliers. On peut dire que

---

[1] Voir " La Renaissance et l'art moderne," par Louis Réan, Paris 1936, p. 190.

pendant un siècle " le Refuge " a fourni aux états protestants de grands architectes, beaucoup de peintres et de sculpteurs, et de véritables tribus de tapissiers, de teinturiers, d'orfèvres, d'horlogers.   On a quelquefois surestimé leur talent car on a tendance à donner aux réfugiés l'auréole des persécutés, mais on ne doit pas oublier l'influence prépondérante qu'ils ont exercé dans toute l'Europe protestante.

En Allemagne, c'est l'électorat de Brandebourg et le land-graviat de Hesse-Cassel qui recueillirent le plus grand nombre de refugiés.   C'est à *Paul du Ry* que Cassel doit les embellisse-ments qui en font une des plus magnifiques résidences alle-mandes.   A Berlin, le Grand Electeur Frédéric Guillaume nomme *Jean Cayart* ingénieur général ; *Philippe de la Chaise* commence la façade du château de Potsdam.   Sous le roi de Prusse Frédéric Ier *Jean de Bodt* participe aux embellissements de Potsdam et construit l'Arsenal de Berlin, edifice aux lignes sévères, un peu alourdi par les trophées de la balustrade. L'œuvre des sculpteurs et des peintres français réfugiés en Allemagne est moins connu que celle (durable) des architectes, mais cependant très importante.   D'autre part des réfugiés et des descendants de refugiés deviennent graveurs des monnaies royales, fondateurs de fabriques de porcelaines, d'éventails, de manufactures de toiles peintes, de tapisseries, de jouets.

Comme les états protestants d'Allemagne la Hollande accueille les réfugiés qui viennent y introduire et développer toutes sortes d'arts, de métiers et d'industries.   *Daniel Marot*, fils de Jean Marot, est architecte de Guillaume d'Orange (qu'il suivra en Angleterre) ; il dirige les travaux du château de Voorst et de la Maison Royale de Loo, fait les plans et dessins de la grand Salle des États de Hollande à la Haye, dessine le tombeau de Cohorn, le Vauban hollandais, élevé en Frise dans l'église de Wickel.   Les réfugiés sont à la tête d'industries prospères : ils établissent de grandes fabriques de chapeaux, de rubans, de moires, de brocarts, de velours brochés.

Beaucoup de calvinistes exilés gagnent aussi la Suède où ils étaient attirés par la cour et l'aristocratie de Stockholm ; un plus grand nombre encore s'installe au Danemark, surtout à Copenhague qui eut deux sculpteurs célèbres : *Abraham César Lamoureux*, auteur de la statue équestre de Christian V. érigeé sur la Place Royale, et son frère *Claude Lamoureux*.

L'Angleterre reçoit surtout des peintres. *Jacques Rousseau* est chargé par le duc de Montagu d'une partie des décorations du magnifique hôtel qu'il se fait construire à Londres. *Jacques Parmentier*, retiré dans le comté d'York peint des portraits et des compositions historiques, un retable pour l'Église de

Hull, un autre pour l'Église Saint Pierre à Leeds. Le parisien *Hénri Gravelot* est l'ami intime de Hogarth et facilite le talent de Gainsborough. *Philippe Mercier* travaille à la cour ; ses tableaux rappellent beaucoup la manière de Watteau. Le sculpteur *Hubert le Sueur* avait travaillé à Londres avant la Révocation ; il avait exécuté quelques tombeaux dans Westminster et avait été surtout au service de Charles I. Beaucoup plus tard, le sculpteur lyonnais *Louis François Roubillac*, élève de Couston, vient à Londres et sculpte des bustes qui ne méritent pas la grande réputation qu'on leur a faite. *Jean Tijou* exécute sous la direction de Wren la plupart des travaux de ferronnerie de la nouvelle cathédrale Saint Paul. Grâce aux réfugiés la sculpture sur ivoire, l'horlogerie, l'orfévrerie, les industries de la soie deviennent florissantes.

De nombreux artistes calvinistes se réfugièrent en Suisse, surtout, à Genève où l'art genevois avait déjà reçu de l'éclat par tous les artistes contraints de quitter la France pendant les persécutions religieuses du XVIe siècle. Après la Révocation une seconde vague de réfugiés provoque un nouvel essor. On trouve là les plus célèbres peintres sur émail, nombreux à Genève où cet art brillaît alors d'une vraie splendeur : *Jean Petitot* qui avait été miniaturiste de Charles Ie d'Angleterre puis de Louis XIV., les frères *Huaud* aux quels on doit de luxueux boitiers de montres émaillées avec des portraits, des scènes mythologiques, quelquefois des sujets religieux empruntés de préférence à l'Ancien Testament.

Dans tous les pays protestants d'Europe l'influence des artistes français réfugiés s'est étendue très au delà de la première génération, jusqu'au milieu du XVIIIe siècle, mais elle ne fut réellement française et calviniste que pendant les cinquante premières années du " Refuge." Après, le goût français commence à se perdre, les exilés deviennent riches au moment où le calvinisme s'altère de plus en plus, où l'arminianisme et le rationalisme s'installent dans l'Église. Or, l'ennemie de toute grandeur c'est la satisfaction qu'on y prend. Le grand style classique, par la perfection de l'ordre (cette soumission de l'homme, cette humilité acceptée) avait résisté au baroque de la Contre-Réforme. Quand la trame calviniste commença à s'user dans toute l'Europe protestante, le baroque prit toute sa revanche : ce fut le désordre " rococo."

B. *L'élégante indifference du XVIIIe siècle*

Dès le second quart du XVIIIe siècle on ne trouve plus guère dans l'art de traces calvinistes vraiment caractéristiques. S'il y a encore des calvinistes qui peignent, sculptent, con-

struisent, ils n'appartiennent guère à l'Église Réformeé que
par leur naissance et leur art ne se distingue plus de tout ce
que créent leurs contemporains. Comme les autres ils cherchent
à plaire à une clientèle élégante et raffinée, pleine de caprices
exquis. Ce maniérisme, caractérisé par l'esprit frivole d'une
époque irréligieuse, est né d'une faillite de la simplicité et de
l'ordre consécutive au système de Law.

Dans la France catholique quelques artistes réformés se
réintroduisent ; ce sont tous des portraitistes mondains, des
graveurs ou des ébénistes distingués dont le talent est apprécié
par la souriante clientèle des salons du bel air. Très peu sont
français, ce sont en général des artistes étrangers à la mode,
ce qui incline à la tolérance vis à vis de leurs origines religieuses.
C'est aussi vers ce moment que la France accueille tous les
réformés qui jouent un rôle de premier plan dans les industries
d'art des étoffes imprimées : indiennes, cretonnes et toiles de
Jouy. Il y a des fabriques célèbres réparties en trois princi-
paux centres : la Normandie (Rouen et Bolbec), la Haute
Alsace (Mulhouse et Wesserling), Jouy en Josas où *Christophe
Philippe Oberkampf*, industriel de grande envergure, recrute
les meilleurs artistes, aussi bien graveurs que dessinateurs,
qui créent des milliers de modèles avec une fertilité d'imagination et une science du coloris uniques dans la décoration des
tissus. Oberkampf est le premier à employer le procédé
coûteux de la gravure sur cuivre ; c'est ainsi qu'ont été exécutées
en rouge sur blanc les plus belles toiles de Jouy à personnages.

Si de France on passe à Genéve, on trouve au milieu du
XVIIIe siècle la Réforme de Calvin très altérée, l'Eglise
glissant vers le moralisme et le rationalisme, l'art sans caractères
distinctifs et cherchant surtout à imiter l'élégance et le goût
raffiné de Paris et de Versailles. Après avoir voyagé dans
toute l'Europe, le sensuel *Jean Etienne Liotard* devient peintre
de Louis XV., fait les portraits de la famille royale et celui
de la Pompadour. *Wolfgang Adam Töpffer* est " le Boilly
de Genève " ; l'impératrice Joséphine le nommera son maître
de dessin et lui achètera pour la Malmaison une " sortie de
Temple " qu'un pendulier de l'Empire transformera en horloge.

En Angleterre ce sont les meilleurs moments de l' " Ecole
Anglaise," la période des grands portraitistes : *William
Hogarth, Joshua Reynolds, Gainsborough, George Romney*, et
de l'excellent paysagiste *Richard Wilson* qui ne doivent pas
faire oublier ses brillants successeurs *Constable* et *Turner*.

En Amérique du Nord, quelques portraitistes, plus ou
moins formés aux leçons de la France et de l'Angleterre, se
spécialisent, non sans naïveté, soit dans les effigies un peu
guindées de dignes puritains, soit dans des portraits de colons

nouveaux riches et plus soucieux d'élégance. Vers cette même époque se constituent, en Amérique du Nord et en Afrique du Sud, deux genres d'architecture assez particuliers et dûs aux colons réformés.

C. Le chaos du XIXe siècle

En France, avec le Concordat de Bonaparte, les réformés retrouvent leur liberté, mais après un siècle et demi de persécutions ils ont perdu leurs traditions liturgiques comme leur discipline ecclésiastique et leur unité doctrinale. Au cours du XIX° siècle, malgré quelques grandes figures et d'admirables activités, les Eglises Réformées, dans presque toute l'Europe, ont glissé vers l'arminianisme, quelquefois même fonder dans le rationalisme ou une vague philanthropie. Au milieu de ce chaos il est très difficile de parler d'artistes calvinistes.

Au début du siècle, le retour à l'Antique se manifeste dans tous les arts, depuis l'architecture religieuse jusque dans les sujets des toiles de Jouy. Les sculptures architecturales du genevois *James Pradier* ont un réel intérêt ; il a travaillé à Nîmes et surtout à Paris où il a exécuté quatre renommées pour l'Arc de Triomphe de l'Étoile et le tombeau de Napoléon aux Invalides. Ary Scheffer devient le peintre favori de la famille d'Orléans ; parce qu'il a peint un Calvin on l'a quelquefois cité comme calviniste alors qu'il faut le rattacher au sentimentalisme libéral de son ami et admirateur, le pasteur Athanase Coquerel fils.

Les classiques puisaient leurs thèmes dans l'antiquité gréco-romaine, les romantiques se tournent vers le moyen-âge, la renaissance ou l'orient. A Pau, un peintre qui avait connu la gloire un court moment, *Eugène Devéria*, se convertit au calvinisme, mais à une époque où son talent est déjà terni ; cependant Devéria a été l'un des plus grands noms du romantisme.

Pendant la deuxième moitié du XIXe siècle beaucoup de réformés français, suisses, anglais, hollandais, allemands, ont peint de grandes compositions religieuses ou historiques, mais tout cela est médiocre et ne mérite guère qu'on s'y attache. Tout autres, et bien plus profondes, sont les influences qu'exercent sur la peinture un jeune français, Frédéric Bazille et deux hollandais qui passèrent en France la plus grande partie de leur vie, Jean Barthold Jongkind et Vincent Van Gogh.

Le montpelliérain *Frédéric Bazille* a été tué à l'âge de vingt neuf ans pendant la guerre de 1870. Son œuvre s'est vite affirmée comme l'une des plus hardies du XIXe siécle. Ses toiles entrèrent au musée de Montpellier et au Luxem-

bourg, sa gloire grandit, les toiles du Luxembourg passèrent
au Louvre et en 1935 l'exposition organiseé à Paris par les
étudiants protestants eut la valeur d'une confirmation.   A
cette occasion Pierre du Colombier écrivit un long article
sur la place de Bazille (qui s'est imposé sans bruit, sans spécula-
tion, par son évidence même) et sur l'importance de son œuvre
par rapport à Manet et Monet.[1]   Vers ce même moment Albert
Marie Schmidt publia ces lignes lucides : " Où Bazille atteint
la perfection de son art, là où il apparait irremplaçable, c'est
dans son Ambulance improvisée (un petit tableau où l'artiste
a peint son ami Monet blessé) : pitié pour la fragilité du corps
humain, sentiment évangèlique de l'éminence des vocations,
recherche de la beauté des ustensiles familiers, y servent une
stupifiante virtuosité du pinceau, une densité incomparable
de la matière plastique, un goût presque trop curieux pour la
poursuite des ondes lumineuses dans les coins et dans les
recoins, enfin ; une conscience artistique de la plus rare
qualité.   Le tableau le plus ' protestant ' de Bazille." [2]

Le paysagiste, *Jean Barthold Jongkind*, n'est guère réformé
que par son enfance et les alliances pastorales de sa famille ;
vers la fin de sa vie sa conduite fut parfois douteuse, il devint
un goinfre et même un ivrogne.

Peu de peintres ont eu une vie où les conflits de la vocation
furent aussi douloureux et aussi inexplicables humainement
que ceux qui bouleversèrent la courte existence de *Vincent
Van Gogh*.   D'abord il s'interesse à la peinture, puis une
insistante vocation de ministre évangélique prend le dessus ;
ensuite l'effondrement vient vite, et le désespoir, et la foi
ruinée ; mais peu à peu une irrésistible et saisissante vocation
de peintre s'empare de cet homme, et quand enfin il semble
engagé dans la plenitude de son œuvre, œuvre d'une originalité
unique, la folie le cerne, et bientôt il se tue.   Toute sa pauvre,
folle et courte vie qu'il aurait voulu donner aux hommes en
leur préchant l'Evangile, ne la leur a-t-il pas donnée quand
même dans la magnificence de son amour pour la nature et
la couleur ?   Lorsqu'il peignait avec des ors un bouquet de
tournesols, ne parlait-il pas du Créateur mieux que le mauvais
sermon d'un fade peintre religieux ?   Et quelques uns de ses
paysages, par exemple des oliviers tourmentés surgissant d'une
terre comme en mouvement, ne font-ils pas penser aux soupirs
de la création selon Romains viii. 18 à 25.   Calvin a défini
une doctrine des vocations ; Van Gogh a accompli sa vocation
de peintre : c'est pourquoi, s'il y a chez lui du calvinisme,
ce n'est pas dans la théologie de l'étrange évangéliste

[1] *Candide*, 4 fevrier 1935.
[2] *Le Semeur*, juin 1935.

influencé par Arminius et Tolstoï, c'est uniquement dans sa peinture.

La France accueillit aussi l'américaine *Mary Cassatt* qui fut le peintre impressionniste de la femme et de l'enfant.

A la fin du XIXe siècle et au début du XXe siècle, deux peintres réformés d'origine suisse présentent un grand intérêt. *Ferdinand Hodler*, bernois de naissance et genevois d'adoption, soumet sa fougue germanique et populaire aux règles de l'ordre latin ; aucun peintre n'a eu sur la jeune peinture suisse une influence comparable à la sienne. *Felix Vallotton* [1] a laissé des nus et surtout des portraits d'une exécution admirable et qui font penser à l'influence que Holbein exerça sur cet artiste culturé, observateur aigü et un peu amer. Son œuvre n'a pas encore obtenu l'élan de sympathie du grand public, mais il ne faut pas oublier que s'il y a trente cinq ans Vallotton parut rétrograde à l'époque où régnèrent le néo-impressionnisme et le pointillisme, puis le fauvisme, il se révéla au contraire comme un peintre avancé dès que la peinture évolua vers un sentiment plus exigeant de la construction et des volumes ; après avoir fait figure de réactionnaire, alors qu'il était un précurseur, il fut peut-être dépassé au moment où il aurait dû apparaitre comme un peintre d'avant-garde.

Il n'est pas possible de préciser maintenant l'activité des artistes calvinistes qui sont nos immédiats contemporains. Disons simplement que nous connaissons, en France et en Suisse, des peintres, des sculpteurs, des architectes et des décorateurs dont les œuvres significatives s'affirment parmi les plus attachantes de notre temps. Depuis dix ans, plusieurs d'entre eux sont liés aux pasteurs qui leur ont appris, en suivant Calvin, à écouter attentivement la Parole de Dieu et à comprendre sur quel roc l'Eglise Réformée est édifiée. Ces liens renoués entre quelques artistes et théologiens, nous devons nous en réjouir et y voir une promesse.

Paul Romane-Musculus.

[1] Voir " Félix Vallotton " par Charles Fegdal, et compte-rendu dans *Foi et Vie* (mars 1932). Un admirateur de Vallotton, le suisse René Auberjonois, a écrit : " Quelques journalistes ignorants l'ont condamné d'un mot ; peinture protestante ! La critique se transforme en éloge. Protestant, oui ! Mais de bonne marque. Rien de commun avec certains de nos peintres qui encombrent nos églises de souvenirs affadis du quattrocento italien. Protestant, il l'était par une conscience assez àpre—un dépouillement de formes allant jusqu'à la tristesse—une simplicité qu'eussent pu lui envier ses amis impressionnistes. Plût au ciel que nous eussions chez nous quelques protestants de cette race ! " (*Aujourd'hui*, 13 février 1930. Numèro consacré à Félix Vallotton).

RÉSUMÉ OF A PAPER

By Pastor MUSCULUS

ON

THE CALVINISTS IN THE HISTORY OF THE ARTS

INTRODUCTION

THIS is a rapid review of the place of Calvinists in the general history of the plastic arts and not an essay simply upon the painters of Biblical scenes or the architects of churches.

An important place, not only in countries where the Reformed Faith gained the majority, but also in France. (We shall insist on this point.)

The persecutions were less unfavourable to Reformed Art than were the divisions and heresies which filtered into the Church.

I. THE SIXTEENTH CENTURY

A. France had great Calvinist sculptors rather than great painters. (Richier, Goujon, Pierre Bontemps, Barthelemy Prieur.)

B. The Minor Arts in France

They shine with striking brilliance.

The Enamellers.—The character of their art—much under the influence of the Old Testament.

The Medallion workers.—The great printers and the engravers on wood and copper.

The Tapestry workers.

II. CALVINIST ARCHITECTS IN FRANCE IN SIXTEENTH AND SEVENTEENTH CENTURIES

A. Civil architecture of the Calvinists

Plays a part of first rank—creation of the " Grand Architectural Style "—importance of arcades.

B. The Androuets du Cerceau and Salomon de Brosse

This great family of architects enjoyed considerable prestige in the reigns of Henry III., Henry IV., Marie de Medicis and Louis XIII. Remarkable works at the Louvre, the Tuileries, at Fontainebleau and at the Luxembourg.

C. Art of laying out cities and gardens

Royal parks and gardens organised by Calvinists.

III. PAINTERS OF THE SEVENTEENTH CENTURY

A. The Calvinists and the Royal Academy

The Academy—its dictatorial administration and defects. Controversies with Abraham Bosse, Celebrity of Sebastian Bourdon.

B. Rembrandt and Calvinist Holland

The two periods in the life of Rembrandt : (1) Glory, riches, the influence of Baroque ; (2) suffering, poverty. Rembrandt read his Bible as the WORD OF GOD. The painter's faith. The Calvinism of his work.

The Dutch School—portraits, landscapes, intimate studies of the home (Frans Hals, Vermear of Delft, Nicolas Maes Ruysdael), Jordaens of Anvers, the painter, convert to Calvinism.

C. Calvinism and the Counter-Reformation

Dutch Calvinist Art and its expansion. Resistance to the Baroque of the Counter-Reformation throughout Northern Europe. In France Calvinists and Jansenists also resist.

IV. SINCE THE REVOCATION OF THE EDICT OF NANTES

A. Expansion of French Art by " The Refugee "

Throughout Protestant Europe refugee Calvinists construct city squares and public buildings, lay out parks, create manufactures and raise workshops.

Germany (mainly great architects : also introduction of artistic industries).

Holland.

Scandinavian lands.

England (mainly painters with some sculptors).

Switzerland (at Geneva brilliant miniaturists in enamel : Petitot).

After the second generation Calvinistic characteristics disappear. Arminianism and rationalism assert themselves in the Church.

B. The elegant indifference of the eighteenth century

The works of the Calvinists have lost all distinctive character. Art becomes mundane—period of mannerisms and irreligion. In France brilliant beginnings of the art of printed fabrics. (Oberkampf and the workshops of Jouy.)

At Geneva Calvinism had changed. Imitation of the sensuous elegance of Paris and Versailles.

In England : the English School ; great portrait painters ; the first landscape-painters.

Creation of a " Colonial " art in North America and South Africa.

C. *The chaos of the nineteenth century*

The return to antiquity.

Romanticism.

Importance of the painter—Frederic Bazille.

Vincent Van Gogh and his agonies over his vocation.

With Hodler and Felix Vallotton we reach the twentieth century.

To-day several painters, sculptors, architects and decorators have links of friendship with Calvinist ministers.

Promise of this recent collaboration of artists with theo-- logians.

Friday, 8th July 1938

A second public evening meeting was held in the Free Church Assembly Hall. Professor Maclean presided and introduced the speakers.

1. The Rev. Dr. KROMSIGT, Amsterdam, Holland

It is for me an honour and a pleasure to speak of Calvinism in Holland and of the general condition of our churches, especially since I have had some connection with Scottish history, through my dissertation on John Knox as Reformer in his relation to Calvin. Also I have pleasant memories of my visit to Edinburgh in 1914 as deputy of the Classes of Amsterdam to the Assembly of the Church of Scotland.

At the Calvinistic Congress of 1934 at Amsterdam I gave a survey of the growth of orthodoxy, especially of Calvinism in the Dutch Reformed Church owing to the influence of Professors Kuyper and Bavinck. In these later years we may observe a continuing growth. Especially in the Dutch Reformed Church there has been a remarkable revival in *ecclesiastical* life in the strict sense of the word. Formerly we had to complain of a " non-ecclesiastical spirit " amongst us, but this has now been ameliorated remarkably. " The Church " receives much more theological attention. This is true not only in circles interested in the Œcumenical Movements.

Many feel that the National Church must clarify its ecclesiastical position among our own people.

There are many influences. Next to the Œcumenical Movement the theology of Karl Barth has been of importance. Whatever may be our opinion about this theology (I have many scruples myself, especially in regard to his view of Scripture) this honour must be given to him—that he has recalled more than anyone else the whole Church to self-consciousness and to new thinking about her principles. It is therefore no wonder that Barth has become the spiritual leader of the Confessional Church in Germany. This has also had a great influence in the Church of Holland. Many have begun to think about the position of the Church among the people and have come to feel (very late, indeed, but not too late, I hope) that Church Government is not a thing of no importance, but ought to be in harmony with the essence of the Church and according to the principles of Scripture. So, many who never thought about these things or who were in opposition have suddenly, to our surprise and gladness, proclaimed the necessity of presbyterial government for our Church, and have joined the small group of " Confessionals " who, for more than half a century, have fought for that government.

Just when we left Holland a most important Report of Reorganisation was the object of discussion in our forty-five Classes. It must hereafter be brought up in Synod and Provincial ecclesiastical governments, so that the issue of voting is still very uncertain. Even if the Report were rejected, as I hear it *has* been rejected by twenty-five Classes as against twenty, we are thankful that there is now so mighty a movement for reorganisation that it cannot be finally restrained.

In theology, too, there have been many changes during the last years. Alongside much apostasy from Christianity there is a great and important movement towards Christian belief and life. In politics our Prime Minister, Dr. Colyn, stands in the first rank, and he is a convinced Calvinist. We have now a Christian government in the general sense, and in it several Calvinists have important places. With deep gratefulness we remember the example given to her people by our Queen Wilhelmina.

There is also a tendency to more scriptural thinking among the Modernists. Professor Heering of Leiden has exercised great influence in this way through his book, *Faith and Revelation*. There remains, however, a fundamental difference between modernists and orthodoxy. Meantime there is more unity among orthodox groups through the struggle for presbyterial Church government. Organisation will only avail if the Holy Ghost come, in answer to our prayers, to revive all things.

2. Rev. STEWART M. ROBINSON, D.D., U.S.A.

My Christian Friends, we in North America—Canadians and citizens of the United States—are your children in the common faith, and the vast multitude of us believe with deep conviction that those spiritual blessings that are ours in the lands in which we live are, under the Grace of God, due to the influences of those great truths which are our concern in this Congress.

I believe that the great day of Calvinism is not a past day but a future day. We have heard more than once already in our Congress, and here in this room last evening, most impressively stated, that it is among the youth of the world that there is to-day love for and seeking after the truth that John Calvin formulated that it might save the world of his day. Though looking forward too, I am going to ask you to look backward that we may remind ourselves that the John Calvin whose name is so often on our lips was a mere youth when he struck off that great document which has come down to us as the " Institutes of the Christian Religion ".

Calvin's Conversion

John Calvin reached his twenty-fourth birthday anniversary on 10th July 1533. What a remarkable generation lay just behind the young man standing in the flowing tide of his maturing manhood. Columbus, da Gama and others had sailed into the uttermost reaches of ocean wastes and discovered not only new ways to old treasure-lands, but new lands incomparably more vast and rich. Copernicus had brought the Ptolemaic theory of the solar system to an end and revealed a more wonderful creation than the mind of man for the past twelve hundred years had realised. Erasmus, the scholar, had published his Greek Testament in 1516 and opened to scholarship the unsearchable riches of God's Word in the original. Hebrew learning had been similarly released from bondage by other scholars, one of the most notable of whom had been Calvin's own teacher. Finally, Luther was making Europe ring with discussion of the nature and meaning of the Gospel. Calvin was a youth who had been gently nurtured amid comfort, so he was alert to the significance of the new world of commerce and trade. He was an exact and careful student, so that the discoveries of the great minds would be eagerly sought by him. Most of all he was a youth of pious and godly disposition, so that the searching sermons and treatises of Luther and of others provoked him to deep thought.

Episcopal palaces, chapter meetings, lecture halls, student conversations in Paris, Bourges, Orleans, at Meaux, Senlis, Noyon, were full of the New Learning, the New World, the New Evangelicalism. The effect of all this upon Calvin is very significantly marked by the progress of his avowed purpose in life. His father, an advocate, well connected with the civil and ecclesiastical life of his city, friend of the Montmors, a local noble family of distinction, had first designed his son for the Church. That impulse gave way to the study of the law. That, in turn, gave way to the pursuit of letters. In 1532 Calvin was the proud author of *A Commentary on Seneca's De Clementia*, writing to his friends to know how it was being received in the learned world, and on " pins and needles " to hear of its reception, whether men praised it or not. It was a fine piece of work, because Calvin, even as a youth, ranked among the very first scholars in a world of masters. He was an intellectual genius, an indefatigable worker, and of blameless life and manners. He was a student contemporary of Ignatius Loyola in the College Montaigne in Paris, but he never shared his superstition. He was a contemporary of Rabelais, but he never shared his cynicism. The world, represented by the Church, the Law, and Literature, successively failed to satisfy Calvin ; whereas the Word of God as it was opened to him through his Greek and Hebrew studies became increasingly fruitful of joy and satisfaction.

The period of crisis in this progress of Grace in the heart of Calvin may be set, with a fair degree of certainty, as the summer of 1533. Dean Doumergue makes bold to place the time between 23rd August and 1st November 1533. It seems safe to say that 1st November 1533 marks the day when Calvin was an evangelical Christian after the Reformed pattern, because this is the date when Nicholas Cop gave his Rectorial Address before the University of Paris in the Church of the Mathurins. This momentous discourse, which shook the world, was undoubtedly the work of Calvin. It contains this passage :

" Nothing is sweeter or more precious to a Christian than the certainty of his salvation. If you do not have this you wander in the mazes of error. Long may the heart question : Is it a matter of ceremony, of piety, or religious devotion ? It is for this reason that Paul in Romans takes the whole matter out of the range of our doubt by demonstrating by many reasons that our justification, or reconciliation with God, depends neither on our dignity nor on our merits."

On 23rd August 1533, Calvin went from Orleans to Noyon to assist the Cathedral Chapter in a special service of intercession over the pest then raging in Paris. After the unwholesome fashion of the time, Calvin had long been a pensionary of cathedral funds as titular vicar or curate of some dependent benefice connected with the diocese. These bursaries were secured then, as scholarships are now, for the behoof of studious young men. Calvin was an ideal type to hold such an honorarium. But, through the years, the family's relation to the Church had become more and more strained. Part of the tension was caused by Calvin's growing evangelicalism.

In the preface to the *Psalms*, Calvin was later to declare that his sudden conversion took place during the time of his law studies. This has been referred to the time before 1531, but it might refer to even a later time. For Calvin was in Orleans as late as 1533. It is most reasonable to believe that in the case of Calvin two processes were at work. On the one hand, through his Biblical studies, under the guidance of the great minds of the master scholars who were his teachers, the Bible was becoming a living Word of Divine Truth which shone like a star in the midst of the murky firmament of ecclesiastical theology and tradition. On the other hand, Calvin's conscience was seeking a place of rest, reaching out for a place like that so victoriously declared in Cop's All Saints' Day address before the University of Paris. The writing of that address marked the crystallisation of Calvin's intellectual search, and the arrival of his soul at the port of rest in the finished work of Christ and the Grace of God.

Ten years before, on 8th August 1523, Jean Valliers had been burned at Paris. Less than three weeks later, sensing the correct root of evangelicalism, the Sorbonne declared it wrong to distribute Bibles. A secret Protestant Church was founded by Faber that same year. On the night of 31st May–1st June 1528, a statue of the Virgin Mary was overturned on the rue des Rosiers at the rue des Juifs. In 1529, Louis de Berquin was burned on the Place de Grève. Calvin knew of these and many other events. The record of the Marbourg Colloquy had been carefully studied by Calvin as early as 1529. It may be said that nothing important in the Reformation movement missed the thoughtful consideration of this great young man.

From 1st November 1533, Calvin's voice is clear. He had to flee the city in the furore which arose about Cop's Rectorial Address. He sought refuge in Santoigne, where the friendly hospitality of Marguerite of Navarre, the king's sister, sheltered him and many another evangelical. Few now realise how great was the prestige of the Reformed position on that 1st November 1533. Francis I. was strongly swayed to Reformed views. The king's brother and his sister openly backed evangelicals. The Bishop of Paris and the Bishop of Senlis (the king's confessor) were both sympathetic. Indeed, it may be said that the most learned, the most pious, the most just were inclined to be evangelical. This explains the fact that Calvin wrote that remarkable preface to his *Institutes* and addressed it to Francis I. In time the professionals, the monks and the Papal emissaries swung the organisation back into line. The Council of Trent created the modern Roman Catholic Church, which never existed until the Reformation was in full progress. Some of the most conspicuous elements of modern Roman belief, like the authority of the Pope, the Immaculate Conception of the Virgin Mary, would not have won half the bishops in Calvin's time.

Perhaps the most beautiful witness to Calvin's conversion is his attitude towards his literary work. In 1532 we found him on tiptoe to hear the reaction of the world of learning to his maiden effort as a scholar. In 1536, at Basle, he gave to the world the first edition of the *Institutes*, a work which just men of all parties, Catholic and Protestant, have united in calling one of the greatest treatises of its kind in all the world of literature. But we find not so much as a word from Calvin concerning it. Indeed, it appeared without a name for a time. Calvin was busy at Basle watching over a little flock of believers. He was rejoicing in the " assurance of his salvation." He was holding everything under God. He did not care about what men might say of him. One of Calvin's favourite verses was Job xvii. 12 : " Post tenebras spero lucem." Later that came to be shortened in the motto of Geneva, " Post tenebras lux." So Calvin found the great salvation. If we would be truly Calvinistic, we must put the positive note into preaching and believing. We do not seek ; we have found. Our security is not in ourselves, or our system or our ceremonies, but in our God, the Father of our Lord Jesus Christ, " who loved us and gave Himself for us."

3. Rev. Dr. J. B. Souček, Czechoslovakia

Dear brethren, I have been asked by our Chairman to say a few words to-day on behalf of the younger men on the Continent, especially in Central Europe, on how we stand in regard to Calvinism to-day.

This is certainly no easy task. Central Europe—as Europe
and the whole world generally—presents no united picture to
the observer. Quite on the contrary, it is a picture of a great
confusion, uncertainty, even chaos. That is clear enough in
the political sphere—but the reasons are deeper. They are
spiritual. Central Europe is now in a deep crisis, in which the
crisis of mankind is made apparent. All older authorities
seem to be losing their hold on the minds and consciences of
men. The family, the State, the dynasties, the social prestige,
the authority of science, and to a very large degree the authority
of the Church too, have been undermined or have utterly dis-
appeared. This was to be observed ever since the end of the
War. But soon it became clear that men and women cannot
remain indefinitely in chaos and in complete lack of any firm
authority. Thorough license is unbearable. That has been
discovered soon enough even in Soviet Russia—even there
new authorities have been speedily created. And the same is
true of the whole Central and Eastern Europe—nay, after all,
of all Europe, America and Asia ! We are in the midst of a
time when—old social authorities being shattered—the vacuum
is being felt and people are frantically seeking new authorities !
    The tragedy of the present era is that they are seeking in
the wrong places and in a wrong fashion. To say it in other
words : the tragic thing is that in the present turmoil real,
vital, living Christianity is so very little felt, that it seems not
to be present, at least as far as the great masses of people are
concerned. New authorities are badly needed, and are being
sought with all the passion of which a desperate human heart
is capable.
    But they are being sought in the creations if not of human
hands, then of human minds and human organising forces.
Instead of a living and loving sovereign God, new idols are
being erected and worshipped passionately. And the results
are what they always have been : the idols are turning quickly
into Molochs who devour the sons and daughters of men.
That is the deep mystery—a mystery of iniquity !—of the
great passionate political movements which infest the Continent
of Europe—of Communism quite as much as of Fascism, and
particularly Naziism. These are religions—false religions,
idolatries, with all the fanaticism, with all the horrors and
miseries which real idolatrous religions always had in their
train. These movements take hold of the minds of men
because they promise to fill the great void ; they promise to
offer a real new authority in the place of the old ones. But
they do not bring real authority which could be acknowledged
with freedom and gladness ; they appear—and they must do

so—as tyrannies which thwart every trace of freedom and enslave the bodies and minds of men.

There are, of course, still countries even on the Continent where these modern idolatrous tyrannies have not gained ascendancy ; but we all know that these free and democratic countries—and that is true not only of the Continent—seem to be strangely paralysed, they seem to have lost most of the faith in their cause, and have too frequently been mistaking license for freedom.

That is the situation in which we live. Everywhere, but most of all in the centre of Europe. How does Calvinism come into that picture ? First of all as a great necessity. As I tried to show, the tragedy of European nations to-day is that they seem to be torn asunder between license and tyranny, between mistaken and misused freedom and misused, false authority. This tormented mankind of to-day needs sorely the return to the only authority which at the same time makes free—to the authority of the living, sovereign, severe God who is at the same time our loving Father in Jesus Christ. He who has the absolute right on our complete obedience and devotion, He whose revelation in His word is the highest standard of what is true and good, He who does not wish the death of the sinner but that he may repent and live : He is the only hope of the present generation. In God the Father of Jesus Christ is the absolute authority—but at the same time to obey Him makes man ultimately free from human authorities, because human authorities can never be absolute and ultimate. To serve God means to be free from the idols and Molochs with all their cruelty and horrible dangers.

Only relatively few men in present Europe see this clearly. Many are unhappy in their license and in their slavery and they are groping after deliverance. But few are finding the right way yet, probably not without the guilt of organised churches—the guilt of our lack of real faith, of courage, of foresight and of loving understanding of the troubles and difficulties of men at the present time. Be it as it may, we cannot say that organised Christianity of any form would be very triumphant and successful at the present moment. But in spite of all, some men and women see and realise what is the need of the day. There are in all churches those who turn for new authority to the Word of God and who seek with new eagerness the face of the sovereign and loving God in Jesus Christ. And among younger men in the ministry there are many who devote themselves with new zeal to the searching of the treasures of the theology and piety of the Reformation for light and help in their present tasks and struggles. And above all a new understanding of the significance and truth of the fundamental doctrines of Calvinism is arising.

For the sovereignty of God which unites true authority with true freedom and which seeks to submit all life to itself —that is the characteristic doctrine of Calvinism. Those who have eyes to see must to-day be deeply impressed by signs that some of the principles of the Lutheran reformation seem not to withstand the pressure of the present evil days. I do not intend in the least to depreciate the value of Lutheranism ; I know very well that the wealth of personal piety and real saintliness found among the best representatives of Lutheranism cannot easily be surpassed, or even reached, in other denominations. But undoubtedly there is in Lutheranism a certain tendency towards exaggerated dualism between individual, personal piety and the social and political duties of man ; dualism between the kingdom of God which is concerned with remission of sins and eternal life, and the ethical tasks of men in society, states, economic life. This tendency to dualism seems to be frequently fatal to Lutheranism, making it of little resistance to the presumptions of the State. Or, if it resists, it does so only in the form of noble martyrdom —and that is something for which all Christians must prepare themselves !—but the possibility of moulding actively the life of society seems completely to escape its mind. Much of the present grave difficulty of the Church in Germany may be explained by this dangerous tendency towards exaggerated dualism between spiritual and temporal.

On the other hand, everybody ought to see that much of the modernistic piety and thought has gone to the other extreme of concerning itself nearly exclusively with this earth, with the tasks of politics and economics—forgetting that, after all, the first and last task of the Christian Church is to preach repentance and remission of sins, and so to prepare men for another life. The extreme of modern secularistic religion is still more dangerous than that of Lutheran dualism.

And against both these extremes the real, original Calvinism is a very wholesome corrective. It is a very balanced doctrine which knows that the kingdom of God is not of this world, but that God's rule, His demands and His laws are meant for this world also, and that it is one of the tasks of the faithful to work and fight for Christ's sovereign rights on this earth. Calvinism knows very well that Church and State are two separate bodies with different tasks and distinct authorities, and it does not attempt to subject the State to the domination

13

of the organised Church. But it never can admit—as some Lutherans seem to do—that the State could be a sphere wholly exempt from the reach of God's laws of justice and love.

These are elements which must be recovered anew if Christianity is to play its necessary rôle in the renewal of mankind—nay, if European mankind is to be saved at all from its present terrible plight. I said that these fundamental principles of Calvinism must be recovered anew. That means that it is not enough only to repeat the words and formulas which our Reformation fathers formed in their day. No mere return to the past will do. We must return to our fathers and learn very humbly at their feet ; but then we must rise and do the work of our own day. That is very much in the spirit of John Calvin, who did not wish a Church or a theology to be named after him, who wanted only to be a guide to the truth of the Scriptures, and the outcome of his labours to be " ecclesia verbo Dei reformata et semper reformanda." Semper reformanda !—that is a challenge to us all. We are not only free, we are obliged to seek new solutions of all moral, political, social problems in the light of the Word of God ; and we are entitled and obliged to seek even new formulations of the fundamental contents of our faith. We are free to do so—so long as we do it not out of our own will and by our own wisdom, but in utter obedience to God and in eager listening to His Word. The task is difficult, because our problems are all but overwhelming, but it can be solved if we trust and obey the Lord.

Another observation : it seems to me that the call " back to Calvinism " to-day must not be raised in any sectarian, denominational and negative spirit. It is not directed against Lutheranism or any other Protestant denomination. It is a positive task. Negations of some errors of other types of theology may be necessary, as I showed in regard to the dualistic tendencies in Lutheranism, but the chief emphasis must be positive and inclusive. This seems to me to be the lesson of the present church situation in Germany, where the recrudescence of denominational exclusiveness on the part of some Lutherans has proved to be very detrimental to the cause of the Confessional Church. Significantly, the Reformed brethren in Germany have not joined with this exclusive denominationalism which denied the Communion of the Lord's Table between Lutheran and Reformed. That was not only because the Calvinists are a minority inside the German Church. No—it was in accord with the genuine spirit of John Calvin, who never regarded himself as a foe of Luther ; who tried sincerely and persistently—even if without full success—to save the unity of Protestantism.

You will understand that this irenic aspect of our task is quite particularly the burden of my heart if I tell you that I come from a country and a Church where the unity of all Protestant denominations has always been a great desire and goal. In Bohemia the struggle for the purity of the Word of God began with John Hus, a full century before the Reformation of Luther and Calvin. The Czech Reformation, with its noblest representative, the Unitas Fratrum, has learned much from both great reformers and their followers. And in the sixteenth century it became increasingly apparent that the Unitas was particularly near to the Reformed, Calvinistic doctrine. In the doctrine of the Lord's Supper, in the unceasing efforts after strict Church discipline, in the incessant attempts to submit all life to the rule of the Divine law, the Brethren of Bohemia felt themselves at one with Calvin. In fact, in the catechisms of the Unitas, in their confessions of faith, in the marginal glosses of their translation of the Bible, which up to this day remains the " Authorised Version " of our Church, an unmistakably Calvinistic doctrine is to be found. But the Brethren were always conscious that their origin was older than the Western Reformation and that they have their own distinct treasures to keep. Among other things an all-but-passionate recognition of the unity of all churches which were reformed by the Word of God belongs to the heritage of the Bohemian Reformation. It was with a great distress that the leaders of the Unitas saw the fierce interdenominational fights in the midst of German Protestantism in the last quarter of the sixteenth century. And the last great representative of the old Unitas, John Amos Comenius, never ceased to deplore these fights and to pray and admonish for a better understanding and final union between Lutheran and Reformed. This heritage is a very living one in my own Church, the renewed Evangelical Church of Czech Brethren. In fact, in this Church Reformed and Lutheran elements are fused in a complete union on the basis of the old Brethren's conviction about the fundamental unity of all churches which arose out of the Reformation by the Word of God. It is in this spirit that we joyfully take part in the hopeful efforts to renew and to recreate the fundamental tendencies of the Calvinistic theology and to mould them for the pressing needs of our difficult and stormy, but certainly great, times.

4. Rev. W. H. HAMILTON, M.A., General Secretary of
the Presbyterian Alliance, Edinburgh.

AUTHORITY

I am asked to speak, especially for our younger people, on the
subject of Authority, and I have only ten minutes. We shall
therefore go no further back than the Apostle St. Andrew.
He met and knew and loved Jesus and was constrained to
leave all and follow Him—the first disciple of us all. *What*
constrained him ? No answer is necessary. Would that
there were no need to go further forward with our discussion !
And indeed it is the impression that Jesus Himself makes on
each human heart in which we find the sole ultimate Authority
for the Christian life and walk and citizenship. We think that
if we could meet Him here and walk with Him, hear Him speak,
see Him work, we too should be " constrained," require no
other authority, and the miracle and call would be renewed
and obeyed. We believe, too, that He lives, and that this *does*
happen to men and women, and to youth above all, in this
twentieth century, so often as Jesus is met and faced.

But we are puzzled in the natural man, and our problems
make us wary and afraid. We have felt the burning full
humanity of the Son of Man and our hearts burned within us
as we gazed on Him. We have read and listened to the great
devout expositions of noble preachers on this aspect of His
nature, and bowed before Him and sought to follow our Prince
and Example, who makes us thereby also the very sons of
God and without shame calls us His younger, lowly brethren.
Aye, but we have striven too, to follow all History's human
thought of Him, and thereby feel—even as we feel for ourselves—that there is something more here than Man, and that
it is not only the perfection of His humanity, as for a time we
sought to argue, that makes Him Divine. We read the
theologians and assent to what they say of Divinity in
Him, even though we recognise with them that they are trying
to express for us something that cannot be told in words.
And then we are afresh puzzled sorely and need Authority—
and often our fierce demand for this Authority seems to take
the form of rebellion against all Authority. It is not really such
—it is only that we can brook no false authority, no fabricated
or simulated dogma, no mere expository cogitation. What,
oh what, we cry, is the full and final and irrefutable authority ?

No theologian of them all has ever shown us, nor assayed
to explain, the nexus between the human and the divine in

Jesus.   They confess under the last pressure of our questioning that it is, and must be, a mystery still.   And that is not cogent enough for the man in the street, the doubting Thomases of this thorny, intractable, implacable life ; not clear enough, perhaps, for eager-eyed, eager-hearted youth.   A visitor from another planet, or even the untheologically-minded among ourselves, might be excused for thinking that the expositors' portraits of Jesus as Man and of Jesus as God were portraits of two different beings.   O that we knew where we might find *Him* !

Reverence and even Faith may sometimes be able to rest in this sublime, inexplicable duality.   It always comes to that, we think, in the end.   Yet there are times, there are moods, there are problems, in which it isn't enough.   There are problems—the question raised by war, as it now is, and patriotism, for example—when the devout thought of Jesus as man and example would lead us one way in fervent *imitatio Domini* : we would follow the way He trod, though it should bring us where it brought Him.   And then that desperately humbling conviction of His otherness seizes us again—*we*, forsooth, follow *Him* ! *We*, forsooth, bear the cross He bore ! *We*, forsooth, humbly share in His passion to redeem ! *We*, whose very virtues and penitence are such that they should ever be among the causes and subjects of our next prayers for pardon !   I am all unrighteousness !   Depart from me, O Lord, for I am a sinful man ; and every thought and part of me, without and within, is muddy, muddy at the best !

Yet His call *is* to follow and obey, to drink His cup, to bear His baptism ; and we want and need Authority that will *convince*, if we are to understand its meaning.

We *could* try to follow the Man, try to regain something of the human image of God in which we were made, if we could but always see Jesus.   Yes, but our theologians doubt, nowadays, if it is possible even from Scripture to derive any sure portrait or connected story of Jesus, the Man of Nazareth, *per se*.   You *can't* purge Paul out of Christianity.   It is the Lord God Almighty in Jesus Christ that the Scriptures reveal and to whom the Holy Spirit witnesses.   It is not Jesus the Man with whom we can fraternise, but the Divine Word by which we must somehow be possessed and fulfilled.   This is all terribly, overwhelmingly perplexing—and I am no theologian, nor greatly care to be, but only a journalist (and my friends of the press would contemptuously add, " a hybrid one at that ").   Can *I*, then, usefully say any word on Authority to others, younger, as puzzled (and at least as devoted) as myself ?

The Churches represented in this Congress have a profound

and perfervid respect for the historic Confessions and Catechisms of our history—Heidelberg, Westminster and the rest—
and this, I imagine, we are willing to share. We sometimes
have our misgivings, I suppose, if our minds are alive and open
and growing. We know that it is easier to demur, however,
than to reconstruct ; and we control our revolt (if the word is
not too strong) because the confessions, after all, are but our
subordinate standards. We may feel that their original framers,
like Balaam's wise and faithful companion, sometimes " lost a
grand opportunity of holding their peace." They have, we are
tempted to think, pronounced, with the facility and naïveté of
a less complicated age, on subjects about which we feel no
mortal man can ever dare to hope to say the final word. And
sometimes, too, we feel that it is not so much this, as something in their whole general attitude, that is unsatisfactory,
unsatisfying, dubious. Should not the great symbols and
expressions of our Faith rather figure our rescued and redeemed
humanity, with its bestowed gift of Divine sonship, placing
itself utterly at God's disposal in His Divine determination,
purpose and intention to work out and complete that actual
Divine redemption of all mankind guaranteed by the submission and work of Jesus Christ our Lord ? It may be so—
but that only raises again the poignant dilemma to which I
have already referred. It remains a mystery, and it baffles us,
both in thought and in behaviour.

I am constrained to urge that the source of the strongest
Authority we can find on earth is, and must always be, the
Holy Scriptures. We Calvinists, of many Churches and races,
would assert this, no doubt, with various intensity and meaning. Different temperaments and judgments find different
things possible, sufficient for reason, necessary for comprehension. Labels are dangerous and vain. Few of us, very
probably, would admit that the Reformers of 400 years ago
simply replaced the disappointing idea of an infallible Church by
that of an infallible Book, in the vulgar sense of the term. It is
Jesus the Word that we know to be alone infallible.

But, whatever differences of attitude there may be within
—even as without—our fold, let us be rid of a certain common
unconscious cant that in these times widely prevails. Without
the written gospels, where should *we* have any knowledge of
this Jesus at all, or how recognise

> That gentle voice of His we hear,
> Soft as the breath of even,

when His Holy Spirit speaks to us ?

Oh, I am fain to confess, if you like, that the natural man

in myself also kicks, kicks hard, kicks violently, kicks obstrep-
erously sometimes, when fundamentalist or neo-Calvinist or
any other presumes to limit Almighty God in His chosen
means of approach to the human heart and mind and soul ;
refuses defiantly to acknowledge any theological dictator in
the liberty wherewith Christ hath made us free, or any who
would usurp the paramount claim of His Holy Spirit to blow
even as the winds of God list, we know not whence, we know
not whither, we know but *why*. Surely God has spoken to
me in Nature and by the mouth of his servant William Words-
worth, in humanity through Robert Browning, in poetry by
channel of John Milton, in history, in beauty, in the fair work
of His inspired creatures.   I could conjure my dear German
comrades, in the bowels of all the prophets, whether God Himself has not spoken to them, as to me and to millions, in the
music of their Beethoven and Bach and Brahms ! Yes, yes—
but what is all this " storm in a teacup " *about* ?   Would we
have *known* that Voice in any or all of these revelations,
had we been ignorant of what the Scriptures tell of man's
gropings and questions, in Job and the Prophets and the
Psalms and the story of Israel, or of that answer and fulfilment
to them all that we have heard and read in the Gospel story
and the very words recorded of Jesus ? And are we any the
worse for knowing and pondering what St. Paul or St. John
reflected concerning it ?   I trow not.   Let us get back to our
Bibles and listen, listen.   The Authority we seek, we shall most
likely find by humble, ardent, open-eyed following of this course
and meditation ; and it may be that, like the youth who
long ago sought in vain for his father's asses but found a
crown and a kingdom, we too shall find there more and other
than we seek—not orders and commands, but a spirit not of
our own to possess us, and the peace of God that passeth
understanding, the one and only Authority that *is* authoritative,
and irresistible because it approves itself true in experience
and needs not even be questioned nor *can* be.

And if more is desired, the Reformed Confessions are
surely worthy study ; but I, personally, should rather first of
all commend to you perusal and careful study of that very
winsome, beautiful, gracious, human-hearted treatise which
fools, who have not read it or have glibly read it amiss, dare
to call the expression of an ogre spirit—the tender, wise and
humble *Institutes* of John Calvin of Geneva—so delicate, so
gentle, so fine, so glad.   *So* read—and we shall ask no submission
to any Authority imposed by man, to no tyrannic dogma that
it is the very spirit and genius of our Protestantism to revolt
from ; but we shall ask you only to consider honestly whether

here or hereabouts you have not found, by God's good leading, that Word of His whose very essence it is that He who hears admits its potent sway forthwith and cries, My Lord and my God ! No Protestant will ever be satisfied with, or seek for others, any Authority but that self-authenticating Word of God. But let none of us miss it through Sloth or Dishonesty or closing of the ears or hardening of the heart against it.

For there is none of all our dogmas so well attested as this—that our Sovereign God, having been pleased to bestow upon His children the tremendous prerogative of moral choice, has set them at an handsbreadth from Himself that, with all the kingdoms of the world in sight, they may still freely and frankly choose Him before (and in spite of) all—and that He will coerce none against his will by any force, but wills and waits to be our " chosen " God and our portion for ever—just as there is none of the ineffable mysteries so sublime and lovely as the fact that they who, so seeking, find Him through Jesus Christ the Son, His Word incarnate, come every one of them to Him with the glad cry, " Not I chose Him, but He most wondrously hath chosen me." This is the quintessence of Calvinism. For the love of Christ constraineth us. It is the Lord's doing, and it is marvellous in our eyes.

Sing, O ye heavens, for the Lord hath done it ; shout, ye lower parts of the earth ; break forth into singing, ye mountains, O forest, and every tree therein : for the Lord hath redeemed Jacob and glorified himself in Israel.

Saturday, 9th July 1938

The Congress met in the Martin Hall at 9.30 a.m., Dr. Maclean presiding. After an opening Psalm, and prayer by the Chairman, the Rev. William C. MacDonald, M.A., Church of Scotland, gave an exposition of Matthew vii. 7, as follows (abbreviated) :

" Ask, and it shall be given you ; seek, and ye shall find ; knock, and it shall be opened unto you."—Matt. vii. 7.

This morning I think it is fitting that we should consider the place of prayer in the Calvinistic view of life. If John Calvin was a thinker and a man of action, he was also a man of prayer.

These words sum up our Lord's simple doctrine of prayer. Jesus is not repeating here the same idea three times. He is laying down the fundamental conditions of answered prayer. He tells us of three things that are necessary when we pray to God, if we want to be assured that our prayer will be answered. 1. There is a necessity for faith : " Ask." 2. There

is a necessity for thought: " Seek."   3. There is a necessity
for action : " Knock."

Let us look at the text from this threefold point of view.
Let us begin with the elementary fact of asking.

All prayer is asking. That needs to be emphasised to-day,
for at the present time there is a dangerous tendency to speak
disparagingly of petitionary prayer. Some people think that
to ask God for definite things is a crude and childish form of
prayer which ought to be outgrown as we progress in the
Christian life. But to suppress the petitionary element in
prayer is to destroy prayer altogether. The only kind of
prayer that will help men and women in the day of sorrow,
in the hour of temptation, in the time of poverty and distress,
is the prayer that expresses the deepest need of their heart to
God, and which allows them to ask God for definite things.
The only kind of prayer that will help us in the hour of need
is the prayer that expresses the longings and feelings of our
heart, for our feelings are ourselves.   What we feel, we are.
If prayer does not express the secret desires of our heart, it
will cease to bring us to God.

Prayer not only brings us to God ; it reveals our true self.
Nowhere do we give ourselves away more completely than when
we are praying. If you were allowed one request, and knew
for certain that this request would be granted, and if you had
the courage to write it down on a slip of paper, that slip of
paper would contain the truth about yourself. It would show
you your goal, and reveal your aim—the kind of person you are,
and what you are living for.

This kind of prayer is very different from repeating morning
and night prayers that we have learned by heart. This kind
of prayer requires faith and courage. We must come to God
believing that He is at liberty to answer our prayer. We
must recover Calvin's conception of the greatness and majesty
of God. We must never get into the way of thinking that
God is a prisoner in His own universe.

Surely this Calvinistic faith in God is not so hard to come
by ! Have we not all, again and again, asked and received ?
We have asked for courage to persevere in spite of difficulty
and bad health, in spite of poverty and hardship ; and we
have obtained courage. We have asked for victory over ourselves. We have asked for power to discipline the body, and
control our thoughts, and check our tempers ; and we have
been more than conquerors.

But faith is not the only condition of answered prayer, so
Jesus adds, in the second place, " Seek, and ye shall find."

Our Lord here seems to admit that the prayer of faith is

not always answered. Millions of men and women pray in childhood and youth ; and later they stop praying. Why? Because they say their prayers were not answered.

That is a serious problem. But there is something more serious than the problem of unanswered prayer, and that is the problem that would arise if every prayer were answered. Just think of the chaos the world would be in if every fervent prayer were granted !

But we hear at times this objection : I prayed to God earnestly and sincerely, but my prayer has not been answered. To that objector Jesus would say : " Seek, and ye shall find." More than faith is necessary. To faith we must add thought. We must think about the situation and search for reasons why our prayer has not been granted.

Sometimes the obstacle is in ourselves. Jesus told us that if we harbour hatred or anger in our hearts, our prayers cannot be answered. Or, again, the answer may have come, but we have failed to recognise it. We expected it in one form, but God sent it in another.

Or, again, the answer may be withheld because we are not prepared for the gift we are asking. Multitudes are praying for peace. But are we ready for peace ? Are we prepared to pay the price of peace ? May it not be that before God sends peace, He is waiting for the nations of Europe to perform acts of justice which are obviously necessary ? How can there be peace when all over Europe injustices are crying to heaven to be righted ?

Or, we may discover that our prayer is denied because we do not know how to pray. Here is a mother who prays for her sick child, but she does not know how to avail herself of the healing agencies God has put at our disposal. Here is a father who prays that his children may be protected from temptation, that they may be saved from making mistakes in their career or their marriage ; but he does not know how to surround his children with the fortifying influences of the Church and the Gospel.

Whenever we begin to think the matter through, and to search out the situation, we soon come to the reason why our prayer was not " answered." So, to faith we must add thought : " Seek, and ye shall find."

But something else is necessary if our prayers are to be answered, so our Lord adds : " Knock, and it shall be opened unto you." When faith fails, and when thought fails, we must take refuge in action.

That was what our Lord Himself did. In the garden of Gethsemane His prayer was denied. He prayed that the cup might be removed ; but He had to drink the cup. His prayer was denied, but He rose from the ground and went straight to Calvary. He found the answer to His prayer in action.

And this is what we must do. We must try to answer our prayers by action. " Knock, and it shall be opened unto you." When faith fails and thought fails, we must take refuge in action. We must take an active part in the evangelical crusade for the bringing about of the Kingdom of God.

When the word of God comes, " Whom shall I send, and who will go for us ? " we must reply, " Here am I, send me." There will always be need of reformers to attack the strongholds of evil. Let us reply, " I shall be a reformer." There will always be need of missionaries to carry the good news of the Gospel to other lands, and of men and women who will give of their means to send the Gospel. Let us say, " I shall be one of these." There will always be need of prophets to speak for God and to herald the Golden Age. Let us say, " I shall be a prophet."

In this way we shall help God to answer our prayers. It is not enough to have faith and thought : there must also be action. We must do something to help God to answer our prayers. " Knock, and it shall be opened unto you."

I should like to close by quoting the text which John Calvin himself quoted for years in his pulpit in Geneva after every sermon he preached, no matter what the subject was. Here is Calvin's text : " If God be for us, who can be against us ? "

As there were no arrears of discussion to be overtaken, the Congress adjourned to allow members to visit places of interest in Edinburgh and the vicinity.

In the evening members of the Congress were accorded a Civic Reception in the City Chambers. The Senior Magistrate present welcomed especially those who were strangers in Scotland to the city of John Knox, assuring them of the respect in which his memory is held. Professor Maclean replied, thanking the Corporation for their hospitality.

Sunday, 10th July 1938

By courtesy of the British Broadcasting Corporation, a symposium by four members of the Congress was included in the Scottish Regional Programme. The speakers were the Very Rev. Dr. R. J. Drummond, Edinburgh ; Professor Lecerf, Paris ; Dr. Nagy, Hungary ; and the Rev. Dr. Stewart M. Robinson, U.S.A.

Monday, 11th July 1938

The Congress assembled at 9.30 a.m., Professor Maclean presiding. After Praise and Prayer by the Chairman, the Rev. Archibald MacFadyen gave an exposition of Romans viii. 17, of which the following is a summary :

" If children, then heirs, heirs of God, and joint heirs with Christ, if so be we suffer with Him, that we may be also glorified with Him."

The children's inheritance is conditioned, it is true, but also assured, by union with Christ Jesus. His is the inheritance ; they who become sons, with Him, share in the inheritance.

What are the marks of their sonship ?

The indwelling spirit proves the sonship by prompting the " Abba Father " (Rom. viii. 15).

Likeness to the Father is another mark : " As the elect of God, holy and beloved " (Col. iii. 12).

The convincing, subjective evidence is believing in Christ : " As many as received Him, to them gave He power to become the Sons of God " (John i. 12).

Nor is this a portioned-out inheritance, as in human succession. The inheritance of each child of God knows not diminution because of fellow-believers. The inheritance is of God ; is indeed of God Himself. " The Lord is the inheritance of Israel and Israel is the inheritance of God. So testified Moses : " The Lord hath taken you to be unto Him a people of inheritance " (Deut. iv. 20). David, on the other hand, declared : " The Lord is the portion of my inheritance " (Ps. xvi. 5), while Paul particularises : " Thou art an heir of God through Christ " (Gal. iv. 7).

The earth belongs to the Lord, the nations thereof being to Him as the small dust of the balance. " But all things are yours " (1 Cor. iii. 21).

The inheritance promises safety : " Fear not, I am thy shield " (Gen. xv. 1). It makes wise. " If any man lack wisdom, let him ask of God " (James i. 3).

The inheritance, not diminished by sharing, is in truth enhanced ; the sharing is with Christ. All the glory that the Son had with the Father before the Incarnation, the subsequent glory of the Atonement, the Resurrection, the Ascension are to be shared with His brethren, " if so be that we suffer with Him "—not in the bitterness which was unapproachable, but there is " a filling up behind " (Col. i. 24) involved in our experience of obedience. Christ suffered in that He was obedient ; obedience in His fellow-heirs cannot be without some—it may be heavy—cost : affliction ; opposition of the world ; the very sight of sin ; these in countless forms take toll of Christ's people as they journey through life ; yet in every trial are to be found traces of Christ having passed that way.

> " I do not know
> The road by which my feet must run the race,
>   But I do know,
> Though rough it be, though steep in many a place,
> That He has said, ' Sufficient is My Grace,'
>   As on I go."

Paper No. 10

By Rev. Dr. J. de SAUSSURE, Pasteur, Église Nationale de Genève

CONNAISSANCE DE LA FOI et COMPREHENSION DE L'INTELLIGENCE

INTRODUCTION

NOUS voudrions essayer d'éclaircir ici les conséquences intellectuelles de ce que nous croyons être la foi réformée authentique.   En d'autres termes, nous voudrions tenter de préciser les relations entre la connaissance spirituelle et la compréhension intellectuelle, entre la théologie et la philosophie, telles qu'elles nous semblent découler du véritable point de vue calviniste.   Il nous a paru, en effet, au cours de nos précédentes rencontres, que les divergences entre les écoles actuelles qui se réclament du Réformateur provenaient, en dernière analyse, d'une différence dans la façon de concevoir ces rapports et que la mise au point de ceux-ci faciliterait notre commun accord.

Ajoutons que nous ne nous occuperons ici que de la face cognitive de la foi, puisqu'il ne s'agira que de ses rapports avec l'intelligence, mais que cela ne nous fait aucunement oublier ses éléments affectifs et volitifs.   Nous tenons à faire cette remarque, afin qu'on ne nous reproche pas de nous en faire une notion purement " intellectualiste."

I

LA FOI, ORGANE DE LA CONNAISSANCE CHRETIENNE

(1) *La Parole de Dieu.*   Le point de départ de la théologie réformée est la Parole de Dieu, telle qu'elle est consignée dans

la Bible. Dieu, inaccessible à nos facultés naturelles,[1] inconnaissable en soi,[2] ne peut donc être connu que pour autant qu'il s'est donné à connaître, pour autant qu'il s'est révélé, pour autant qu'il a parlé. Les limites de l'Ecriture déterminent très exactement celles de notre ignorance et de notre savoir au sujet de Dieu : nous devons connaître de lui tout ce qu'il nous en a dit là, et nous ne pouvons en connaître que cela.[3]

Je prends ces thèses pour accordées et ne m'attarderai pas à les démontrer, puisque la théorie de la connaissance a pour objet son organe subjectif et non son contenu objectif. Je ne referai donc pas ici une théorie de la Révélation ; je n'exposerai pas la doctrine réformée de la Parole de Dieu. Je préciserai seulement que la source et l'objet de la connaissance chrétienne sera pour nous ce que d'autres études nous amèneraient à reconnaître comme constituant la Parole de Dieu.[4]

(2) *Le Témoignage du St.-Esprit.* Et j'en viens directement à ce qui, du point de vue réformé, constitue l'organe subjectif de la connaissance chrétienne : la foi. Qu'est-ce qui suscite la foi ?

La Parole de Dieu : " la foi vient de ce qu'on entend, et l'on entend quand la Parole de Christ est prêchée." [5] Mais la Bible, où est consignée la Parole de Dieu est souvent lue sans que cela produise la foi : beaucoup d'incrédules connaissent fort bien l'Écriture. La Bible ne devient donc pour moi la Parole de Dieu que du moment où Dieu m'interpelle personnellement par elle ; autrement dit, pour autant que je n'y vois plus seulement des *paroles* de Jérémie, de Matthieu ou de Paul *sur Dieu*, ni même des *paroles* adressées autrefois, par quelque divinité inconnue de moi, *à Jérémie, à Matthieu, ou à Paul,* mais bien des *paroles* que m'adresse *aujourd'hui, à moi* personnellement, le Dieu qui m'atteint et se fait donc directement connaître à moi par Jérémie, Matthieu ou Paul. Dès lors, mais dès lors seulement, ces textes deviennent pour moi la parole *de Dieu.* Et comment Dieu m'atteint-il personnellement ? Par son St.-Esprit. Comment me fait-il trouver Sa Parole dans la Bible ? Par le témoignage que le St.-Esprit rend en moi à la divinité de cette Parole consignée dans ses textes ; par le témoignage que Dieu lui-même rend en moi par son Esprit à Sa Parole dans la Bible. " Ce qu'aucun oeil n'a vu, ce qu'aucune oreille n'a entendu, ce qui n'est monté au cœur d'aucun homme," par exemple la divinité de certaines paroles, que ne peut reconnaître aucune de nos facultés naturelles

[1] 1 Tim. vi. 16.   [2] *Instit.* p. 10.
[3] *Instit.* p. 560.   [4] *Instit.*, pp. 17, 189.   Cf. *Ecole,* p. 174.
[5] Rom. x. 17.   Cf. *Connaiss. relig.* pp. 18, 275–6.

(figurées ici par l'œil, l'oreille, le cœur), " Dieu nous l'a révélé par son Esprit, car l'Esprit sonde tout, même les profondeurs de Dieu " et " ce qui est en Dieu, personne ne le sait que l'Esprit de Dieu." [1]

Cette doctrine du *Testimonium Spiritus Sancti internum* est cardinale dans la théologie des Réformateurs. C'est de son oubli que proviendra l'erreur littéraliste qui revient à confondre, pour reprendre ici des termes bien calvinistes, le signe et la réalité signifiée. Le littéralisme commet à l'égard de la Bible la même erreur que le catholicisme à l'égard de l'hostie : il confond le signe matériel et la réalité spirituelle, à l'inverse du modernisme qui va jusqu'à les séparer, soit à propos de la Bible, soit à propos des Sacrements. En saine doctrine réformée, le signe est le gage certain de la réalité divine, mais il ne doit jamais être confondu avec elle ; (a) de plus, il ne la communique qu'à la foi, par le seul témoignage interne du St.-Esprit ; il ne saurait jamais être prouvé divin pour des raisons extrinsèques, d'ordre historique, rationnel, philosophique ou esthétique, comme sans cesse le littéralisme a tenté de le faire à l'égard de l'Écriture, ou le catholicisme à l'égard des sacrements.

A l'inverse, il ne faut jamais séparer le témoignage du St.-Esprit de la Parole de Dieu, et, au nom de soi-disant " inspirations," aller jusqu'à rejeter des éléments ou l'ensemble de la Bible.[2] C'est l'erreur de l'illuminisme qui commet à l'égard de l'Écriture la même faute que le spiritualisme moderniste à l'égard des sacrements : à force de séparer la réalité du signe, il aboutit à l'abandon de celui-ci. Et de même que l'oubli du nécessaire *Testimonium Spiritus Sancti internum* fausse la notion de la Parole de Dieu, l'oubli du lien entre ce témoignage et la Bible fausse l'idée qu'on se fait de l'Inspiration. L'illuminisme en fait une Révélation, ajoutée ou même opposée à la révélation scripturaire et confond ainsi l'œuvre du Verbe, seconde personne de la Trinité, qui seul parle, et celle de l'Esprit, troisième personne divine, qui persuade, στεναγμοῖς ἀλαλήτοις.[3]

On ne demeure donc sur l'authentique terrain de la théologie réformée que pour autant que l'on distingue toujours

(a) Etant donnée l'absolue véracité de Dieu, partout où apparaît le signe existe *en soi* la réalité divine ; mais *pour nous*, elle n'existe que là où elle suscite notre foi. Toute la Bible est *en soi* Parole de Dieu, mais *pour* chacun de *nous*, elle ne le devient, d'une façon vivante, que là où le St.-Esprit nous en convainc. Pour l'application de cette distinction au Sacrement, cf. mon étude sur *la Notion calviniste des sacrements* dans les *Études sur Calvin et le Calvinisme*, p. 261, Lib. Fischbacher, Paris, 1935.

[1] I Cor. ii. 9–11.
[2] Cf. *Instit.*, p. 25. *École de Calvin*, p. 44.
[3] Rom. viii. 26. Cf. *Instit.* p. 27 ; *École*, p. 44 ; *Connaiss. relig.*, pp. 39–40.

mais ne sépare jamais Esprit et Parole de Dieu, Parole de Dieu et Bible, Révélation et Inspiration ; pour autant qu'on se rappelle que seul l'Esprit certi-fie l'Écriture, nous rend certain de son caractère de Parole de Dieu, et que seule la Bible véri-fie nos inspirations, nous fait distinguer lesquelles sont vraies, authentiquement divines et lesquelles ne sont qu'imagination humaine ou même instigation satanique (a). Comme Calvin le dit, en une de ces formules aussi riches que concises, dont il a le secret, "l'Écriture est l'école du St.-Esprit" ;[1] inversément, seul le St.-Esprit nous fait discerner la divinité de l'Écriture ; et tout cela parce que notre état de péché et de déchéance nous rend incapables de distinguer par nous-mêmes la révélation divine.[2]

En conclusion, c'est l'Écriture, et elle seule, qui nous confère la connaissance de Dieu et de sa volonté ; mais cette connaissance demeure morte tant que le St.-Esprit, ne nous y fait pas reconnaître, en la vivifiant en nous, la Parole de Dieu. C'est le St.-Esprit qui éveille en nous la conviction religieuse ; mais cette conviction reste confuse et incapable de nous conférer une connaissance de Dieu tant qu'elle n'est pas clarifiée par le témoignage nettement énoncé et invariable de la Parole de Dieu.[3] C'est donc par la Parole de Dieu que le St.-Esprit nous parle, et par le St.-Esprit que la Parole de Dieu nous persuade.

Avant d'aller plus loin, une remarque encore, analogue à celle que nous avons faite sur la foi, et destinée comme elle à réfuter d'avance l'objection d' "intellectualisme" : ne traitant ici que du problème de la connaissance, nous n'avons pas à donner une doctrine complète de l'œuvre du St.-Esprit, mais uniquement de son rôle dans la formation de la connaissance chrétienne ; cela ne nous fait pas oublier d'y voir aussi "le consolateur" de notre cœur ni l'agent de sanctification de notre volonté.[4]

En résumé, la source unique de la connaissance chrétienne se trouve :

1°. dans le témoignage de la Parole de Dieu, inscrit dans la Bible et qui fournit à cette connaissance ses *données*, précises et immuables ;

2°. dans l'action du St.-Esprit qui confère à cette donnée son *évidence*, certaine et inébranlable. Cette évidence suscite en nous cette "ferme conviction" qui s'appelle ;

(a) Pour plus de détails sur ce sujet, cf. mon étude sur *l'Inspiration de la Sainte-Écriture* dans l'ouvrage *Die Kirche Jesu Christi und das Wort Gottes*, herausgegeben von D. W. Zoellner und Dr. W. Stählin, Furche-Verlag, Berlin.

[1] *Instit.*, p. 469.　　　　　[2] Cf. *Instit.*, p. 202.　*École*, pp. 180 sqq.
[3] Cf. *École*, pp. 40 sqq.　　　[4] Cf. *Instit.*, pp. 263–4.

3°. la Foi.

Subjectivement parlant, cette évidence marque donc le com-
mencement premier de la connaissance chrétienne qui ne peut
avancer d'autre raison de son bon droit que l'irrésistible
puissance de persuasion du témoignage intérieur du St.-Esprit.
Mais toute connaissance repose sur une évidence première,
sensorielle, rationnelle, morale, esthétique ; aucune donc, y
compris la connaissance scientifique, ne peut se prétendre en
meilleure posture que la connaissance chrétienne ; c'est même
le contraire qui est vrai, puisque, parmi toutes ces évidences,
celle qui émane de Dieu lui-même, bien loin d'être plus con-
testable que celles qui découlent de nos sens, de notre raison
ou de notre conscience, est infiniment plus certaine qu'aucune
autre ; disons même, vu les bonnes raisons que nous avons de
douter du témoignage des sens, de la raison ou de la conscience
humaine, que l'évidence divine est la seule certaine, la seule
fondée à engendrer une conviction absolue.

En d'autres termes, Dieu seul est preuve de Dieu, et c'est
vouloir confirmer la réalité par le néant que de chercher à
le prouver par des démonstrations rationnelles ou morales.

" Nous ne cherchons point," écrit donc Calvin,[1] " ou argumens ou
verisimilitudes, ausquelles nostre jugement repose : mais nous lui
[à la Parole de Dieu] submettons nostre jugement et intelligence,
comme à une chose eslevée par d'essus la nécessité d'estre jugée. Nompas
comme aucuns ont acoustumé de recevoir legièrement une chose
incongneuë : laquelle apres avoir esté congneuë leur desplaist. Mais
pourceque nous sommes trescertains d'avoir en icelle la vérité inex-
pugnable : nompas aussi comme les hommes ignorans ont acoustumé
de rendre les espris captifz aux superstitions : mais pour ce que nous
sentons là une expresse vertu de la divinité monstrer sa vigueur, par
laquelle nous sommes attirez et enflambez a obeyr sciemment et
voluntairement, néantmoins avec plus grand efficace que de volunté
ou science humaine. *C'est donc unetelle persuasion, laquelle ne requiert
point de raisons : toutefois, une telle congnoissance, laquelle est appuyée
sur une tresbonne raison. C'est à scavoir d'autant que nostre esprit ha
plus certain et asseuré repos, que en aucunes raisons.*
Sy nous n'avons cette certitude plus haulte et plus ferme que tout
jugement humain : en vain l'auctorité de l'escriture sera approuvée par
raisons, en vain elle sera astablie par le consentement de l'Église, ou
confermée par autres argumens. Car si ce fondement n'est premierement
mis, elle demeure toujours en suspendz.

(3) *La Foi.* De ce qui précède, il résulte que la Foi est donc
une ferme adhésion à la Parole de Dieu, suscitée par le surnaturel témoignage que l'Esprit de Dieu rend en notre âme à
cette Parole.

A ce titre, en tant qu'adhésion convaincue de tout notre
être à la Parole de Dieu, la foi est quelque chose d'éminemment

[1] *Instit.*, pp. 21–22.

14

personnel. Non pas en ce sens qu'elle consisterait en l'invention, en la découverte de trésors spirituels nouveaux, qui nous permettrait d'ajouter de nouvelles connaissances sur Dieu à celles communiquées par l'Écriture ; non pas donc dans le sens que le libéralisme donne à ce mot de " personnel," lorsqu'il prétend que chacun doit se forger " sa vérité " et l'exprimer en " croyances," variables d'un siècle à l'autre et d'un individu à l'autre. Mais bien en ce sens que le croyant doit s'appliquer personnellement, appliquer à son être particulier et à sa situation concrète l'invariable Parole que Dieu lui adresse, toujours identique à elle-même éternellement et universellement et formant l'immuable objet de la foi ; [1] et en ce sens encore, que la foi engage tout l'être du croyant, toute sa personne, non pas seulement sa pensée. En ces deux derniers sens, la foi se distingue, comme étant toujours personnelle et concrète, de la connaissance scientifique, abstraite et impersonnelle. Mais cela ne veut pas dire qu'elle soit normalement plus variable que celle-ci ; les fluctuations de la foi ne découlent que de l'imperfection de l'adhésion des divers croyants à l'immuable objet de leur foi.

Pour le calvinisme, c'est donc la foi, fruit surnaturel de l'œuvre divine du St.-Esprit en nous, et non pas la raison naturelle, qui constitue l'organe de la connaissance chrétienne. On ne saurait trop insister sur ce point qui constitue l'originalité foncière de la théologie réformée vis à vis de toutes les théologies, ou plus exactement de toutes les philosophies chrétiennes qui font de nos facultés naturelles, raison, intelligence ou conscience, l'organe de la connaissance doctrinale. Identifier la théologie réformée à un rationalisme quelconque, intellectualiste ou moraliste, c'est prouver que l'on n'a pas saisi, ou que l'on oublie toujours à nouveau—car rien n'est plus facile—le caractère surnaturel de ce qu'elle appelle la foi son caractère transcendant par rapport à tous les organes naturels des connaissances humaines. C'est précisément la singularité paradoxale de la foi, d'être en même temps une réalité surnaturelle et cependant intérieure à l'esprit humain, en même temps un don miraculeux de Dieu et pourtant un trésor personnel au croyant. Et c'est la particularité essentielle de la théologie réformée, particularité que l'on oublie trop souvent lorsqu'on en discute, de faire de cette réalité paradoxale qu'est la foi le siège et l'unique siège de la connaissance chrétienne. [2] Or c'est cette particularité même qui, fidèlement observée, protège notre dogmatique de l'esprit de système où sombrent si facilement les autres " théologies " et assure en même temps sa stricte fidélité à la Révélation dont elle ne veut

[1] Cf. *Connaiss. relig.*, p. 19.   [2] Cf. *Instit.*, p. 236.

être que l'exposition ordonnée. On ne saurait donc trop insister sur ce point.

La seconde considération—fidélité à la Parole de Dieu—nous importe encore plus que la première—résistance à la tentation de systématiser. Et d'ailleurs celle-ci se ramène à celle-là, car l'esprit de système entraîne fatalement des infidélités à l'Écriture. Soulignons donc encore combien une théologie de la foi est plus conforme que toute théologie de la raison, ou de la conscience, ou de l'expérience, aux affirmations bibliques comme celle de l'Epître aux Hébreux (xi. 3) : " C'est par la *foi* que nous *reconnaissons* qu'une Parole de Dieu a formé le monde," ou comme les nombreux passages sur la " justice obtenue par la foi," car le salut accordé à la foi, c'est le salut total, impliquant tous les éléments de notre être, s'étendant à tous les domaines de notre vie, assurant la justesse à notre pensée aussi bien que la justice à notre existence : " Etant ainsi justifiés par la foi, ayons la paix avec notre Seigneur Jésus-Christ," [1] aussi bien la paix de la pensée que celle du cœur ou de la conscience. Comme chrétien, je ne crois pas seulement la résurrection de l'esprit, mais " je crois la résurrection de la chair," [2] c'est-à-dire de tout notre être terrestre, de toutes nos facultés naturelles, de notre corps charnel, de notre âme charnelle, et aussi de notre pensée charnelle et de notre conscience charnelle, ou, si l'on préfère, naturelles.

La théologie réformée étudie donc la Parole de Dieu, dont elle entend procéder exclusivement, au moyen de l'organe par lequel cette Révélation elle-même indique qu'elle doit être connue, et ainsi, cette théologie se montre fidèle à la révélation de Dieu non seulement dans son contenu, mais aussi dans sa forme.

S'il en est ainsi, si toute la pensée réformée est mise en œuvre par la foi et la foi seule, il importe avant tout d'être parfaitement au clair sur ce que nous entendons par ce terme. Reproduisons donc ici la définition de la foi telle que Calvin la donne dans l'*Institution* : " Nous avons une pleine définition de la foi si nous déterminons que c'est une ferme et certaine connaissance de [la] bonne volonté de Dieu envers nous, laquelle, étant fondée sur la promesse gratuite donnée en Jésus-Christ, est révélée à notre entendement, et scellée en notre cœur par le St.-Esprit." [3]

Ce que nous venons de dire coïncide-t-il vraiment avec cette définition ?

Cette expression " la bonne volonté de Dieu . . . est

[1] Rom. v. 1.   [2] Symbole de Apôtres.
[3] Pp. 191–2. Cf. Catéch., 18e *Dim. Connaiss. relig.*, p. 18.

révélée à notre entendement " ne contredit-elle pas ce que nous avons affirmé, à savoir que, selon le calvinisme authentique, l'organe de la connaissance chrétienne n'est pas la raison, l'intelligence, ni aucune de nos facultés naturelles, mais bien la foi ? Pour élucider cette question, analysons un peu les précisions dont Calvin fait suivre immédiatement sa définition de la foi : " Quand nous l'appelons connaissance de la volonté de Dieu, nous n'entendons pas une appréhension telle qu'ont les hommes des choses qui sont soumises à leurs sens." [1]

Cette " apprehension des choses soumises aux sens," c'est ce que nous appelons aujourd'hui la compréhension ; cette compréhension, c'est le rôle distinctif de ce que notre langage moderne appelle l'intelligence scientifique, qui s'applique précisément au domaine sensible, aux " choses soumises à nos sens " et au monde abstrait qu'elle en tire ; cette compréhension consiste à saisir le " comment " des choses et à en donner l'explication. Il résulte donc de cette première précision de Calvin que le connaissance due à la foi est d'un *autre ordre* que cette compréhension intellectuelle.

" Car," poursuit-il, " [cette connaissance] surmonte tellement tout sens humain, qu'il faut que l'esprit monte par dessus soi pour atteindre à icelle." [2]

De cette seconde précision, il découle que la foi est transcendante à toute faculté humaine. Elle constitue bien une connaissance intérieure à " l'esprit " humain, mais surnaturelle et procédant de la Révélation divine, et non pas d'aucun raisonnement intellectuel, c'est-à-dire dû à cette faculté humaine et naturelle que nous appelons tout à l'heure l'intelligence (*a*). Calvin ne le dit-il pas d'ailleurs en autant de termes : " Quand nous sommes tirez [par l'Esprit de Dieu] nous sommes totalement raviez *pardessus nostre intelligence* ? " [3]

Donc, " il faut que l'esprit monte par dessus soi pour atteindre " à la connaissance de la foi, " et même," continue Calvin, " y étant parvenu, il ne comprend pas ce qu'il entend ; mais ayant pour certain et tout persuadé ce qu'il ne peut comprendre, il entend plus par la certitude de cette persuasion que s'il comprenait quelque chose humaine selon sa capacité." [4]

Ce verbe " entendre " nous explique l'usage du terme " entendement " employé précédemment, mais, du même

---

(*a*) De même, puisque la connaissance de la foi " surmonte tout sens humain " (ou, comme nous l'avons dit : est transcendante à toute faculté humaine), elle ne procède d'aucun raisonnement moral, dû à la conscience humaine, ni d'aucun raisonnement esthétique, fondé sur notre sensibilité naturelle. Ainsi, la doctrine reste aussi étrangère au moralisme et à l'esthétisme qu'à l'intellectualisme.

[1] *Instit.*, p. 191. Cf. *École*, p. 171.   [2] Cf. *Instit.*, p. 191 ; cf. p. 203.
[3] *Instit.*, p. 203.   [4] *Instit.*, p. 191.

coup, cette phrase achève de nous prouver que " entendre "
ne signifie pas " comprendre "—" il ne comprend pas ce qu'il
entend "—et que " l'entendement " dont parle Calvin ne doit
pas être confondu avec l'organe de la compréhension que nous
appelons l'intelligence et dont la " capacité " s'applique aux
" choses humaines."

" Donc," termine le Réformateur, " nous concluons que
l'intelligence de la foi consiste plus en certitude qu'en appréhension." Ainsi, la connaissance due à la foi, la connaissance
chrétienne, doctrinale, est faite de *certitude que* et non de
compréhension du *comment*. Mais nous développerons ce
point, lorsque nous parlerons de la connaissance qui découle
de la foi. Pour le moment, disons encore, en nous permettant
une paraphrase du texte d'Hébreux, xi. 1, qui nous semble
autorisée par la remarque de Calvin que " Dieu est invisible,
non seulement à l'œil, mais aussi à l'entendement " [1] : " La
foi est une certitude des choses que l'entendement ne voit
pas." Et achevons notre mise au point en soulignant encore
une différence fondamentale entre la connaissance de la foi et
la connaissance intellectuelle, à savoir que la première a un
caractère éminemment personnel, dans le troisième sens que
nous avons indiqué tout à l'heure, à savoir qu'elle engage
notre personne tout entière ; ce caractère, elle *doit* l'avoir si
elle veut constituer un authentique acte de foi et non pas une
simple croyance de tête ; tandis que la caractéristique de la
connaissance intellectuelle est, au contraire, d'être impersonnelle ; elle *doit* tendre à l'être le plus possible si elle veut
constituer un acte de science et non pas une simple opinion
facultative. Calvin souligne bien ce trait de la connaissance
chrétienne, lorsqu'il écrit : " Ici gît le principal point de la
Foy : que nous ne pensions point les promesses de miséricorde,
qui nous sont offertes du Seigneur, être seulement vraies hors
de nous, et non pas en nous, mais plutôt qu'en les recevant
en notre cœur nous les fassions nôtres." [2]

La foi consiste donc en une vivante et personnelle appréhension, je dis bien une appréhension et non point une compréhension, de la miséricorde divine, et, par elle, du salut et
de la vie éternelle.[3] " La Foi est une possession certaine et
assurée des choses qui nous sont promises de Dieu." [4]

4. *La Foi, un don de Dieu.*—Puisque c'est le témoignage
intérieur du St.-Esprit qui suscite la foi, celle-ci représente
donc un *don*.[5] Elle n'est donc en nous ni une faculté innée,
ni une acquisition de l'homme, ni une réponse qu'il apporte

[1] *Instit.*, p. 212 ; cf. p. 211.   [2] *Instit.*, p. 193 ; cf. *Ecole*, p. 171.
[3] Cf. *Ecole*, p. 172 ; *Instit.*, p. 199.   [4] *Instit.*, p. 211.
[5] Cf. *Ecole*, p. 182.

à la grâce de Dieu de son propre mouvement. Et puisque le St.-Esprit, ce n'est pas l'Esprit des spiritualistes, aussi bien humain que divin, puisque ce n'est pas un simple esprit de sainteté, une qualité qu'atteindrait l'esprit humain élevé à son plus haut degré,[1] mais bien une réalité *divine*, la troisième personne de la Trinité, l'œuvre du St.-Esprit en nous ne peut être que surnaturelle ; la foi qu'il produit en nous est, par conséquent, un don *surnaturel*. En affirmant cela, Calvin sait fort bien que cette vérité heurte de front l'opinion courante que l'humanité se fait de la foi, l'opinion qui renaîtra toujours en nous aussitôt que, cessant d'adhérer à la Parole de Dieu, à la vérité telle que Dieu nous la révèle, nous retomberons au niveau de notre pensée naturelle et spontanée, qui subsiste et reparaît sans cesse chez le chrétien, comme les œuvres du " vieil homme " subsistent et reparaissent sans cesse dans sa vie : " C'est . . . un singulier don de Dieu que la foi," écrit le Réformateur ; " il est bien vrai que c'est une opinion fort étrange au monde, quand on dit que nul ne peut croire au Christ, sinon celui auquel [cela] est donné particulièrement." [2]

N'empêche que cette " opinion," si " étrange " soit-elle au " monde," est la seule conforme à la Révélation biblique qui constitue notre seule autorité ; nous nous y tiendrons donc, en admirant le courage des Réformateurs à la maintenir envers et contre tout bon sens humain et tout raisonnement mondain, uniquement par fidélité à l'Ecriture. Ne dit-elle pas, en effet, dans une déclaration dont la phrase de Calvin n'est, pour ainsi dire, qu'un écho : " Personne ne peut venir à moi, si cela ne lui est donné par le Père ? " [3]

La conviction de la foi s'établit donc " par dessus tout jugement humain." [4] L'évidence chrétienne se produit à la lumière surnaturelle du St. - Esprit, comme l'évidence intellectuelle ou morale se produisent à la lumière naturelle de l'entendement ou de la conscience humains.[5]

Dans l'économie actuelle, la foi représente même une réalité doublement surnaturelle. " Dans l'état d'intégrité avant la chute," la foi était déjà surnaturelle en ce sens qu'elle était déjà un don de Dieu à sa créature, " une création de Dieu " en elle, mais elle était alors naturelle à l'homme, en ce sens qu'elle formait, dans cet état, " un élément intégrant, essentiel de la nature humaine." [6] Tandis que, depuis la chute,

---

[1] Cf. p. ex., ces définitions d'Elie Gounelle (*Christianisme social*, Mars-Avril 1933, p. 208) : La grâce, " c'est l'humanisme à la plus haute puissance " ; la grâce " est la parfaite antithese du péché, mais non pas de l'humanité."

[2] *Instit.*, p. 202.

[4] *Instit.*, p. 21 ; cf. *Ecole*, p. 181.

[6] *Connaiss. relig.*, p. 49.

[3] St. Jean, vi. 65.

[5] Cf. *Contrad.*, pp. 175 *sqq.*

elle est devenue surnaturelle en ce second sens qu'on ne peut plus dire qu'elle soit habituelle à l'homme déchu et fasse partie intégrante de sa nature actuelle.   En effet, alors que l'homme déchu est un intellectualiste-né, même lorsqu'il est fort inculte, et un moraliste-né, même lorsqu'il est fort immoral —je veux dire : alors qu'il se place d'emblée au point de vue de son intelligence naturelle et de sa conscience naturelle pour juger, à tort, des choses de Dieu—la foi authentique " est un don singulier," bien rare et qu'il lui est fort peu naturel, hélas ! d'accepter.

Ainsi la foi n'est *pas de nous*, puisqu'elle procède du St.-Esprit et cependant elle est bien *notre* puisque pour être authentique elle doit revêtir ce caractère personnel dont nous parlions tout à l'heure.

(5) *Le Principe de l'Analogie de la Foi.* Ayant établi maintenant la genèse de la Foi, sa définition et ses caractères propres nous pouvons étudier son fonctionnement comme organe de la connaissance chrétienne.

C'est selon le *principe de l'analogie de la Foi* que la *fides qua creditur*, dont nous avons parlé jusqu'ici, formule les données de la *fides quæ creditur* ou, si l'on préfère, de la doctrine chrétienne.   Ce principe, M. le professeur Lecerf le définit ainsi : [1]

" D'après l'Ecriture (Jean vii. 18 ; viii. 50), le seul critère intrinsèque, ou, pour parler avec Calvin, la seule pierre de touche qui puisse être une " marque de divinité " est la foi elle-même dans sa tendance vitale.   Il s'appelle, d'ailleurs, le *principe de l'analogie de la foi*.   L'intuition qui conditionne la foi est, avons-nous dit, celle de notre *dépendance* à l'égard de Dieu. . . . *Pour elle, est religieuse une proposition dogmatique dans la mesure où elle met en évidence le caractère unique de la souveraineté et de l'indépendance de Dieu d'une part, et l'absoluité de notre sujétion à lui d'autre part.*"

M. le professeur Lecerf signale que, ce principe, Calvin le formule très nettement dans son Epître à François Ier et dans son Commentaire à l'Évangile de St. Jean, vii. 18 et viii. 50.   Et il ajoute [2] : " Ainsi, le signe de la présence d'une révélation divine, et la clef qui permet d'en ouvrir les sceaux et d'en comprendre le sens, c'est la présence d'une doctrine conforme à ce que nous avons appelé l'analogie de la foi . . . La vérité religieuse ne peut avoir d'autre critère intrinsèque qu'un critère religieux.   Et ce critère, c'est la conformité avec la foi.   La foi est le principe interne de la dogmatique, comme l'Ecriture en est le principe externe."

Nous tenons donc là le principe gouverneur qui, dans le

[1] *Connaiss. relig.*, p. 42.   [2] *Ibid.*, p. 43.

domaine surnaturel de la foi correspond à ce que sont, dans les domaines naturels de la morale et de la science humaines, les principes que, dans une étude antérieure, j'ai appelé le principe de moralité et le principe de vérité, qu'il vaudrait d'ailleurs mieux nommer le principe d'intelligibilité.[1]

Entre ces divers principes gouverneurs de notre pensée, il intervient, d'une part, une différence radicale, puisque celui de l'analogie de la foi informe une intuition *surnaturellement* communiquée et se trouve produit lui-même par ce don *surnaturel*, tandis que les autres informent *naturellement*, par des moyens humains, le sens moral *naturel* et le sens intellectuel *naturel*, c'est à dire innés à l'homme. Mais, d'autre part, quant au rôle que chacun joue dans son domaine propre, en tant que principe gouverneur de la connaissance particulière à ce domaine, ils se correspondent exactement. De même que le sens moral ou le sens intellectuel se précise, se formule en principe de moralité ou en principe d'intelligibilité, de même la foi se détermine, s'informe, en vue de la connaissance chrétienne, en principe de l'analogie de la foi (*a*).

Ce principe va fonctionner, comme ceux de moralité et d'intelligibilité dans leurs domaines respectifs, comme *principe de triage* au sein de la multitude, infiniment variée et contradictoire, des données religieuses naturelles, c'est à dire des croyances issues du sentiment religieux naturel (*b*). Ces multiples croyances de l'humanité, si belles soient-elles, si probable soit leur contenu, nous ne pouvons jamais savoir si elles sont religieusement *vraies*, si elles représentent d'authentiques étincelles de la grâce subsistant parmi les cendres du sentiment religieux naturel,[2] en d'autres termes nous ne pouvons jamais savoir, si elles correspondent à l'objectivité divine, jusqu'à ce que nous en jugions selon l'analogie de la foi. " L'homme spirituel," l'homme animé du St.-Esprit lui rendant témoignage de la Parole de Dieu, l'homme qui juge du seul point de vue de la foi, cet homme " juge de tout," nous dit St. Paul,[3] et lui seul le peut à bon droit puisqu'il se fonde

---

(*a*) Dans les *Contrad.*, étant encore sous l'influence de Frommel et pas encore de Calvin, j'ai encore identifié, comme le fait ce théologien, les domaines religieux et moral ; mais il suffit d'appliquer entre le domaine moral et le domaine religieux les mêmes distinctions que j'ai indiquées alors entre celui-ci et le domaine intellectuel pour que l'ensemble de la thèse développée dans cette étude reste vrai. J'avais d'ailleurs prévu cette éventualité dans la Remarque I. de la, p.58.

(*b*) Pour la différence entre ce sentiment religieux naturel et la foi, nous nous permettons de renvoyer à l'ouvrage de M. le professeur Lecerf, *Connaiss. relig.* pp. 18, 44 *sqq.*, 162. Ce que M. Lecerf appelle ainsi correspond à ce que Calvin nomme un " sentiment de divinité." Cf. p. ex. *Instit.*, p. 4.

[1] *Contrad. relig.*, pp. 162 et 164.

[2] Cf. *Instit.*, p. 6 ; cf. *Connaiss. relig.*, p. 41.   [3] 1 Cor. ii. 15.

uniquement sur la Révélation objective de Dieu.   Tandis que
l'homme naturel, livré à son sentiment religieux spontané, ne
peut jamais savoir si ses croyances, si sublimes soient-elles,
correspondent à la réalité ou ne constituent que des fictions et
des illusions.   Il a même, de par son péché, une fatale propen-
sion à ne pouvoir recevoir les vérités divines : " l'homme
naturel," (a) ajoute l'Apôtre, " n'accepte pas les choses de
l'Esprit de Dieu . . .' il ne peut les connaître parce qu'elles
demandent à être jugées avec l'Esprit."   Seule donc la
foi, fruit du St.-Esprit, peut juger savamment de la vérité
religieuse (b).

Mais, si le principe de l'analogie de la foi nous offre un
principe de triage à l'égard de toutes les croyances humaines,
vis à vis de la Révélation divine il ne représente plus qu'un
principe d'adhesion. Comme le souligne M. le professeur
Lecerf " la foi est pure réceptivité." [1] Comment d'ailleurs
en irait-il autrement puisque c'est de cette Révélation même
et de cette Révélation uniquement que procède la foi ? Elle
ne peut que se reconnaître dans la Parole dont elle est issue.
Puisque " la foi vient de ce qu'on entend " et que " ce qu'on
entend est produit par la parole de Christ," " La brebis reconnaît la voix de son Maître dans toutes ses paroles.[2] Il n'est

(a) *Trad. Stapfer.*   Littéralement psychique, mais la $\psi\nu\chi\eta$ correspond bien
à ce que nous appellerions l'âme naturelle de l'homme and 1 Cor. ii. 14.

(b) Remarquons que tout ce que professe le libéralisme est juste à l'égard
des religions naturelles ; son erreur est d'ignorer la différence entre la foi
surnaturelle et le sentiment religieux naturel er de ramener la première au
second ; cette erreur découle de ce que le libéralisme ne tient pas compte de
la chûte.   Sa théorie faisant des croyances religieuses le produit d'une intellectualisation des sentiments religieux est juste, mais n'atteint que les
croyances naturelles, qui sont dues, en effet, à l'élaboration de ces sentiments
par l'intelligence naturelle et n'ont donc rien de commun avec les doctrines
surnaturellement révélées à la foi par la Parole de Dieu certifiée par le St.-
Esprit.
Il faut donc simplement raisonner à l'inverse du libéralisme.   Parce
qu'il retrouve chez St. Jean le Λόγος des philosophes alexandrins ou chez
St. Paul l'idée d'expiation professée par mainte religion païenne, il ne voit là
chez ces apôtres, que philosophie humaine dont dépouiller leurs écrits
pour retrouver le " pur Evangile."   Tandis qu'au contraire, puisque ces
doctrines du Λόγος et de l'expiation se trouvent dans la Parole de Dieu et
nous sont donc révélées par elle comme conformes à la réalité divine, nous
reconnaissons, sur ces points-là, dans la philosophie hellénistique ou dans
telle religion païenne des " étincelles " de la vérité divine jaillies parmi toutes
les erreurs religieuses dont elles fourmillent.   Nous ne pouvons savoir qu'il
y a quelque vérité divine dans ces théories grecques ou ces idées païennes que
dans la mesure où nous les voyons ratifiées par la Parole de Dieu.   En
l'absence de ce critère, nous ne pouvons que mettre un grand point d'in-
terrogation sur toutes les croyances humaines ; mais par la Parole de Dieu
illuminée à nos yeux par le St.-Esprit, autrement dit en tant qu' " hommes
spirituels " nous pouvons " juger de toutes " ces opinions religieuses de
l'humanité.
[1] *Connaiss. relig.*, p. 18.   [2] Rom. x. 17 ; St. Jean x. 4.

donc pas question, au nom du principe de l'analogie de la foi, d'aller m'ériger en juge de la Parole de Dieu ; si nous avons saisi la genèse de la foi, cette prétention ne peut même avoir aucun sens à nos yeux. Ainsi, " l'homme spirituel juge de tous " les produits du sentiment religieux, il " examine tout et retient ce qui est bon " [1] parmi eux, c'est à dire ce qui est conforme à l'analogie de la foi, mais il ne peut que se laisser juger lui-même par la Parole de Dieu.[2]

La grâce révélatrice, illuminatrice de notre pensée, tout aussi bien que la grâce régénératrice, inspiratrice de notre cœur, de notre conscience et de notre volonté, nous est accordée, non pas en considération de notre dignité, mais bien plutôt et uniquement en considération de notre misère.[3] Si, conformément à la doctrine de notre corruption totale, nous avons reconnu cette misère de notre pensée aussi bien que de nos facultés pratiques, nous ne pourrons voir dans la foi qu'une " pure réceptivité," ou, comme le dit encore le professeur Lecerf, une pure " aptitude à reconnaître la réalité divine." [4] Tant que nous ne sommes pas convaincus de cette misère totale de notre intelligence pécheresse, pécheresse d'un péché foncier, radical, originel, tant que nous conservons la moindre confiance dans notre propre jugement, nous inclinons à voir dans la foi un principe de triage même vis-à-vis de l'Écriture, c'est à dire inévitablement un principe de rejet de certains éléments bibliques—et c'est ce que fait le libéralisme, dans sa confiance en la raison. Mais, par là-même nous faisons obstruction à certaines données de la Révélation, nous nous appauvrissons d'autant et, pire encore, nous nous condamnons d'une façon générale par cette attitude orgueilleuse. " Dieu résiste aux orgueilleux," [5] tout aussi bien sur le terrain de la pensée que sur celui de la vie. Tandis qu'une fois persuadés de notre misère totale, nous nous abandonnons enfin à l'œuvre objective de la Révélation et elle nous fait connaître la vérité divine, car " Dieu fait grâce aux humbles " [6] dans ce domaine aussi. Nous ne recevons donc pas plus la révélation dans la mesure où nous possédons certaines capacités à la comprendre et à en juger que nous ne bénéficions de la régénération dans la mesure où se trouvent en nous certaines qualités préparatrices ou je ne sais quelle dignité d'être renouvelés ; mais, au contraire elle ne nous est accordée que dans la mesure où nous avons abdiqué toute prétention d'être pourvus de telles capacités, pour autant que nous nous en sommes reconnus totalement dépouilles et avons cessé, par là, de conditionner

---

[1] I Thess. v. 21.
[2] Cf. St. Jacq. iv., 11–12.
[3] *Instit.*, p. 357 ; *Ecole*, p. 178.
[4] *Connaiss. relig.*, p. 18.
[5] St. Jacques, iv. 6.
[6] St. Jacques, iv. 6.

la Grâce ; car elle ne reste Grâce et ne peut donc se communiquer comme Grâce qu'en tant qu'elle demeure inconditionnelle.

II

Caractères de la Connaissance Produite par la Foi

1. *Une Certitude.*—Nous l'avons dit : il n'est pas question de com-prendre, d'embrasser, de déterminer l' " objet " divin —*finitum non capax infiniti*—mais bien de se laisser comprendre, envelopper, déterminer par le Sujet divin, de se laisser toucher et persuader par Sa révélation ; il ne s'agit pas d'en acquérir, mais d'en recevoir la connaissance.   Dans ces conditions, la connaissance chrétienne revêt la caractère d'une *certitude que* et non pas d'une *compréhension comment*.[1]

Comprendre comment : c'est le propre de la connaissance intellectuelle ; et elle n'y parvient qu'en expliquant, c'est à dire en déterminant, en mettant ses divers éléments en relations les uns avec les autres.   Elle ne peut donc qu'avoir un caractère déterministe et relativiste.

Croire que : c'est le propre de la connaissance chrétienne. Convaincue de chacun de ses éléments par leur révélation, elle n'a donc pas besoin, et doit même se garder de les rattacher, de les relier à autre chose qu'eux-mêmes, par exemple aux objets de notre connaissance sensible, intellectuelle ou expérimentale ; elle doit éviter à tout prix d'y ramener, quitte à les fausser, ses propres données.   Elle ne saurait donc qu'avoir un caractère absolu, *absolutus*, délié de toute relation, exempt de tout relativisme.

Ainsi, la connaissance qui découle de la foi est tout autre qu'une connaissance intellectuelle ; c'est une connaissance spirituelle, c'est à dire suscitée par le St.-Esprit.   On ne saurait trop y insister, soit vis-à-vis des intellectualistes qui se croient orthodoxes, soit vis-à-vis des anti-intellectualistes qui, parce que nous adhérons aux doctrines de la Révélation, nous traitent d'intellectualistes.   Non, répondrons-nous avec St. Paul aux uns et aux autres : " ce que Dieu nous révèle nous n'en parlons pas dans les termes qu'enseigne la sagesse humaine, mais dans ceux qu'enseigne l'Esprit, exprimant ce qui est spirituel en style spirituel." [2]

Mais nous sommes toujours trompés à nouveau par l'apparence intellectuelle des termes de la pensée religieuse.   Aussi, est-ce pour éviter cette confusion et pour exprimer jusque dans le langage la radicale différence du spirituel et de l'in-

[1] *Instit.*, pp. 191–192 ; cf. *Ecole*, p. 171.   [2] 1 Cor. xi. 13.

tellectuel que j'ai proposé, dans une précédente étude, d'appeler " idées " les notions religieuses et " concepts " les notions intellectuelles.[1] En effet, les unes et les autres forment bien des notions, vu que, dans les deux domaines, il y a bien, à proprement parler, connaissance ; et *noscere* signifie précisément connaître. Mais seules les notions intellectuelles constituent des concepts—de *concipere*, concevoir, prendre ensemble, contenir—car n'est compréhensible que ce qui est intelligible. Tandis que les notions spirituelles ne représentent que des idées—de *ἰδέα*, *idea*, image—car elles ne nous fournissent guère que des images de données, certes connaissables, mais non compréhensibles, et seulement " imaginables " par voie d'analogie. Ce qui nous explique la constante préférence de Jésus pour la parabole, dans l'Évangile, et le fréquent emploi de l'image dans le langage religieux.

Pour exprimer cette distinction dans le vocabulaire de M. le professeur Lecerf, nous dirons que la dogmatique, c'est à dire l'exposé de la connaissance due à la foi, forme une science canonique et non pas spéculative, " parce que " comme il le dit à la suite de Bavinck, " cette discipline détermine ce que l'on doit croire, sur l'autorité de Dieu, au lieu de se borner à traduire en formules intellectuelles les expériences subjectives d'une individualité religieuse." [2]

2. *Une connaissance analogique.*—Cette connaissance doctrinale, produite par voie d'analogie, selon le principe de l'analogie de la foi, revêt donc un caractère analogique. Mais soulignons aussitôt que cela ne signifie pas du tout la même chose qu'un caractère symbolique, au sens moderniste de ce terme. Nous arrivons peut-être ici à l'une des mises au point les plus nécessaires à faire dans notre débat avec le libéralisme.

Calvin lui-même emploie, exceptionnellement, le terme de " symbole," [3] mais, lorsqu'il le fait, c'est visiblement dans un autre sens que le modernisme (*a*). Il importe de le préciser, et pour faire plus constamment sentir la différence, il vaut mieux se servir de deux mots : laissant celui de " *symbole* " au libéralisme qui lui a donné pour longtemps la signification qu'il revêt aujourd'hui dans la plupart des esprits, nous nous en tiendrons, pour exprimer la pensée réformée sur ce point, au terme d' " analogie."

La plus rigoureuse orthodoxie ne fait aucune difficulté d'admettre que la connaissance doctrinale ne peut être qu'analogique, et non pas ontologique. " Dieu," nous dit, par

(*a*) Pour plus de détails sur se sujet, voir mon article sur la différence entre le terme moderniste de " symbole " et le terme calviniste de " signe " dans les *Cahiers protestants*, September 1934, pp. 383 *sqq.* Cf. aussi Dominicé. la *Sainte-Cène*, pp. 8 *sqq.*

[1] Cf. *Contrad.*, p. 85.   [2] *Connaiss. relig.*, p. 287.   [3] P. 4 : *Instit.*, p. 632.

exemple, M. le professeur Lecerf, " se connaît lui-même parfaitement (theologia archetypica) ; . . . il est capable de
communiquer, sous le mode analogique, cette connaissance
aux créatures duées d'intelligence, en particulier à l'homme
(théologia ectypica)," c'est à dire tirée (εκ) de son archétype,
mais non plus identique à lui-même comme la connaissance
que Dieu en a.[1] " Calvin " lui-même, relève encore le même
auteur " a expressément indiqué l'analogie comme procédé de la
connaissance de Dieu. Voir, par exemple, *Commentaire sur
Jérémie*, xxiii. 5. J. Zanchi (*De natura Dei*) en a formulé la
théorie, d'après Thomas d'Aquin. H. Bavinck les suit." [2]

On ne peut nier, en effet que, pour se révéler à l'homme,
Dieu n'utilise des idées humaines, et que, pour exprimer ces
idées, il n'emprunte une langue humaine. Entre la réalité
divine et la connaissance que peut en recevoir l'homme, il
intervient donc en tous cas un double décalage, sans même
parler ici des autres causes d'inadéquation de la pensée
humaine aux données divines. Que valent, par exemple, nos
idées de " père " et de " fils " pour exprimer l'intimité de la
première et de la deuxième personnes de la Trinité, telle que
l'évoque St. Jean au premier verset de son Evangile ?

Mais si, dans cette double traduction inévitable qu'implique
la Révélation, Dieu choisit l'idée la plus apte à rendre la
réalité, et le mot le plus propre à exprimer cette idée, toute
autre idée et tout autre mot auxquels nous recourrions pour
définir cette réalité ne sauraient être que moins justes, moins
vrais, et devant donc être rejetés par quiconque croit à ce
qui s'appelle vraiment une révélation. Toute doctrine produite par ce processus divin, bien que n'ayant qu'une valeur
analogique, possède donc un caractère nécessaire et normatif,
c'est à dire que le mode de sa production ne pouvait être
que ce qu'il a été et qu'elle en a reçu un caractère contraignant
pour nous. Une *analogie,* divinement imposée, est donc
tout autre chose qu'un *symbole* choisi par les hommes pour
exprimer à leur idée un sentiment religieux ou même une
inspiration authentiquement divine. Car, dans le cas du
symbole, rien ne garantit la perfection du choix fait parmi les
diverses idées et les divers termes possibles ; il conserve donc
un caractère facultatif et l'homme reste libre de lui en substituer d'autres. Par exemple, bien que le terme de " Père "
n'ait, à l'égard de Dieu, qu'un caractère analogique, il n'est
aucunement licite de la remplacer par celui de " Mère,"
malgré la préférence de beaucoup d'esprits humains, notamm-
ent parmi les hindouistes, pour une notion féminine de la
divinité. Tandis qu'un drapeau, symbole de la patrie plus

[1] *Connaiss. relig.*, p. 22. [2] *Ibid.*, p. 222, *n.* 2.

ou moins arbitrairement choisi par les hommes, peut être légitimement changé.

Pour traduire par une image notre pensée, nous pourrions dire qu'entre l'analogie et le symbole subsiste la même différence qu'entre un cours d'eau occupant, dans un terrain donné, le seul lit correspondant à sa propre force de propulsion, et un canal dont le tracé est plus ou moins librement choisi par les ingénieurs, et probablement pas sans erreurs, parmi plusieurs projets interchangeables.

Sous cette différence entre l'analogie et le symbole, nous retrouvons la divergence des deux positions fondamentales possibles à l'égard de la doctrine : celle de l'orthodoxie qui y reconnaît le produit d'une révélation de Dieu à l'homme, et celle du libéralisme qui en fait le résultat d'une invention, d'une découverte de Dieu par l'homme à partir de quelque ineffable inspiration. Même en donnant toute son importance à l'écart intervenu entre la réalité divine et la doctrine exprimée en langue humaine, nous restons en pleine orthodoxie en concevant leur rapport de façon analogique ; tandis qu'en l'envisageant sous le mode symbolique, nous sommes déjà en plein libéralisme (a).

(3) *Indépendance de la Dogmatique*. La connaissance constituée de la façon que nous avons décrite est, on le voit, complètement indépendante de la connaissance intellectuelle, soit scientifique, soit philosophique.

Nous avons reconnu, en effet, qu'elle ne procède pas, comme les croyances des religions humaines, de l'intellectualisation de sentiments religieux, mais uniquement de la réception par la foi de la révélation divine Elle produit une théologie, à proprement parler, tandis que de telles intellectualisations conduisent à des philosophies religieuses, ce qui est bien autre chose et tombe seul sous la critique du libéralisme, juste à leur égard mais complètement déplacée à l'égard de la dogmatique authentique (b). Car celle-ci, comme le dit M. Lecerf en une formule lumineuse dans sa brièveté, " est une science de la foi par la foi," [1] ou elle n'est plus dogmatique.

En deuxième lieu, l'indépendance de la dogmatique à l'égard de la connaissance intellectuelle se marque dans le fait que les jugements spirituels diffèrent du tout au tout des

(a) Pour plus de précisions sur la valeur cognitive de analogie. Cf. Lecerf, *Connaiss. relig.*, pp. 223–225.

(b) Certains titres de livres reflètent d'une façon frappante cette confusion faite par le libéralisme entre dogmatique et philosophie religieuse. P. ex.: H. Bois, la philosophie de Calvin. Cette confusion provient de l'intellectualisme foncier du XIXᵉ siècle qui n'a pu concevoir de connaissance autre qu'intellectuelle.

[1] *Connaiss. relig.*, p. 27.

jugements intellectuels. Il n'est pas possible de reproduire
ici toute la démonstration de cette différence que j'ai longue-
ment développée ailleurs ; (a) contentons-nous donc de rappeler,
en résumé, qu'entre les jugements relevant de ces deux ordres
de connaissance :

1. Les *termes* diffèrent, puisque, pour reprendre la distinction établie tout à l'heure, dans un cas ce sont des " idées "
et dans l'autre des " concepts." Pascal nous fait bien sentir,
par exemple, que le même mot " Dieu " recouvre un tout autre
contenu suivant qu'il est employé du point de vue spirituel ou
intellectuel, lorsqu'il écrit : " Dieu d'Abraham, d'Isaac et de
Jacob, non des philosophes et des savants." [1]

2. Les *critères* commandant ces jugements diffèrent,
puisque celui du premier domaine est le principe de l'analogie
de la foi, tandis que celui du second est le principe d'intelligibilité (b).

Seules, les *formes* purement logiques demeurent communes
aux jugements de tous les ordres de la pensée. Mais elles
ne peuvent, à elles seules, déterminer aucun contenu ; elles
ne gouvernent que la forme de la pensée, le contenu de celle-ci
et les rapports concrets entre les éléments de ce contenu ne
pouvant être établis que par le critère propre à chaque
domaine. [2]

Dans ces conditions, il nous est impossible de voir dans
la pensée doctrinale une adaptation au domaine religieux de
tel ou tel système *philosophique* ni une prolongation métaphysique de morales autonomes.

La première méthode est celle de la théologie catholique,
reprise par la théologie libérale ; (c) tandis que le romanisme
applique au christianisme la philosophie d'Aristote, le modernisme y adapte celle de Bergson, par exemple. Le second

(a) *Contrad. relig.*, pp. 84 *sqq.*: Pour la raison que j'ai indiquée ci-dessus
[p. 216 (a)] il importe de substituer, tout au long de cette démonstration, le
terme " spirituel " aux termes " moral " et " éthico-religieux."

(b) Cf. Lecerf, *Connais. relig.*, p. 43 : " La vérité religieuse ne peut avoir
d'autre critère intrinsèque qu'un critère religieux. Et ce critère c'est la
conformité avec la foi."

(c) De plus en plus convaincu de l'étroite parenté de ces deux sortes de
théologie qui, à première vue, semblent si opposéer l'une à l'autre, nous avons
été très intéressé de voir cette similitude fortement soulignée par M. le professeur Gut, de Zurich, en ces termes: " Es wird oft zu wenig beachtet, dass
liberale Theologie mit ihrer Verbindung von Christentum und Philosophie
grundsätzlich dem katholischen Denken nàher steht als reformatorischen
Glaubensverständnis, so gross im übrigen die Unterschiede sein mögen. Sie
beide verbindet ein Vertrauen an die Vernunft und ihre Leistungsfähigkeit zur
Erkentnis Gottes, wie es von einer evangelisch-reformatorischen Theologie
nicht geteilt wird " (*Schweizerische Rundschan*, Novemberheft, 1937, p. 618).

[1] Cf. *Contrad. relig.*, pp. 84 *sqq.*
[2] Cf. *Contrad.*, pp. 102 *sqq.*

procédé est celui de toutes les théologies moralistes qui relèvent de Kant. Ni l'une, ni l'autre de ces façons de faire ne correspond à la nôtre, et cela nous permet d'échapper aux critiques de l'histoire des religions qui atteignent ces " théologies " ou plus exactement ces philosophies chrétiennes avec justesse lorsqu'elles y montrent l'expression religieuse de la pensée d'une époque, destinée à changer avec celle-ci.

Quant à nous, ce que nous avons dit de la constitution de la doctrine nous fait conclure à l'erreur foncière de la méthode qui consiste à choisir une philosophie, puis à voir comment faire entrer la foi chrétienne dans ses cadres ; cette manière de faire ne peut aboutir qu'à tronquer les données de la foi qui n'arrivent pas à rentrer dans le système ou au contraire à ajouter des éléments à la révélation divine pour ne pas laisser de vides dans cette synthèse. La seule méthode juste consiste à développer la doctrine chrétienne selon le jeu de ses propres lois, d'une façon organique, puis à trier parmi les systèmes humains, parmi les religions, les morales et les philosophies, ce qui est conforme à l'analogie de la foi, pour l'assimiler, et ce qui ne l'est pas, pour l'éliminer. Alors, dans la mesure où ce procédé est strictement observé, on évite de mettre la doctrine à la remorque de l'histoire des cultures humaines. Il est évident que nous traçons ici un idéal et que, comme nous le verrons en terminant, ce triage, opéré par des esprits pécheurs et donc sujets à l'erreur, est, en pratique, toujours à refaire, d'époque en époque. En fait, il faudra donc, au cours des siècles, apporter à nos dogmatiques des changements de tonalité et leur faire subir des adaptations de langage, mais, en droit, leur contenu même demeure immuable. L'histoire des doctrines conservera donc toujours son rôle légitime dans la mesure où elle se bornera à expliquer par les circonstances et les conceptions de l'époque les modalités et l'expression données à un dogme par ses divers expositeurs, mais pour autant qu'elle prétend expliquer par là le fond même de ce dogme, elle outrepasse ses réelles possibilités et prouve son ignorance de la genèse véritable d'une doctrine authentique. A l'égard de celle-ci, une seule question se pose en vue de son admission ou de son rejet : non pas si elle date du XIIe, du XVIe ou du XXe siècle, mais si elle est vraie ou fausse, c'est à dire conforme ou non, selon l'analogie de la foi, à l'éternelle réalité de Dieu. La vérité n'a pas d'âge.

(4) *Constitution organique de la dogmatique.*—La dogmatique se constitue donc en une connaissance ordonnée, d'une façon organique, c'est à dire dans les formes logiques communes à tous les domaines de la pensée humaine et appliquées à celui-ci selon le principe de l'analogie de la foi. Ainsi, cette connaissance

se développe selon des nécessités spirituelles, comme les morales et les sciences humaines se constituent organiquement, les unes sur la base du principe de moralité, les autres sur la base du principe d'intelligibilité, c'est à dire selon des nécessités morales dans un cas et intellectuelles dans l'autre (a).

Qui dit organisme dit hiérarchie d'organes complémentaires et interdépendants.   Et de fait, Calvin admet une hiérarchie de doctrine.   La tâche du dogmaticien consiste donc à dégager d'abord les dogmes fondamentaux, puis à en déduire les dogmes secondaires qui se fondent sur les premiers et auxquels il se trouve conduit, non par des raisonnements intellectuels, mais par ce que nous venons d'appeler des nécessités spirituelles (b).

III

DU RAPPORT DES DIVERS ORDRES DE CONNAISSANCE ENTRE EUX

(1) *Leur incommensurabilité.*—La dogmatique, avons-nous dit, conserve une complète indépendance vis-à-vis de la science, de la philosophie, de la morale, de l'esthétique, bref vis-à-vis de tous *les ordres de pensée* propres à chaque domaine de l'esprit, vu que les termes qui constituent ses jugements et le critère au nom duquel elle les porte diffèrent complètement des termes et des critères propres à chacun de ces autres domaines.

Il ne saurait donc pas plus y avoir contradiction qu'accord entre les connaissances nées de ces divers ordres de pensée, car pour qu'il y ait contradiction entre deux jugements il faut que les termes (sujet et prédicat) soient les mêmes et le point de vue le même dans les deux propositions ; [1] on ne peut donc établir une contradiction, ni d'ailleurs non plus statuer un accord, entre deux jugements portés de points de vue différents, ce qui est le cas lorsqu'ils sont régis par deux critères différents, comme, par exemple, le principe de l'analogie de la foi et celui d'intelligibilité.   Les divers ordres de connaissance sont donc, comme on dit en mathématiques, incommensurables entre eux (c).

N'empêche qu'il *semblera* toujours y avoir des contradictions entre eux, parce que souvent de mêmes mots servent à

(a) Ce que j'appelle ici " nécessité spirituelle " me semble correspondre à ce que M. le professeur Lecerf nomme "instinct de la piété " (*Connaiss. relig.*, p. 280).

(b) Pour plus de détails, cf. *Contrad.*, pp. 224 *sqq.*, en y faisant les modifications indiquées ci-dessus, p. 216 *n.a.*

(c) Pour plus de développements ; cf. *Contrad.*, pp. 287 *sqq.*

[1] *Contrad.*, p. 60.

désigner, par exemple, les idées religieuses et des concepts intellectuels. Ainsi, le même mot " Dieu " recouvre, pour la foi et pour la philosophie, deux contenus complètement différents (a).

C'est donc l'intellectualisation de termes spirituels, le fait de prendre de tels termes pour des concepts intellectuels, qui fait naître la contradiction, non pas une apparence de contradiction, mais une contradiction bel et bien réelle du point de vue intellectuel. Certains jugements doctrinaux, parfaitement logiques du point de vue spirituel, deviennent contradictoires lorsqu'ils sont pris pour des jugements philosophiques gouvernés par le principe d'intelligibilité. Et c'est pourquoi, suivant la remarque de St. Paul déjà citée,[1] " l'homme naturel " qui juge des " choses de Dieu " du point de vue de son intelligence naturelle, " n'accepte pas les choses de l'Esprit de Dieu ; il les taxe de folie ; il ne peut les connaître, parce qu'elles demandent à être jugées avec l'Esprit," selon le critère spirituel et non pas intellectuel. La doctrine chrétienne ne pourra jamais sembler qu'une " folie " à l'homme naturel, c'est à dire à l'intellectuel qui n'est pas doublé d'un " homme spirituel." On ne la rendra jamais intelligible sans l'altérer et la mutiler. Ce qui ne l'empêche pas de constituer dans son ordre une science réelle, mais spirituelle et non pas intellectuelle. Aussi, pour reprendre encore les termes de St. Paul, " exposons-nous ce qui est spirituel dans un language spirituel . . . et non dans les termes qu'enseigne la sagesse humaine," c'est à dire dans un langage intellectuel.[2] Cette conséquence, remarquons-le, découle directement des versets précédents, 9 à 11, sur lesquels nous fondions, en commençant, la doctrine, typique de la théologie réformée, du *Testimonium Spiritus Sancti internum*. Oui : puisque le contenu de notre foi nous est " révélé par l'Esprit," puisque nous le discernons à la seule lumière de l'Esprit de Dieu et non point à celle de l'évidence intellectuelle, la seule forme qui convient à l' " exposer," c'est celle " qu'enseigne l'Esprit " et non point celle " qu'enseigne la sagesse humaine," c'est à dire l'intelligence naturelle.

(2) *Leur commun caractère logique.*—Mais affirmer qu'un ordre de pensée n'est pas intelligible ne signifie pas qu'il ne soit pas logique. Sans pouvoir reprendre ici toute la démonstration que j'ai tentée dans le livre auquel j'ai déjà fait allusion, il ne faut du moins en rappeler ceci pour justifier une telle distinction de l'intellectuel et du logique :[3] l'usage général confond ces deux termes parce qu'il ne prend pas garde que, dans un jugement intellectuel, intervient, en plus de la pure

(a) Pour plus de détails ; cf. *Contrad.*, pp. 293 *sqq.*
[1] Cor. ii. 14.   [2] Cor. ii. 13.   [3] *Contrad.*, pp. 112 *sqq.*

forme logique, un critère particulier, le principe d'intelligibilité ; exactement comme, dans un jugement doctrinal intervient, en plus de la même forme de pure logique, le critère
propre à ce domaine, le principe de l'analogie de la foi ; ou
encore comme, dans un jugement moral, s'ajoute à la pure
forme logique, commune à tous les domaines, un critère
proprement éthique, le principe de moralité (a). Si l'usage
commun fait cette confusion, c'est parce que nous sommes
des intellectualistes-nés et qu'inconsciemment nous nous
plaçons d'emblée, dans nos jugements, au point de vue
intellectuel.

Mais, en réalité, il importe de distinguer, dans tout jugement, sa forme au sens large du mot, c'est à dire englobant
tout ce qui n'appartient pas au contenu de ce jugement et
incluant, dans ces conditions, un critère particulier—et sa
forme au sens étroit du mot, c'est à dire purement logique,
dépouillée de tout critère spécial.[1] Alors, si, par une telle
distinction, on rend la logique vraiment formelle, au sens
étroit de ce terme, on est en droit de dire qu'elle s'applique à
tous les domaines, spirituel, moral, esthétique, aussi bien
qu'intellectuel. Mais dès lors, elle se réduit à quelque chose
de si abstrait qu'elle demeure inutilisable sans l'intervention
d'un critère particulier. Ainsi, la logique pure gouverne tous les
domaines, mais ne peut, à elle seule, constituer aucun ordre
de connaissance particulier. Ou bien, entendu selon cette
définition, elle demeure générale, elle vaut alors pour tous les
domaines, mais elle reste inapplicable ; ou bien, elle se
spécialise par l'adjonction d'un critère, elle devient dès lors
applicable concrètement, mais du même coup ne vaut plus
que pour le domaine correspondant à ce critère.

La logique pure peut me dire : A exclut non—A ; mais
quant à savoir si B est du type non—A et se trouve, par
conséquent, exclu par A, ce n'est plus la logique qui peut
me le dire, mais seul le critère propre au domaine auquel
appartiennent A et B. Ce n'est donc pas la logique, mais
bien le principe d'intelligibilité, par exemple, qui m'avertit
que le concept A—disons : la sovueraineté d'un Dieu philosophique—*exclut* le concept B—disons : telle notion philosophique de la liberté humaine, tandis que selon le principe
de l'analogie de la foi, l'idée A—la souveraineté du Dieu de la
foi—*inclut* l'idée B—la liberté chrétienne. Lors donc qu'un
jugement spirituel s'avère intelligible, c'est à dire que ces

(a) On pourrait sans doute en dire autant de l'esthétique, qui doit aussi
avoir sa logique propre constituée par les pures formes logiques, communes à
tous les domaines de la pensée, appliquées à celui-ci selon un critère proprement esthétique, le principe de beauté.
    [1] *Contrad.*, pp. 102 *sqq.*

termes étant, à tort, conçus intellectuellement, s'excluent comme contradictoires, cela ne signifie pas que ce jugement soit absurde, c'est à dire illogique ; et, de fait, il ne l'est pas si ses termes s'accordent selon le critère spirituel.

Il peut sembler curieux que les adversaires de la doctrine nous reprochent à la fois d'être des intellectualistes et des gens qui arguent de ce que " la folie de Dieu est plus sage que les hommes " pour maintenir toutes sortes d'absurdités. Mais la possibilité de critiques aussi contradictoires sortant de la même bouche s'explique par la confusion signalée tout à l'heure. Par contre si cette confusion permet les deux reproches opposés, que l'on nous fait, la distinction que j'ai indiquée nous rend possible de les écarter tous les deux : car elle nous a montré d'une part combien doctrine et intellectualisme sont choses différentes et même incompatibles, et d'autre part combien la dogmatique a bel et bien sa logique, tout aussi rigoureuse que la logique intellectuelle. Répudier le critère intellectuel dans le domaine spirituel n'équivaut donc nullement à se permettre toutes les absurdités, mais garantit bien plutôt le respect du critère propre à ce domaine.

IV

DE l'INEVITABLE CONFUSION DES DIVERS ORDRES DE PENSÉE DANS LA PRATIQUE THÉOLOGIQUE ET DE LA NÉCESSITÉ QU'ELLE ENTRAÎNE DE RÉVISER CONSTAMMENT TOUT SYSTÈME THÉOLOGIQUE

(1) *Caractère fatal de cette confusion.*—Tout ce que nous avons dit jusqu'ici est vrai en théorie, et demeure en droit la seule vérité. Mais, en fait, hélas ! il en va bien autrement. Car la pratique de la théologie se trouve bien plutôt constituée par le drame quotidien dû au fait que nous reglissons sans cesse d'une notion spirituelle des choses de la foi dans une notion soit intellectuelle, soit morale, soit même esthétique.

Pourquoi cela ? Tout simplement parce que nous sommes des intellectualistes-nés, des moralistes-nés, des sensitifs, tandis que nous ne sommes pas des spirituels-nés. Et, à son tour, pourquoi cela ? Parce que l'intelligence, la conscience, la sensibilité forment nos facultés naturelles, innées, tandis que la foi, comme nous l'avons dit, représente un don surnaturel. Or, comme, en bonne doctrine réformée, le pécheur subsiste dans le chrétien, comme l'homme spirituel conserve, tant qu'il se traîne ici-bas, " les reliques " de l'homme naturel, bien que nous devions demeurer dans la foi, nous n'évitons pas en pratique, de retomber sans cesse de la grâce dans la nature, ce qui veut dire, quant au domaine qui nous occupe ici, que nous n'évitons pas, dans la pratique, de retomber sans cesse d'un ordre de pensée gouverné par le seul principe de l'analogie de la foi dans un ordre de pensée commandé par le principe d'intelligibilité.   Et cela d'autant moins qu'en fait la distinction des deux domaines se présente d'une façon bien moins tranchée que nous ne l'avons décrite, d'une manière schématique, pour la clarté de l'exposé.   Pratiquement la transition de l'un à l'autre s'opère par toute une gradation, ou plutôt une dégradation de nuances insensibles, entraînant l'esprit des pures idées spirituelles aux purs concepts intellectuels, à travers une série de notions intermédiaires, toujours moins doctrinales et toujours plus intelligibles.

Il en va donc exactement de même, pour le chrétien, sur le plan de la pensée que sur le plan de la vie.   Exactement comme sa foi se dégrade inévitablement dans l'exercice même des œuvres qui en découlent, elle se déforme fatalement dans l'exercice même des pensées qui en dérivent.

Le problème est même plus délicat encore : car, ces œuvres, pratiques ou intellectuelles, qui la font dégénérer, la foi a l'absolu devoir de les engendrer.   Sous peine d'infidélité à elle-même, la foi doit se traduire en œuvres, bien que cette traduction ne puisse que la trahir—Il en va là comme de nos congrès internationaux où pour nous comprendre, nous sommes obligés de nous traduire nos pensées, d'une langue dans une autre, tout en sachant que ces traductions mêmes n'évitent jamais d'être une source d'incompréhension. La foi doit mettre en œuvre l'intelligence du chrétien, tout comme elle doit mettre en œuvre sa volonté et sa sensibilité ; mais, en principe, elle doit, pour rester pure, en demeurer distincte, alors qu'en pratique elle n'évite pas de s'y mêler et de s'y dégrader. C'est le drame quotidien où le chrétien se trouve engagé, aussi bien dans sa pensée que dans sa vie : chaque fois que, devant Dieu, il dissout de nouveau ses œuvres pratiques ou intellectuelles, pour ressaisir le salut par la foi seule, par la foi pure, il *doit*, à nouveau, exprimer cette foi par des œuvres, et il n'évite pas alors de l'y compromettre.   En principe, cette déformation n'est pas nécessaire, et c'est pourquoi. il en est toujours coupable, mais en pratique, elle est inévitable, car, bien que *semper justus* par la foi, il est *semper peccator* dans ses pensées et dans sa vie, même mise au service de la foi.

Ainsi, soumis au devoir d'exprimer la foi chrétienne en une pensée qui, normalement, doit demeurer purement spirituelle, en fait nous tendons toujours fatalement à substituer une philosophie religieuse naturelle à la doctrine révélée, et une morale naturelle à la morale révélée. C'est dans ce glisse-ment qu'il nous faut trouver la cause de la substitution à la vraie doctrine de tant de philosophies " chrétiennes " qui se prennent à tort pour des théologies et de tant de moralismes " chrétiens " qui se prennent à tort pour des morales chrétiennes. Aucun dogmaticien, pas même Calvin, n'a complètement échappé à ce danger, et, d'après ce que nous venons de dire, ce serait tout à fait anticalviniste de penser le contraire au sujet de notre réformateur.

Dans la piété chrétienne, le seul remède aux trahisons de notre foi, inévitables au cours de sa traduction en œuvres, est de remonter sans cesse, par la prière, au principe de cette incarnation de l'Esprit de Dieu dans notre vie, à la source de la foi, à la Grâce même de Dieu. De même, dans la pensée chrétienne, le seul remède aux altérations intellectualistes, moralistes, ou même esthétiques de la doctrine, qui se pro-duisent fatalement lors de son élaboration en un système complet, est de remonter sans cesse au principe de toute théologie fidèle, à la seule source de toute dogmatique authen-tique, à la Parole même de Dieu. Et c'est pourquoi, d'époque en époque, il nous faut constamment nous confronter à nouveau avec l'Écriture, vérifier sous l'égide de sa seule autorité, et réviser dans leurs éléments non-bibliques toutes nos théologies y compris celle de Calvin ; d'avantage, il nous faut, d'année en année, critiquer de la même façon notre propre dogmatique, si nous en avons une.

Bref, le calviniste authentique, c'est à dire vraiment soumis à la seule autorité de l'Écriture, ne pourra jamais concevoir les lignes directrices de sa théologie comme les rayons d'un cercle fermé et immuable, une fois constitué ; il les envisagera bien plutôt comme ceux du soleil, qui émanent toujours à nouveau d'un centre fixe, mais dont les aboutisse-ments varient forcément avec les accidents du paysage qu'ils pénètrent. Si nous prenons au sérieux-même à l'égard de Calvin, et de nous-mêmes !—le *semper peccator*, nous ne pourrons imaginer aucun paysage psychologique ou historique sans de tels accidents, ni, par conséquent, les points d'incidence de nos théologies comme définitivement acquis, mais cela ne nous fera nullement verser dans le relativisme moderniste si, par ailleurs, nous ne prenons pas moins au sérieux l'autorité absolue de la Révélation scripturaire, centre fixe de notre pensée doctrinale, et fixe à jamais, selon la parole de notre Seigneur : " le ciel et la terre passeront, mais Mes paroles ne passeront point." [1]

En conclusion : sera vraiment calviniste toute théologie

[1] St. Matt. xxiv. 35.

concentrique à celle du Réformateur, même si elle ne coïncide
pas en tous points avec la périphèrie de sa dogmatique. Tandis
qu'une théologie qui reproduirait, point par point, le détail de
cette périphérie, mais les grouperait sur un autre centre, ou
encore sur deux centres, par exemple, la Révélation et la
Raison, ne saurait légitimement se prévaloir du titre de
calviniste.

(2) *Calvinisme fermé et calvinisme ouvert.*—Pourquoi ai-je
pensé utile de soumettre ces réflexions à notre Congrès ? Parce
que, depuis quelques années que j'observe les diverses écoles
qui se réclament du Réformateur, il me semble que c'est
précisément cette question qui les sépare, et que, si nous pouvions
l'élucider ensemble, un grand pas serait fait vers l'unité de nos
différents mouvements.

Il me semble que les uns, voyant dans l'intelligence le
siège de toute connaissance, tendent à faire du calvinisme un
système intellectuel adéquat à son objet doctrinal et par
conséquent définitif jusque dans ses moindres détails ; tandis
que les autres, reconnaissant dans la foi l'organe de la connaissance dogmatique, admettent que toute expression plus ou
moins intellectualisée de la doctrine réformée ne peut que lui
être plus ou moins inadéquate et ne possède de ce fait qu'une
valeur plus ou moins provisoire, si bien que, tout en restant
entièrement fidèle à cette doctrine, on peut en réviser les
développements plus philosophiques que théologiques ; je
dirai même : que, *par fidélité* à la doctrine réformée, l'on *doit*
l'épurer sans cesse de ces développements.

C'est cet intellectualisme qui a faussé le calvinisme dès le
XVIIe siècle ; mais déjà chez le réformateur lui-même, comme
d'ailleurs chez tout théologien, l'on peut en trouver quelques
traces par ci par là. Je crois donc que certains exposés du
calvinisme qui paraissent, à première vue, très orthodoxes
parce qu'ils reproduisent littéralement les points particuliers
du système, sont en réalité très peu calvinistes dans leurs
principes essentiels. Je pense ici, par exemple, au livre du
professeur Loraine Boettner, *The Reformed Doctrine of Predestination* qui énumère et expose, sans doute, les fameux
" Five Points of Calvinism," [1] mais qui, tout au long, en appelle,
pour justifier ses arguments, à la double autorité de la Bible
et de la Raison ; (*a*) et je n'hésite pas à dire que cette façon

(*a*) Cf. p. ex. p. 1 : " The purpose of this book is . . . to show that [Cal-
vinism] is beyond all doubt the teaching of the Bible and of reason."   P. 49 :
" This view alone is consistent with Scripture and with what we see in the
world about us."   P. 59 : " In this section, we shall examine each of these
[points], giving the Scripture basis and the arguments from reason which
support them," etc.

[1] P. 59.

de faire intervenir une seconde autorité à côté de l'Écriture relève non pas de la dogmatique réformée, mais bien plutôt de la théologie catholique, ou libérale (puisque, à cet égard, celles-ci coïncident).

Par contre, si nous avons saisi à quel point l'originalité de la doctrine calviniste réside dans le fait que, pour elle, le *seul* organe de la connaissance chrétienne, c'est la foi, et qu'ici comme partout ailleurs, elle nous enjoint de procéder *fide sola*, nous serons prêts à admettre comme authentiquement réformée telle ou telle théologie qui s'en tient fidèlement à ce principe fondamental, même si, sur tel ou tel point de détail, elle croit devoir corriger Calvin par obéissance à l'Écriture. Je dirai même : d'autant plus que sur de tels points elle rectifiera l'exposé du réformateur, si c'est vraiment par obéissance à l'Écriture qu'elle le fait ; car, à l'occasion, fausser compagnie à Calvin pour rejoindre la Bible, c'est encore être calviniste, c'est être vraiment calviniste.

Je voudrais donc que nous voyions d'abord, tous ensemble, si nous sommes d'accord sur ce point fondamental que l'unique organe de la connaissance chrétienne, c'est la foi définie comme elle l'a été plus haut, en sorte qu'à nos yeux à tous la dogmatique soit, " selon la lumineuse formule de M. le professeur Lecerf, " la connaissance de la foi par la foi " et par la foi seule. Si cet assentiment peut être obtenu, mes désirs seront comblés, car je pense qu'après cela nous pourrons envisager comme des calvinistes authentiques tous ceux qui partagent cette conviction et fondent sur elle toute leur théologie, même si celle-ci diffère un peu de la nôtre dans certaines de ses conclusions. Alors, comme les apôtres à la conférence de Jérusalem, nous n'hésiterons plus à " nous tendre la main d'association " [1] entre adhérents aux diverses théologies réformées qui renaissent aujourd'hui et le but, tout pratique, de cet exposé sera atteint, pour ma plus grande joie, car une telle entente ne pourra que favoriser puissamment l'expansion de nos efforts communs au service de l'Évangile.

Comment on this paper was made by Lieutenant-Colonel L. M. Davies, who as a geologist and a serious student in other branches of science, pointed out the inconsequence of the jibe made against such men of science as maintained faith in the Bible as revealed truth, namely, that their intelligence must operate within separate watertight compartments. He cited four instances justifying implicit acceptance of God's Word by inquirers after scientific knowledge ; in each of these, present-day knowledge had overcome the age-long

[1] Gal. ii. 9.

ignorance which had persisted in contradiction of Holy Writ.

In reply to an objection put by Dr. Rutgers, Dr. Saussure said : Professor Rutgers, while he declares himself in agreement with my paper generally, wonders if it is inevitable for every theology to be subject to error and therefore transient. We are God's creatures *by essence*, he says, and sinners *by accident*. To affirm the continuance of error, *i.e.* of sin, does that not confer on it an *essential* character ? Once regenerate, cannot faith keep our thought in the truth ?

I wish at once to affirm my full accord with Dr. Rutgers in saying that *quâ* creatures of God we are good by *essence* and sinners by *accident*. I am no Manichæan. But the question is—What degree of gravity do we attach to this *accident ?* While Catholicism admits that the image of God, though shattered, subsists at least partially in fallen man, Reformed theology affirms that it is annihilated. And our doctrine makes still clearer that even the Christian, though regenerated in principle, remains in fact always a sinner here below (*semper justus, semper peccator*). Or if you prefer to express it thus, it recognises that Rom. vii. applies not only to a man before he becomes a Christian but also when he has become a Christian. St. Paul does not say " the good that I would I *did* not (before my conversion) and the evil which I would not that I *did*," but " the good that I would I *do* not and the evil that I *will* not that I *do*."

In principle there is no necessity, no essential constraint, in these backslidings, in this survival of sin in the Christian, and that is why we are always to blame for them. I am not a fatalist in the etymological sense of the word. They happen " fatally " (*fatalement*) in the current sense of the word, *i.e.* not necessarily but unfailingly. Calvin shows at great length in the *Institutes* on one hand, the non-necessity, on the other hand, however, the inevitability of sin for the Christian. That is why Sunday after Sunday in the confession of Sin we acknowledge that "we are unable of ourselves to do good," (not, " any good " but simply " good," *i.e.* without trace of sin), and, for that very reason that " we merit by the just judgment of God condemnation and death."

While we live in Faith our thought will be free from error. I agree with Professor Rutgers, and that is why, in principle, I have assigned a normative and immutable character to a theology which should remain purely spiritual. But as a matter of fact no one lives perfectly and continually in faith, and therefore, practically, every theology contains erroneous elements, perpetually subject to revision.

We have no right, therefore, on the pretext that we cannot avoid error to put from us the duty of expressing our faith in as reflective a manner as possible, and of thus loving God " with all our mind." Nor have we the right to imagine that we have produced a theology exempt from all error and therefore unchangeable.

SUMMARY

KNOWLEDGE OF FAITH AND COMPREHENSION OF INTELLIGENCE

By Pastor SAUSSURE

INTRODUCTION. Our aim : to try to make clear the intellectual consequences of the Reformed Faith, the difference between the contemporary schools which profess it seeming to spring from a different conception of the relation between faith and natural intelligence.

I. FAITH, THE ORGAN OF CHRISTIAN KNOWLEDGE

(1) *The Word of God.*—Forms the only source of reformed theology.

(2) *The Witness of the Holy Spirit.*—The Scriptures only produce faith in us by the witness which the Holy Spirit renders to them and which makes us recognise them as the Word of God. To forget this leads to literalism, which commits with regard to the Bible the same error as Catholicism makes with regard to the Sacrament : it confuses the sign and the reality signified. Christian knowledge, therefore, rests only on the evidence produced by the Holy Spirit.

(3) *Faith.*—The organ of this knowledge is faith, the supernatural product of the Holy Spirit in us, and not natural intelligence. That protects our theology from the spirit of system which inevitably provokes infidelities to Scripture. Thus reformed theology is faithful to the Word of God, not only materially but formally (Heb. xi. 3) — Analysis of Calvin's definition of faith, showing that our doctrine conforms to it.

(4) *Faith, a Gift of God.*—Christian evidence is produced by the supernatural light of the Holy Spirit, as intellectual or moral evidence is produced by the natural light of human understanding or conscience. Although *ours*, faith is not *of us*.

(5) *The Principle of the Analogy of Faith.*—Definition of Professor Lecerf : Regarding faith, a dogmatic proposition

is religious in such measure as it puts in evidence the unique
character of the sovereignty and independence of God on the
one hand, and the absoluteness of our subjection to Him on
the other hand.   It is according to this criterion that faith is
explicit in a dogmatic-ordered knowledge.   This principle
corresponds, in the supernatural order of faith, to the principles of morality and intelligibility in the natural domains of
human morals and science.

Like them, it functions as a principle of selection in regard
to natural data (human beliefs), but in regard to scriptural
revelation it represents no more than a principle of adhesion
(since it is derived from it).

II. Characteristics of Knowledge produced by Faith

(1) *A Certainty.*—Christian knowledge consists in a *certainty that*, not in a *comprehension how*.   As religious ideas are
constantly assuming the appearance of intellectual concepts,
subject to comprehension, it is important always to remember their character as pure analogical ideas.   Dogmatics
is a canonical science, not a speculative one.

(2) *An Analogical Knowledge.*—But not symbolical in the
modernist sense of the term.

(3) *Independence of Dogmatics.*—Spiritual judgments differ
altogether from intellectual judgments :

(*a*) by their terms (ideas, not concepts) ;
(*b*) by their criterion (principle of analogy of faith and
not principle of intelligibility).

The logical form alone is common to both ; but, taken
in the pure sense of the term, this cannot by itself determine any content of the thought ; this (the content) only
becomes concrete by the intervention of a particular criterion
which, at the same time, differentiates from that moment a
spiritual, doctrinal thought from an intellectual, philosophic
thought.

(4) *Organic Constitution of Dogmatics.*—Dogmatics is an
ordered knowledge in logical forms applied, according to the
principle of the analogy of faith, to the data of the Word of God.

III. Concerning the Relation of Different Kinds of Knowledge among Themselves

(1) *Their Incommensurability.*—In the light of II. 3, there
can no longer be either contradiction or agreement between
the different orders of thought.   The unconscious and illegiti-

mate transformation of dogmatic ideas into intellectual concepts often make these appear as if contradictory to this latter point of view (1 Cor. ii. 14 confirms this). Instead of distorting Christian truth to make it intelligible one must take care always to explain what is spiritual in terms of the spiritual (1 Cor. ii. 13).

(2) *Their Common Logical Character.*—But if spiritual and intellectual thoughts are mutually incommensurable, in view of the difference of their terms and their criteria, they are equally logical, inasmuch as logical forms govern them both. A judgment can, therefore, be contradictory from the intellectual point of view, without being, for all that, absurd; that is to say, illogical.

IV. Concerning the Inevitable Confusion of the Different Orders of Thought in Theological Practice and of the Necessity that it Entails of constantly revising any Theological System

(1) *Fatal Character of this Confusion.*—Given that, on the one hand, the natural man is a born intellectualist, a born moralist, a born æsthetician (natural faculties), while he is not a born spiritual being (faith, supernatural gift) and that, on the other hand, the natural man exists in the Christian (Calvin : *Relics of the Flesh*) we cannot avoid, in practice, distorting the expression of our faith into the intellectual, moral, æsthetic, etc., sense, while in principle, the spiritual order remains irreducible to these natural orders.

The problem is even more complex, because just as faith must be translated into practical works, although these cannot but betray it by their sinful character, so it must be translated into intellectual works, although these also cannot but betray it, as they must assuredly contain errors : error being the intellectual form of sin.

According to good Calvinist doctrine we must, therefore, continually revise, in the light of the Word of God alone, the expression of all our theologies, including that of Calvin and including our own.

(2) *Closed Calvinism and Open Calvinism.*—It seems to us that the difference between the various Reformed schools of to-day rests in the fact that some, seeing in intelligence the seat of all thought, find in the systematised thought of Calvin the adequate and, consequently, immutable, expression of his doctrine, while others, making of faith the only organ of dogmatic thought, can only recognise in any system, including

that of Calvin, an expression fatally inadequate (since every Christian is *semper peccator*) of the doctrine which he has striven to interpret (and consequently always subject to revision) according to the criterion of the Word of God alone.

If we can agree on the fact that faith is the only organ of doctrinal knowledge a great step will be made towards an understanding between our different Calvinistic schools and towards their better collaboration for the greater good of our common cause.

Paper No. 11

THE SIGNIFICANCE OF THE OLD TESTAMENT FOR THE CHRISTIAN LIFE

By the Rev. WILHELM VISCHER (Basel)

IT is said to be characteristic of the Calvinistic dogmatic as well as of the Calvinistic ethic that it is determined by the Old Testament. Not seldom is that to be found bound up with the judgment that the doctrine and life of the Calvinist are " characterised by Law." In a good sense, that means that they are earnest and obedient ; in a bad sense, that they are wanting in the evangelical freedom of the children of God. We do not intend to examine now whether the Calvinistic ethic deserves this praise or this censure, nor whether the impress of the Old Testament is a peculiarity of the Calvinists. What must occupy our attention now is the fundamental question as to the significance of the Old Testament for the Christian life. It will be the answer to this question which will set the other questions in the right light.

Our main thesis runs thus : The unique significance of the Old Testament for the Christian life is grounded in the fact that the Gospel proclaims that Jesus is the Christ of Israel, promised and expected in the Old Testament, born in the fullness of time, crucified under Pontius Pilate, and, through the power of God, awakened from the dead, Who will come again to judge the quick and the dead. This message asserts that Jesus is the Head of a body, the members of which the Old Testament points out ; that therefore, Jesus, the Head, has His life not for Himself alone but for His own people and in His own people. This life of Christ Jesus for His own and in His own is the Christian life. As Jesus is preached and known as the Christ only through His relation to the Old Testament, so the relation of the Life of Jesus to the Old Testament alone unlocks the reality of the Christian life.

PART I

In order to make clear the contents of this assertion we must take it into consideration that Jesus can be understood otherwise, and not as the Christ. The question which Jesus Himself once in a decisive hour directed to His disciples, " Whom do the people say that I am ? " has time and again been put to men, in every age, and time and again finds the same answers which are reported to us in rich variety by the Evangelists. We know how to-day within and without the Church all those attempts are being repeated in a modern form, to understand the Life of Jesus as the Life of a great Sage, a religious Genius, a Superman, the Bearer of a new ethic, or also simply as a Man of plain piety, if not, on the other hand, a Destroyer of the highest values and, finally, a Madman. One might hold Jesus as the Standard and the Champion of the most diverse philosophies and conceptions of life, from the most conservative to the most revolutionary. All these interpretations of Jesus have in all their diversity one thing in common, that they regard the Life of Jesus as a life *along side of* other such possibilities, as a life from which other men can more or less learn and receive, perhaps even something that is most important, but besides which there are still, in this way or that, other sources of life. From all these interpretations of Jesus the Gospel-proclamation distinguishes itself, in that it proclaims Jesus as the Christ, and thereby says, There does not exist for any man true and real Life, if Jesus does not give him a participation in His own life.

" The Christ " is not just any explicable title, but signifies the Son of the Living God, the Image of the Invisible God, the First-born of all creatures. In Him is Life. By Him and for Him were all things created, that are in Heaven and that are on Earth, visible and invisible. And He is the Head of the body, the Church (Col. i.). The Christ is He who has been anointed by God Himself as the Priest-King of the chosen people, whose advent all Words of the Old Testament proclaim. For this reason do the preachers in the New Testament constantly appeal to what stands written in the Old Testament. Only so could they proclaim Jesus of Nazareth as the Christ. Only through the reference to the Old Testament can it be shown and acknowledged that He is the Messiah, and only so is it possible to understand the meaning of His Messiahship. What does it mean then ? Simply that He is the Head of a Body, that He has therefore His unique and incomparable

Life not for Himself but for His own. For the Old Testament points out members of this body which live on Him and through Him. The whole body with all its *members*, the whole folk of the Old Covenant, are dead if Jesus is not its Head as the Christ. All the Life-activities of the men reported in the Old Testament are moved by Him and unto Him. The life histories of all these men are parts of His Life history. That is the reason why they were written with so strikingly little biographical interest for individual personalities. What is written of them is properly written of the One, through Whom and in Whom they all live, as part of His biography. Therefore do the witnesses of Christ Jesus in the New Testament ever and again lay their finger upon passages of the Old Testament and say : That and that, which Jesus did, had to happen, in order that what is written there and there may be fulfilled. We should be deceiving ourselves if we thought that this applies only to the few passages especially called " Messianic." For the New Testament the Holy Scripture is a whole. When one touches upon some one passage, the whole Old Testament is involved—as with a living body, the touching of one part is traceable through the nervous system in the whole body.

(A) The Christological interpretation of the Old Testament by the Gospel is by no means a subsequent misinterpretation of those old Scripture-passages. Rather it, and it alone, corresponds to their original and most proper sense. Every other attempt to interpret them only obscures and violates them. It must strike every attentive reader that the Old Testament histories are histories of the future, which happen with a view to an end that is not yet reached in themselves. Called of God men go forth, desert all that they have, and advance to meet the *Promised One*. The commands of God which drive them to actions and passions are always promises. The man who lays hold upon a promise in faith and thereby has given to his life movement and direction, is in the Old Testament " righteous," properly oriented, a " righteous man." The righteous man, according to the familiar word, lives always by faith. That is even expressed in the future. " The righteous man shall live by faith "—so completely has the life of the believer its reality in the future.

Therein is expression also given to the fact that all the people of the Old Testament live, in the proper sense, only as forebears. For that reason the genealogies play such a strikingly great part, and therefore so much weight is laid upon the fact that the line of generations is never broken. It is a great promise, of the Creator and the Redeemer, which forms the reason why Adam along with Eve, " the mother of all living," may beget children. Seth and Shem, Enoch and Noah are the roots of a tree the existence of which is only justified through the fruit which it will some day bear. Abraham's life has its significance altogether in the fact that he will become a father, that he has been promised a son. If " the son of Abraham " is not born and the promise not fulfilled, then is Abraham's life in vain. Isaac is marked out by the Biblical report as a quite unimportant man in and for himself. The more important is he therefore as the first heir of Abraham for all those others who will follow in type after him : " Only in Isaac shall thy seed be called." The " blessing," that is, the proper life-force, which God has given to Abraham, and which rests just upon a promise for the future, Isaac inherits. It is for this blessing and for nothing else that Jacob, the forefather, strives with God and with men. All his descendants carry it on. They wait and hasten to meet the day in which the whole blessing of Abraham will be fulfilled, and a people which is as numerous as the stars in heaven and the sand by the sea will sing praises to the living God. That is why it is so important that in all judgments at least a " remnant of Israel " remains preserved. Moreover, the life of David has no worth in and for itself. What gives him and all who sit upon his throne their significance is the fact that the Lord has given him the eternal promise, " I will build you a house," that he is the first of a dynasty whose last king, " the Son of David," the King of the kingdom of God, will appear. As the righteous people of the covenant live from faith to faith, so do they also die in faith. For that reason their graves are important. The graves of the patriarchs and of David are more than mere monuments of the past, they are signposts of the future. The covenants through which God gave these people time and possibility of life contain all the promises of a new life. Hence the signs of the covenant, the rainbow, the circumcision, the Passover meal and the Sabbath are all pledges of the future, sacramental symbols of the coming kingdom of God. The prophets and Apocalyptists from Isaiah to Daniel are not the first to announce the coming of the Messianic Kingdom as the goal of Israel's history. Already do the historical works of Joshua, Judges, Samuel and Kings stand with good reason under the title " Prophets." It is real prophecy which proclaims the event not as past but as an oracle of the future. The history of Israel is impregnated with the word of promise. The vital functions of the chosen people are the motions of a body which expects to give birth. Everything obtrudes itself upon the " Travail of the Messiah." He, the One Who is " the hope of Israel " (Acts xxviii. 20), must come if the word of the promise, of the blessing, is not to fall to the ground, and all that has been lived and suffered is not to have been for nothing.   The Son of Adam, the Son of Abraham, the Son of David must be born and in His Person as King bring in the Kingdom which all the righteous of the Old Covenant went forth to meet.

Thus Israel lives only in the expectation of the One Who is to come, and so bears along with her existence a promise for the whole world.   For in " that day," in " the last days," which form the horizon of all Old Testament happenings, when the time is fulfilled and " she who travaileth hath brought forth, and the Prince of Israel whose goings forth have been from of old, will come out of Bethlehem " (Mic. v.), then " the heathen " will see the glory which rises up over Israel.   In this way the Old Testament points to the advent glory which issues from Christmas.   " Your father Abraham," said Jesus to the Jews, " rejoiced to see My day.   And he saw it and was glad."   Therefore the voices of the bride and bridegroom were never to become silent.   For that reason the Creator gave the command, and never took it back :   " Be fruitful and multiply, and fill the earth."   Hence the powerful affirmation of this present life through the Old Testament :

" How excellent is Thy loving kindness, O God !
　Therefore the children of men
　Put their trust under the shadow of Thy wings.
　They shall be abundantly satisfied with the fatness of Thy house ;
　And Thou shalt make them drink of the river of Thy pleasures.
　For with Thee is the fountain of life :
　In Thy light shall we see light "—(Ps. xxxvi.)

No one may curse the day of his birth, no one may flee for refuge to another world beyond.   Rather ought each here and now to taste and see how gracious the Lord is.

Life is altogether a gift of grace.   There is no natural right to life, and as little right to dispose of one's life.   Life has its origin and ground in the free will of God.   The eternal God is Father, the Father of His eternal Son.   He does not want to be alone.   He wants to have creatures, whom He can love and who are to love Him.   That is the one, all-determining Law of grace for life.   He is a fool who thinks he can master his own life, who thinks he knows better than God and gets on without Him.   " Who can be joyful and delight himself without Him ? " (Eccles. ii. 25).   He has wisdom of life who has a hearing heart and obeys the word of the Lord in the fear of God.

Life is placed under the right of grace, and so the natural right which the stronger man means to have is questioned.

16

> " Talk no more exceedingly proudly ;
> Let not arrogancy come out of your mouth :
> The bows of the mighty men are broken,
> And they that stumbled are girded with strength.
> They that were full have hired themselves for bread ;
> And they that were hungry ceased :
> So that the barren hath borne seven ;
> And she that hath many children is waxed feeble.
> The Lord killeth and maketh alive ;
> He bringeth down to the grave, and bringeth up.
> The Lord maketh poor, and maketh rich :
> He bringeth low, and lifteth up.
> He will keep the feet of His saints,
> And the wicked shall be silent in darkness :
> For by strength shall no man prevail.
> The adversaries of the Lord shall be broken in pieces ;
> Out of heaven shall He thunder upon them :
> The Lord shall judge the ends of the earth :
> And He shall give strength unto His king,
> And exalt the horn of His Christ."—(1 Sam. ii.)

Thus Hannah, the mother of Samuel, who is to anoint the first king over Israel, sings already the Magnificat of the mother of the Messiah. We see how the advent brightness of the Lord, which shone round about the shepherds in the middle of Christmas night, shines also upon the men in the Old Testament.

(B) It is also quite evident, however, that the shadows of that darkness fall upon them which darkened the whole land on the midday of Good Friday, as the Christ Jesus hung in death's struggle upon the Cross, fall upon the same men.

> " For we are consumed by Thine anger,
> And by Thy wrath are we troubled.
> Thou hast set our iniquities before Thee,
> Our secret sins in the light of Thy countenance.
> For all our days are passed away in wrath :
> We spend our years as a tale that is told.
> Who knoweth the power of Thine anger ?
> Even according to Thy fear so is Thy wrath.
> So teach us to number our days.
> That we may apply our hearts unto wisdom."—(Ps. cx.)

Bitter enough was the sentence of death passed over Adam and all his children. The soil and the life upon it were *cursed*. The man who offends against the Royal Law in one point is guilty of all. He who does not obey the one commandment of life chooses death. The wrath of God is revealed from Heaven against all impiety and insubordination of men, who wish to set themselves in the place of God. Not one can conceal himself nor hide his nakedness from the searching look of the Holy One. Every attempt to glorify man is destroyed through God's Word. They all come short of the glory which they ought to have as men made in the image of

God. There is none that doeth good, no, not one. Over the head of everybody hangs the sword, not only over Cain, but also over Noah, over the Semites as well as over the Hamites and the Japhethites, and first properly over the sons of Abraham, whose first-born lay already bound upon the faggots and felt the sacrificial knife over his neck. The final execution of the sentence is yet delayed ; but the time of their life is purely a *Day of Grace*, a reprieve. Their sins will be unsparingly uncovered in them all. Israel is not called to add to the religions of humanity a new one, perhaps a higher one. The One true God will rather employ her for the purpose of depriving Nature and History of their gods, of their might and their power. And thus it is clear that all human religions are nothing else than attempts of man, out of the fear and longing of his godless heart to form gods for himself which are yet only lies and wind, idols and nonentities. For this reason Israel may enter into no life or cult fraternity with the children of the Land. They must ban them and hang up the slaughtered kings on the tree before the wrath of God in order to make room on earth for the Holy Lord (Joshua and Judges). Their contribution to world history is the great disturbance which leads to catastrophe.

It is not as if Israel were superior. They can only live before the Holy One because in place of their own blood other blood is shed. The blood of the Psacal Lamb delivers them from the death-angel. The Covenant of God is contracted through *sacrifice*. The Israelite order of life is an order of sacrifice. Day in and day out must life be taken, lest the wrath of the Holy One should annihilate the chosen people. The sacrificial precepts form a net over all the spheres of life, both of the nation and of the individuals. They attest : You can only live as those who have been reprieved. It is therefore the grossest misunderstanding when Israel thought the sacrifices were her own performances through which she could justify herself before God. Offered with such a disposition and purpose sacrifice is the worst sin of witchcraft (1 Sam. xv.). The Holy One of Israel repudiates such sacrifice through the Word of His prophets.

> " To what purpose is the multitude of your sacrifices
>   unto me, saith the Lord.
> I am full of the burnt-offerings of rams,
> And the fat of fed beasts ;
> I delight not in the blood of bullocks,
> Or of lambs, or of he-goats."—(Isa. i.)

> " The sacrifices of God are a broken spirit :
> A broken and a contrite heart,
> O God, Thou wilt not despise."—(Ps. li.)

Israel may not wish to set herself with a religion of her own in the place of the banned cults and religions. If she does do this she herself may succumb to the ban. The more she wishes to save herself and to ensure herself against judgment, the more certainly and terribly will she fall into the hands of the Living God. If she will not serve the Living God in pure obedience then she must be sacrificed herself for the revelation of the Holiness of God in this world. " *Israel's End*," then, is proclaimed by the prophets as the goal of Israel's history. " The strange work " of God, the utter demolition of the " City of God " which has become a mass of lies, the overthrow of her chosen royal house, the profanation of the Temple, and all that one might ascribe as Israel's religion, must then reveal the Holiness of God.

We find in Israel no harmonious religious personalities. They are all broken up, wrecked on the " rock of Israel." As with the Forefather Jacob-Israel they are all lamed in the thigh through their wrestling with God. They all *suffer* from God. It is in the depth of their lives, and not in the height, that they are nearest God. The strongest among them are the most broken. The servants of the Lord whom He has chosen for Himself as mediators have no form nor comeliness, they labour and are heavy laden, who can hardly endure to perform their service any longer. " Blot me out of the book which Thou hast written," cried Moses. " Kill me, I pray Thee, out of hand, if I have found favour in Thy sight ; let me not see my wretchedness " (Num. ii. 15). Elijah asks : " Now, O Lord, take away my life for I am not better than my fathers." And Jeremiah lamented : " Cursed is the day wherein I was born " (Jer. xx. 14). " Why is my pain incurable, which refuseth to be healed ? Wilt Thou be altogether unto me as a liar, and as waters that fail ! " From none of these servants is suffering taken away at their complaint ; on the contrary, still more of the Divine burden is laid upon them, and they are told it is the greatest grace when they are allowed to share some of the burden of the endless suffering of God. That is their consolation.

The suffering for the sake of God, the enduring of the darkness and the judgment of God are not spared even to the righteous in Israel. Job and the Preacher are not exceptional men among this people. We only need to open the Book of Psalms ; " There we see," as Luther says, " into the heart of the saints, as into death, nay, as into Hell." They must all pray, they simply cannot live without praying. Prayer for them is not one among other things but the only possibility of life ; for they cannot live without God. They are cast upon

Him from the womb.   And yet even to them is God again and again distant and hidden.   They are troubled in body and soul and suffer from the sickness unto death.   They pant after God, after the living God, as the hart after the water-brooks. Out of the depth and out of the darkness they entreat for the shining of His countenance.

> " I will say unto God my rock,
> Why hast Thou forgotten me ?
> Why do I go a mourning
> Because of the oppression of the enemy ?
> As with a sword in my bones,
> Mine enemies reproach me ;
> While they say daily unto me,
> Where is thy God ? "—(Ps. xlii.)

> " O Lord, rebuke me not in Thine anger,
> Neither chasten me in Thy hot displeasure,
> Return, O Lord, deliver my soul."—(Ps. vi.)

Thus the figures and the words of the Old Testament show us that no man can live before the Holy God.

(C) Nevertheless they *do live* !   In spite of all the menaces, in spite of the punishment and the suffering, the final judgment in the Old Testament is not carried out.   The hope for the great " Turning " (Wendung) lies over all.   It is just the condemned and the victimised who are the strongest witnesses of that.   Job is a typical example of many, when against all right he appeals to the mercy of the Highest.

> " For I know that my Redeemer liveth,
> And that He shall stand at the latter day upon the earth.
> And though after my skin worms destroy this body,
> Yet in my flesh shall I see God :
> Whom I shall see for myself,
> And mine eyes shall behold,
> And not another."—(Job xix.)

When in the end God gives anew to His servant Job his life, doubled possessions, and his family, that is a sign of the great restoration of all things which is promised to all those who suffer now for righteousness' sake.

The creature has been subjected by the Holy God to vanity with a view to hope.   A conqueror is promised to Adam Who will go forth born of the woman, and will tread on the head of the old Serpent which seduces the whole world and accuses the brethren.   The moratorium, which God granted in His covenant with Noah to the world infinitely encumbered with debt, proclaims the possibility of God's cancelling the total debt.   After having surrendered Isaac to the knife Abraham

received him back again as a sign that he has not reckoned in
vain with the possibility of God's power to raise even the dead.
Every Passover celebration of the Children of Israel strengthens
the expectation that once more some blood will be shed which
will bring about the final emancipation of this world from
servitude. Every Sabbath and every Sabbath-year testify to
the fact that once again the great year of release will be proclaimed and the eternal festive day will break, at which all
creatures will sing praises in holy joy to their Creator and
Redeemer. The great disturbance of the world history
through Israel, Israel's own restlessness, in which she must
wander as a stranger throughout the ages and peoples without
finding an abiding-place upon this earth, are the result of,
and are with a view to, the Children of God finding their home
with the Eternal Father ; and with them all pressing and
wrestling of the creature comes to rest in God the Lord. In
and over the destinies of the chosen people it becomes manifest
that God Himself has become the outcast and the stranger of
His earth ; the Unknown sojourns with her and dwells as the
defenceless One in the midst of His enemies until they are
overcome by His love. The Lord made Himself a servant
and took their guilt upon Himself. Do not the thousand and
thousands of thousands of Israel's sacrifices point to the one
sacrifice which God Himself must bring in order that sinners
may be able to live before Him ?

> " Thou hast made Me to serve with thy sins,
> Thou hast wearied Me with thine iniquities.
> I, even I, am He that blotteth out thy transgressions
>   for Mine own sake,
> And will not remember thy sins."—(Isa. xliii.)

The Holy One wants to take upon Himself the sins of the world
that the world may live. In order to make that manifest He
has chosen Israel. This folk is His servant, called to priestly
service. And in spite of all infidelity it abides in its holy
office for the sake of the One Who as the only innocent One in
the midst of the guilty is burdened with and offered up for all
their guilt. The Turning of the Judgment of God through
His grace must be revealed in Israel. For that reason she is
led into Hell and out again. For that reason a remnant is
always preserved which turns away from sin to righteousness,
out of death into life. For that reason the Messianic Light
which the Lord has kindled in the House of David is never
altogether extinguished in spite of all the sin and punishment
of David's house (1 Kings ii. 36 ; Ps. cxxxii. 17). The dark
cloud of the prophetic message of " Israel's End " which

bursts in lightning and thunder and hailstorm over the chosen people is girded round with a silver lining by the sunshine of Easter Day. . . . Above the lament for the dead over Israel the noise of the Spirit is audible to the ear of the prophet ; the dry bones come to life again (Ezek. 37).

The breach of the covenant which it had already suffered at Sinai God covers up in His grace until the last days when He will make it manifest that He had long established a new covenant with His folk in which He might put His Law in their hearts and remember their sins no more (Jer. xxxi.).   The longer the night, the more radiantly shines the " Morning Star " of the Messianic promise.   In the rebel cry, " We want to have a king like the other nations," there is already audible in the historical books of the Old Testament the Hosanna which rings out to welcome the Son of David who comes in the name of the Lord to give glory in the highest and on earth peace.   The kingdom of Solomon, the first son of David on the Messianic throne, gives already (in his glory, and in his power manifested from the City of the Great King unto the ends of the earth) a foretaste of the *Regnum Gloriæ* of the Last One of the House of David to Whom by the resurrection is given all power in Heaven and on Earth.   None of all the inexhaustible possibilities in nature and culture are abandoned.   When the Son of David with understanding heart rules with that Wisdom which was God's agent at the Creation and is ever before Him, then for the first time will all beings and things really display their Divine endowment (Prov. viii. 31 ; 1 Kings iii. 9).   No sin can cover up the promise altogether.   The fire smoulders again under the ashes.   Although Israel could not endure as the Chosen people to be different from all others and to have her citizenship in Him alone Who upturns the world ; although for that reason God drives her out of the holy land of inheritance and scatters her to the four winds—nevertheless He does not allow the minion of the Great King of Persia to succeed in rooting out the Jews or removing this " foreign-body " which disturbs the empire (Esther).   Even Daniel sees how the kingdom of the wild beasts is judged, and in the clouds of heaven One comes upon the earth Who is like unto the Son of Man.   He is given Might, Honour and the Kingdom so that the peoples and nations of all tongues serve Him.

God. wants the world.   He has created it.   It belongs to Him.   Therefore He judges their self-glory and overturns everything.   That is His salutary justice.   For that reason the suffering of His righteous in this world contains the promise of a coming world.   The miserable will inherit the earth.   They may not fly for refuge to the Beyond.   They must hold fast the hope of God's victory for *this* world.

> " They that sow in **tears**
> Shall reap in joy.
> He that goeth forth and **weepeth**,
> Bearing precious seed,
> Shall doubtless come again with rejoicing,
> Bringing his sheaves with him."—(Ps. cxxvi.)

Out of the deepest depth of tribulation and suffering the song of praise ascends in Israel's Psalter from the victims to their Redeemer :

> " Let everything that hath breath praise the Lord.
> Hallelujah ! "—(Ps. cl. 6.)

Thus the Old Testament proclaims the " Turning " from death to life through the miracle of God's grace in the dying and rising of the anointed Head of Israel.   The whole life of the men of the Old Covenant and their environment stands, unconsciously or consciously, in the expectation of this one miracle.   Israel lives by her future.

PART II

(A) The Gospel is the good news : Now is the time fulfilled. The promised and expected One is come.   The Christ Jesus is born.   He is the Head from Whom all the members of God's folk have their life at all times, B.C. not less than A.D.   The Patriarchs, as Augustine says, have preceded as members of Christ's Body, the appearing of the Head, as at the birth of a human being a hand may first appear and still be bound up with the whole body under the head as the unity of life.

In the most evident way the genealogical table at the beginning of the Gospel exhibits the connection of the life of Jesus with the life of the men of the Old Covenant.   For this *biblos geneseos*, this " book of the birth of Jesus Christ," is nothing less than a recapitulation of the Old Testament, which shows how Jesus is born as the Son of David and as the Son of Abraham, and so is the Christ of Israel.   But there arises immediately at this point a very important matter—the fact, namely, that in no natural way does Jesus spring from the genealogical tree.   The connection of His life with the life of His people, whose Head He is, is only established by the miracle of grace.   The Holy Ghost, not nature and history, not even the nature and history of Israel, begot Him,   That an Israelite maiden bears Him is the miracle of the faithful God Who keeps His word which He has given to His chosen people.   Mary the virgin conceived Him of the Holy Ghost.   And Joseph, her betrothed husband, who wants to put her away privately, because he is " just," has, at a special command of God, to legitimise the human birth of God's Son for the House of David and so for all Israel.   Thus, and thus alone, is the connection of the Head with the Body established.   Only through Grace and the obedience of faith does family relationship with Him arise.   Does that surprise us ?   Was it not, then, already shown with sufficient clarity through the Old Testament tradition on from the birth of Isaac, who was the first son of Abraham in the genealogical tree, that this whole line lives only by grace, that all the true sons of Abraham are born of the miracle of grace, and are only so connected together with each other ?   It was just that to which the symbols of circumcision testified.   Everyone who was not circumcised had to be rooted out of Israel.   We hear that Israel during the time of her expectation, while the life of the chosen people was being passed on perceptibly from generation to generation, lived frequently not by faith in grace, but took for granted her existence as lineage and folk, and held this to receive its recognised status entirely through circumcision. But already Moses and Jeremiah had declared that circumcision proved no Israelite to be a true son of Abraham and gave to none the right to life if the heart were not circumcised unto faith in grace.   Through the circumcision of Jesus Christ eight days after His birth it becomes manifest that now the promise of Abraham and the time of expectation are fulfilled. The circumcision has now no more value.   Faith in the grace of God in Jesus Christ must now be the evidence for every Israelite as to whether he is or is not circumcised in heart. " Think not to say within yourselves, We have Abraham to our father," cried John the Baptist.   " God is able of these very stones to raise up children unto Abraham."   To those who resign before Jesus Christ their own right to life and hope for life alone from His grace, He gives the power to become Children of God, which are born not of blood, nor of the will of the flesh, nor of the will of man, but of God.   All who reckon themselves as belonging to God's folk on the ground of blood and of the Law, on the ground of nature and history, are cut off and driven into the wilderness like Ishmael, the son of the slave-girl.   But how many become brothers of Jesus Christ in faith, who are, like Isaac, children of promise, and even when they come out of the most heathen race.   For in Christ Jesus neither circumcision avails anything nor uncircumcision, but a new creation (Galatians).   As a sign of this new Creation baptism in the name of Jesus is now set in the place of circumcision.

The Good News that through the birth of Jesus Christ, as the Son of Abraham and of David, every man who believes on Him will be given the possibility and the right to live through grace alone, the Jews held to be the dissolution of the Old Testament. How difficult it was for the first Christian Church to take in earnest the fact that through Jesus the partition between the Jews and the other people is done away, we learn in the Acts and the epistles of the Apostle Paul. And yet the message that all races of the earth are reprieved through the Christ of Israel is in truth a fulfilling of the Old Testament. For neither Abraham nor Israel was called by God for his own sake. From the beginning it was clearly said that all that God does with His chosen (people) is to serve the salvation of the world and the justification of His forbearance in which He allowed men their life in spite of Adam's sin, and ever and again gave it anew and preserved it. Now the One is born Who, as " the Hope of Israel," gives to all who believe on Him the right to life.

(B) We saw, however, quite as clearly, that the life of man lies under the curse and wrath of God. Jesus cannot, therefore, become the brother of men without bearing this curse. None of them have a right to live if He does not take upon Himself before God the whole burden of their guilt and for them make atonement. That, then, is just what He has done according to the Gospel. Even at the moment when through the baptism in the Jordan He makes known His solidarity with sinners, and again on another occasion when upon the Mount of Trans-figuration He gives His path of life the " Turning " down into the deepest depth, into death, in fellowship with the accursed, even there the Father proclaims from the height that this Man is anointed as the Mediator of salvation : " This is my beloved Son in whom I am well pleased ; hear ye Him." As Joseph, apparently contrary to all justice, had to legitimise the birth of Jesus, so must John, instead of being baptised by Jesus, baptise Him with the sinners-baptism, and so at the same time testify that through this enrolling of the only righteous One among the unrighteous all righteousness is fulfilled.

It seems contradictory that the Body should receive its life through the execution of the Head. Nevertheless, it is logical ; for only when the One does not keep His life for Him-self but for the others can it then be imparted to the many. That is the simple logic of the justice of God ; thus God counts (logizetai) the righteousness of the One unto the unrighteous. That is what neither the Scribes and the Pharisees nor the disciples of Jesus wanted to understand, but what with absolute logic and necessity *had to* come to pass, if the Scripture was to be fulfilled. Before His death and resurrection Jesus had said so again and again to the disciples. All that is written in the Old Testament is only true because Jesus has answered for it with His life. Otherwise the assertions of the Old Testament were such interpretations of life as the anxiety and longing of the human heart produce. But now through the death of Jesus they are believed as God's Word and show forth at the same time the necessity and fruitfulness of His death. Because all men without exception fall short of the glory which they ought to have before God, it is not therefore enough that they should have in Christ the right Teacher who through His Word and example shows them how they ought to live. In the light of His purity are they, and all who behold it, able for the first time to learn their own impurity and damnableness. He must answer for them if they are to be justified even in the light of His life. They show us that the teacher of the holy life must at the same time be their priest who sanctifies them through the offering of His own holy life. Only therein can all that happened in the Tabernacle and the Temple receive its legal justification, in that Israel exercises the priestly office of mediation for mankind. On Him, on the anointed Head of Israel, must the Father's will be done ; He must drink the bitter cup. He must hang on the cursed tree and cry, " My God, my God, why hast Thou forsaken Me ? "

(C) He has accomplished it—quite alone—for all. And no one understood it. They all saw in His terrible death the evidence that God did not acknowledge Him. And is not His End really the evidence that the faith of the Old Testament is an illusion, that this God does not even exist ? No ! God has acknowledged Jesus Christ and awakened Him from the dead. " God was in Christ reconciling the world unto Himself." That is the message of Easter, which also brings to light the secret of Good Friday, and therewith also the secret of Christmas and of the whole life of Jesus. In Him God has made human existence and destiny His own. The man for whom the message of God's action in the dying and rising of Jesus does not take the veil off the Old Testament, reads it simply as a document of human piety. The death of Jesus unveils the breach of the Old Covenant so that the illusion of a religio-historical signifi-cance of the Old Testament is destroyed through the knowledge that all the wisdom and piety of man is done away through the holiness of God. But also the resurrection of Christ Jesus reveals that the Old Testament is God's very Word, and that God's Word can not fall to the ground, that in Christ Jesus all the promises of God are yea and amen.

(D) The crucified and risen One is raised to the right hand of God. From there He has sent the Holy Spirit as His witness on Earth. It was the miracle of Pentecost which first enlightened them so that they could confess and proclaim the act of God's salvation in the life of Christ Jesus. The Holy Spirit taught them the secret which God had purposed to impart in the fullness of times, namely (*anakephalaiosesthai ta panta en Christo*), to gather together in the one Head all creation into the fellowship of Life (Eph. i.). The perception of the unity of the Church hangs upon the perception of the unity of the Old and New Testaments, as the Holy Spirit the hidden Author gives it. Only when we acknowledge the unity of the Holy Scripture of both Testaments can we confess (with the Heidelberg Catechism) : " That out of the whole human race, from the beginning to the end of the world, the Son of God, by His Spirit and Word, gathers, defends and preserves for Himself unto everlasting life a chosen communion, in the unity of the true faith ; and that I am, and for ever shall remain, a living member of the same." This membership in the Body of Christ, this participation in all His treasures and gifts, is the reality and the possibility of the Christian life.

 The Old Testament attests the possibility and the reality of the Christian life in that it gives an account of men who were chosen out to live altogether in the expectation of the coming Christ Jesus, while the New Testament proclaims that He is now come in humiliation, is crucified, and is risen on the third day, and is soon to come again in glory to judge the living and the dead. That is the way in which both Testaments are distinguished from each other within their united and common witness. The distinction would be falsely described should we wish to say that they are one in matter, in their fundamental religious principles, but are distinguished through the Person of Jesus. For the essential nature of their unity consists just in their attestation that the matter itself is nothing else than the Person. It is the personal presence of the Helper which is the help. God establishes through the Person of the Mediator the fellowship of life between Himself and His own. Christ Jesus is Himself the Life, and the Truth and the Way. Any Old Testament conception of Christ whose content is not the living Jesus would be nothing else than the perversion of the Truth into lies. An Old Testament religion for itself or as the preliminary stage of a Christian religion would be nothing but the denial of the one and only revelation of the living God in Jesus Christ. It is just this decision with which the contemporaries of John the Baptist and the contemporaries of Jesus, and at the same time all who read the Old Testament with them, are confronted through the Gospel : Do you know and believe that absolutely everything which you know and have as men of God is only true and your own in Jesus Christ ? Or do you think, for example, that you can be Abraham's Children without believing in Jesus, your Lord and Brother ? Do you mean too that you have but a small spark of Divine life in you or a possibility and a right, to live before God and with God other than through Jesus Christ ? Be converted and believe on the One ! He is the One who should come. He is now here ; now must it be shown whether you have really been expecting Him. All who believe on Him are the true Israel, the people of Christ. The One for the sake of whom Israel had her specially chosen life, and had to propagate it throughout the centuries, is now born, dead and risen. On that account circumcision has become superfluous. Instead of it Baptism has been commanded as the sign that the old man, the Jew as well as the heathen, the religious man as well as the godless, has died and is buried with the crucified One, in order that he might live a new life with the resurrected One. Since Jesus has been offered as the Pascal Lamb, the Lord's Supper must be celebrated in place of the Passover meal as a sign that through His body broken for us, and through His blood shed for us, we are pardoned and are established and preserved in the fellowship of life with Him and with all the elect unto eternal life until we become partakers of His table in the kingdom of His Father.

PART III

Thus the Gospel confirms and actualises to the fullest extent all that is written in the Old Testament, in that it proclaims : " God Who at sundry times and in divers manners spake in times past unto the fathers by the prophets, hath in these *last* days spoken unto us by the Son, Whom He hath appointed Heir of all things, by Whom also He made the worlds " (Heb. i.). " *This day* is this Scripture fulfilled in your ears " (Luke iv.). Believe now as Abraham believed ! Harden not your hearts as the Children of Israel in the wilderness ! *How much more* valid for us " upon whom the ends of the world are come " (1 Cor. x. 11) are the promises and commandments, the consolations and warnings which were spoken to those who lived in the expectation of the coming Christ Jesus. Christ Jesus is the Turning-point of the world. As certainly as the Gospel calls us to be the citizens of the new world, so certainly does its challenge meet us in the old world in which we live from our first breath to the last. And just for that reason all that is written in the Old Testament properly applies to us, now for the first time, and with much greater force. If it was said to those men that they were born as brothers of the One who should be born, how much more does that apply to us now that our life has its unique ground and purpose in that we become brothers of the One, and through Him praise the Father in Heaven and enjoy Him for ever. It is not some imaginary nature that gives us the right and the commandment to live. For the sake of the One Who will not be blessed without us, may we have joy in life, and have no right to throw our lives away in levity or despair. All the ordinances of life, in marriage, family and State must be grounded altogether in grace, and be ordered by the commandment of grace. "Submit yourselves one to another *in the Lord.*" In this commandment lies the true obligation and freedom. Neither marriage nor the family, nor nationality, nor the State, nor the League of Nations, nor science, nor art, has its own purpose, worth or necessity. They have all to serve the one evangelical possibility, that men should hear the Word of God and in the obedience of faith fulfil the law of Love, that is to say the love of Christ. "He who loves father and mother, son and daughter more than Me is not worthy of Me. Whosoever will save his life will lose it ; whosoever will lose it for My sake will find it. There is no man that hath left house, or brethren, or sisters, or father, or mother, or wife, or children, or lands, for My sake and the Gospel's, but he shall receive an hundredfold now in this time, houses and brethren, and sisters, and mothers and children, and lands, with persecutions and in the world to come eternal life." For the man to whom some self-culture and self-indulgence is more important than growth in the grace of Jesus Christ and joy in the Lord, to whom family and nationality and native land and science and art appear more important in life than membership in the body of Christ, whoever pursues a political aim to the cost of the " Politeuma " in the heavens (Phil. iii. 20) can have no part in the kingdom of God.

"But and if thou marry, thou hast not sinned " (1 Cor. vii. 28). "Live joyfully with the wife whom thou lovest. Let thy garments be always white ; and let thy head lack no ointment. Whatsoever thy hand findeth to do, do it with thy might " (Eccles. ix. 8–10). "This I say, brethren, the time is short : it remaineth, that both they that have wives be as though they had none ; and they that weep, as though they wept not ; and they that rejoice, as though they rejoiced not ; and they that buy, as though they possessed not ; and they that use this world, as not abusing it : for the fashion of this world passeth away " (1 Cor. vii. 29–31).

Whoever hears the call of Christ is called to freedom. He takes the yoke of the kingdom of heaven upon himself and is thereby freed from the service of vanity.   He can worship the idols of this world no more ; they have no more right to him, and so no power over him.   Much less than the chosen of the Old Covenant can he be obliged to take part in the building of Babel.   He waits with Abraham and all the confederates of the Promise for the " Polis," whose Founder and Maker is God.   That gives him his status as an alien in this world.   That does not mean a lack of interest in this world.   For it is the chosen aliens who are the legitimate inheritors of the earth. For it belongs to the True God, its Creator and Redeemer, and not to the usurpers and their idol-gods.   It belongs to Jesus Christ and those who are fellow-heirs with Him.   " Rejoice thou little flock for it is thy Father's good pleasure to give you the kingdom." Jesus Christ has repudiated nothing in the creation.   Rather has He retained all in the very act of His being crucified for it.   He has died for the world that it might not be destroyed in the wrath, but live.   The world for which He died the Father has given Him to be His own.   To Him alone belongs everything which is in heaven and on earth.   All that have received sonship through Him are His fellow-heirs.   If they suffer with Him they may partake in His sovereignty. They cannot give up this world.   But it is quite as clear that they cannot tread anything violently under foot in order to possess it and master it.   They receive and hold the Kingdom while they suffer for it.   " The Kings of the Gentiles exercise lordship over them ; and they that exercise authority upon them are called benefactors.   But ye shall not be so ; but he that is greatest among you, let him be as the younger ; and he that is chief, as he that doth serve " (Luke xxii. 25).   As they suffer with Jesus they may hold fast to the great hope which is given for all with the resurrection from the dead.   Thus they are blessed as the poor with Him, blessed as the suffering, the oppressed, those that hunger and thirst after righteousness, the merciful, those who see God with a pure heart, the peaceable, the persecuted—blessed, for theirs is the kingdom of heaven, and they will inherit the earth.   They live as those who are sacrificed with Christ and those who exercise the priestly office which deals out life to the world.   The more unrighteousness abounds, the less the love in them grows cold. They endure in the patience of Christ, persevere in the final affliction and refuse to be led astray through false hopes and false deliverers until their crucified and risen Lord comes again and brings in the kingdom of glory.

It is just they who walk in faith and not yet by sight. They do not attempt to transfigure the world through illusions and to anticipate the kingdom of glory through apparent realisations. If the men of the Old Covenant could not live without praying, the life of these men is far more one altogether characterised by prayer. They may, and must, pray, seek, knock and cry out of the depth for their Redeemer, because Jesus Christ takes them into His prayer. And the Spirit Himself intercedes for them with groanings that cannot be uttered.

We ought not to think, then, that Jesus Christ has come to abolish the Old Testament, the Law and the Prophets. He has not come to destroy, but to fulfil. Through Himself, through His own living and dying and rising again He fulfils it. He brings the One sacrifice through which all becomes true and actual, the one great sacrifice of Love with which God appropriates the world. Therefore He brought the forgiveness into the light, the signs of which were the sacrifices of the Old Covenant. In that He makes manifest, through the sacrifice which once and for all puts forgiveness into operation, He makes obsolete the use of the signs which had preceded it. And just while He as God's Son loves sinners in the name of God and at the same time loves God in the name of sinful men, He reveals and fulfils the one commandment of life in all the commandments for every man who believes in Him. That is the Christian life : participation by faith in the Life of Jesus Christ, so that we are shut up in the Love of the Father to His Son, and in the Love of the Son to the Father, and that we may love each other as brothers even as we are loved by Him.

That is the wonderful possibility for life which the Gospel unlocks to us through the preaching that Jesus is the Christ of the Old Testament. To be sure, Jesus is more than the fathers, but that is just because He is the One for Whom they have been waiting, and not for some other who (might) put them in the wrong with their faith and hope. True, He is more than David and Solomon, but He *is* upon the throne of David and Solomon. He is more than all the Prophets of Israel, but that is simply because He is the One Who was proclaimed by them, in Whose life and teaching, dying and rising, the judgment and grace of the Kingship of God is present. He is the Son of Man, the Lord of the Sabbath. His day is the eternal festive day in which all pressing and wrestling come to rest and all the holy armies in Heaven and on Earth honour their Creator and Redeemer, and in unspeakable joy behold His Face.

It is as members of the Old World that we are confronted with the call of the Gospel, which declares that the Old Testament is fulfilled and we may wait and hasten towards the glorious future of the Lord.   So long as this world-age lasts and the message of the Gospel is sounded out in the world, it holds good for all who want to live as Christians, that they should have themselves instructed through the words of the Old Testament in conversion and repentance, in turning away from the old life and in turning towards the new, and be transformed by the renewing of their minds in order to learn and prove the faith, the love, the hope, the justice and holiness and wisdom, which are in Christ Jesus.   Out of it do we learn the true wisdom of life.   For they are " the Scriptures which are able to make us wise unto salvation through faith in Jesus Christ " (2 Tim. iii. 15), and show us the inexhaustible richness of the only possibility for real life, the life alone through the gracious love of God in Jesus Christ, our Lord and Saviour.

SOMMAIRE

De la Conférence du Pasteur WILHELM VISCHER (Bâle).

LA SIGNIFICATION DE L'ANCIEN TESTAMENT POUR LA VIE CHRÉTIENNE

Introduction.—On entend souvent dire que la vie et la doctrine réformées sont façonnées par l'Ancien Testament. Nous ne voulons pas rechercher maintenant si cela est exact mais plutôt poser la question essentielle : Quelle est la signification de l'Ancien Testament pour la vie chrétienne ?

Thèse Principale.—La signification unique de l'Ancien Testament pour la vie chrétienne repose sur le fait que l'Évangile proclame : Jésus est le Christ d'Israël.   Ce message affirme que Jesus est la tête d'un corps dont l'Ancien Testament nous montre les membres ; qu'il ne vit donc pas pour lui-même mais pour et en les siens.   Cette vie du Christ Jésus pour les siens et en les siens est la vie chrétienne.   De même que Jésus ne peut être annoncé et reconnu comme le Christ qu'en rapport avec l'Ancien Testament, de même c'est seulement la relation entre la vie de Jésus et l'Ancien Testament qui nous rend évident la réalité de la vie chrétienne.

17

Développement : 1e *Partie.*—Toutes les explications de
Jésus qui ne le comprennent pas comme le Christ d'Israël ont
ceci de commun : elles considèrent la vie de Jésus comme une
vie à côté de laquelle il y aurait d'autres possibilites de vie,
alors que la prédication évangélique affirme qu'il est la source
unique de la Vie.

Le Nouveau Testament proclame : Tout ce qui est contenu
dans l'Ancien Testament est accompli en Jésus-Christ. Les
histoires de l'Ancien Testament sont des parties de son histoire.
(*a*) Cela n'est pas une fausse interprétation des écrits de l'Ancien
Testament mais cela correspond à leur sens primitif. Car
tous les événements de l'Ancien Testament tendent vers cet
avenir qui leur est promis. Les hommes de l'Ancienne Alliance
sont des pères et des précurseurs. Ils portent la " Bénédiction." Ils vivent tous dans l'attente de Celui qui doit naître
comme fils d'Adam, fils d'Abraham, fils de David. Leur vie
est éclairée de la lumière de l'Avent. Et c'est pour cela qu'ils
peuvent jouir de la vie ; c'est pour cela que leur vie et chaque
vie ne leur appartient pas naturellement. Elle est un don de
la grâce. Le Seigneur de la vie s'oppose à ceux qui veulent
s'approprier la vie par la violence, mais aux humbles il donne
sa grâce. C'est eux qu'il bénit. (*b*) Avec autant de netteté
l'Ancien Testament montre que la malédiction de la colère de
Dieu pèse sur la vie. Les ombres du Vendredi-Saint tombent
sur elle. Elle est condamnée à mort. Tout temps vécu est un
temps de grâce. Par sa révélation en Israël le Dieu saint réduit
à l'impuissance Nature et Histoire en vainquant leurs dieux.

Israël aussi, justement Israël ne peut fonder sa communion
avec le Dieu saint que sur le sacrifice. Les sacrifices d'Israël
sont des signes du pardon de Dieu. Si Israël croit pouvoir se
justifier par lui-même, c'est lui-même qui est sacrifié ; les
prophètes annoncent la fin d'Israël. Les " Justes " de l'Ancienne
Alliance souffrent par la main de Dieu. Ils ne peuvent vivre
que par la prière. En eux est revélé que quiconque voit le
Dieu saint doit mourir. (*c*) Et cependant ils vivent ! En eux
qui sont jugés est revélé que Dieu par sa merveilleuse justice
change le jugement en victoire. Le seigneur saint prend la
forme d'un serviteur et se charge de la faute du monde, afin
que le monde vive. Toutes les figures et tous les mots de
l'Ancien Testament respirent l'air de Pâques.

2e *Partie* : (*a*) L'Évangile annonce : Celui qu'on attendait
est venu. Il est né, le fils d'Abraham et de David. Mais ce
ne sont pas la nature et l'histoire d'Israël qui l'engendrent :
C'est par grâce qu'il est introduit dans l'arbre généalogique.
Le vrai Israël, ce ne sont pas ceux qui sont circoncis dans leur
chair mais ceux qui croient en Jésus et vivent uniquement de

sa grâce.   La barrière tombe, qui dans les temps de l'espérance séparait Israël des païens.   Israël cesse d'avoir une existence particulière.   (b) Le Chrst Jésus subit la malédiction de Dieu. Il *doit* donner sa vie afin que l'Ancien Testament soit accompli. Il n'est pas seulement celui qui enseigne son peuple, il en est aussi le prêtre et il s'offre lui-même en sacrifice.   Ainsi est abolie toute " religion de l'Ancien Testament."   (c) Par la résurrection de Jésus-Christ d'entre les morts il devient manifeste que Dieu était en Christ réconciliant le monde avec lui-même.   (d) C'est seulement par le miracle de Pentecôte que les Apôtres reconnurent et purent annoncer le Grand-Œuvre de Dieu, dans la vie de Jésus-Christ.   Seulement lorsque par le Saint-Esprit, qui est l'auteur caché de l'Écriture sainte, nous reconnaissons l'unité des deux Testaments, nous pouvons croire et confesser qu'il y a *une* Sainte Église dont Christ est la tête et dont nous sommes les membres vivants.   Cette participation au corps de Christ est la réalité de la vie chrétienne. L'Ancien Testament atteste cette réalité, en nous présentant des hommes qui ont vécu de l'attente de Jésus-Christ ;   le Nouveau Testament, lui annonce qu'il est venu dans l'abaissement et qu'il reviendra dans la Gloire.   C'est là la difference entre les deux Testaments.   Leur unité réside dans la présence du Seigneur vivant.   A la place des sacrements de l'attente sont maintenant institués le Baptême et la Cène.   Le Baptême est le signe que nous sommes mis à mort et ensevelis avec le Crucifié, afin de marcher en nouveauté de vie avec le Ressucité. La Cène est le signe que, par son corps rompu pour nous et par son sang répandu pour nous, nous sommes, en communion avec Lui et tous les élus, soutenus et fortifiés pour la vie éternelle, jusqu'à ce que nous soyons à table avec lui dans le Royaume de son père.

3e Partie.—L'Évangile par conséquent confirme et rend actuel, à l'extreme, tout ce qui est contenu dans l'Ancien Testament.   Toutes les promesses et commandements qui s'adressaient à ceux qui ont vécu dans l'attente du Christ, ont maintenant pour nous sur qui la fin du monde est venu, une valeur *beaucoup plus grande*.   Il leur était dit qu'ils étaient nés, comme frères de Celui qui devait naître un jour ; à combien plus forte raison maintenant le seul sens et but de notre vie doit-il être que nous devenions ses frères et que par Lui nous glorifions le Père qui est dans les cieux.   " Celui qui veut conserver sa vie la perdra ;   mais celui qui la perdra à cause de moi la retrouvera."   Cela est vrai de la vie individuelle, conjugale et familiale, du peuple, de l'état, de l'éducation, de la politique, du commerce, de la science et de l'art.

Celui qui entend l'appel du Christ est appelé à la liberté.

Il doit abandonner l'adoration des idoles de ce monde. Elles n'ont plus sur lui aucun droit, aucune puissance. Il ne doit plus participer à la construction de la tour de Babel. Car, avec Abraham et tous les fils de la promesse, élus et étrangers dans le monde, il attend le Royaume de Dieu. Ces élus, ces étrangers gardent une ferme espérance pour cette terre. Car s'ils souffrent maintenant avec Jésus-Christ pour Dieu, ils ont la promesse qu'ils seront conhéritiers de sa victoire. Ils marchent par la foi, non encore par la vue. Leur vie est prière. En offrant le grand sacrifice de l'Amour par lequel Dieu reçoit le monde dans sa miséricorde, Jésus-Christ a accompli l'Ancien Testament. Il a mis en vigueur et accompli le seul commandement de la Vie, le double commandement de l'Amour.

La participation à sa vie est la vie chrétienne par laquelle nous sommes unis à l'Amour du Père pour son Fils, à l'amour du Fils pour le Père : et c'est ainsi que nous pouvons aimer Dieu et nos frères comme il nous a aimés.

L'appel de l'Évangile à cette vie nouvelle nous atteint en tant que membres du monde ancien. Aussi longtemps que ce monde dure et que l'Évangile est annoncé, il faut que tous ceux qui veulent vivre chrétiennement se laissent instruire par les écrits de l'Ancien Testament dans la répentance et le renouvellement de l'intelligence, dans la foi, l'amour, l'espérance, la Justice, la sainteté et la sagesse qui sont en Jésus-Christ.

Professor N. W. Porteous (Edinburgh), in expressing appreciation of the paper, said that Mr. Vischer had never given a clearer and more satisfactory statement of his distinctive point of view. In the speaker's judgment there had been much too big a gulf between the Old Testament scholar and the preacher, and no one was tackling the problem of bringing these two together in a more original way than Mr. Vischer. At the same time, the question might be raised whether Mr. Vischer took sufficient account of the actual religious beliefs held in Old Testament times and whether the task of discovering them was as hopeless as he seemed to think. It was true, however, that, for the Christian theologian, the ultimate significance of the Old Testament appeared only when he went to it with the New Testament in his hand, and on this fundamental issue the speaker stood with Mr. Vischer over against the pure *Religionsgeschichtler*.

M. le Pasteur J. de Saussure now moved the following Resolution : " At the moment of leaving Edinburgh the participants in the International Calvinist Congress of 1938 desire to express their gratitude to God Whose Providence has permitted this fraternal meeting and has thus given them the opportunity of learning much, one from another.   They wish also, before separating, to thank the organisers of this Congress, particularly its venerable President, his devoted secretary and their principal collaborators, also those persons and families who have afforded them so generous a hospitality.   They rejoice in the brotherly participation in the meeting of the different Churches of this country.   They thank the Press and the B.B.C. for the publicity which they have been good enough to accord to their labours.   They regret profoundly the absence of their German brethren, and hope that their next meeting will take place in their country, if it be God's Will, to Whom belongs the Power and the Glory."

Professor Rutgers, in seconding, said : " The members of the Congress owe a great debt of gratitude to those who organised this Congress, with Professor Maclean as their head and Mr. Rounsfell Brown as their hand, and who took so much care of our spiritual and of our material needs.   And we all love dearly our venerable president, not only for the benevolence of his leadership, but also for its strength, for as Calvinists we do not like weak government."

In closing the Congress, Professor Maclean said : " We have come to the end of our proceedings, and I cannot help feeling somewhat overwhelmed with a sense of gratitude to God for this Congress which will have far-reaching effects in many lands.   We are not in search of a basis of union ; we have it.   We have carried out our work in such a manner as to make it clear to the generation that is now around us that the Reformed Faith is worthy of the respect of the highest intellect and of the devotion of the warmest heart, and that it is fitted to meet the world situation that confronts us.

" I am thankful that we have had the Congress in this city of Edinburgh, for it has brought ministers and professors within this city to meet one another in holy purposes such as might not arise in other circumstances.   We have had, too, good evidence of their brotherhood.   For all the scholars from Britain and Edinburgh who have adorned the proceedings, I am extremely grateful.

" The International Commission that has just been appointed has resolved, at the request of our German friends, that the next Congress should be held in Germany towards the end of July two years hence.   But, if we fail to carry out our purpose and aim in Germany, the Congress will be held in Montpellier, in the south of France.   For the theologians present—and in spite of what Dr. Rutgers said, we *are* theologians, with one or two exceptions—I may say that the subject to be discussed at the next Congress will be " *Ordo Salutis*—The Plan of Salvation."

The Congress was closed with a Benediction.

APPENDIX *A*

SYMPOSIUM

BROADCAST FROM THE B.B.C. EDINBURGH STUDIO ON
SUNDAY, 10TH JULY 1938

DR. DRUMMOND.—The Sovereignty of God, the good, gracious God and Father of our Lord Jesus Christ, is the fundamental principle of the Reformed Faith. In it there is something congenial to the Scottish temper. It sometimes finds expression in strange ways. For instance, there's the shepherd's rebuke to grumblers at the East Wind ; " What ails ye at the East Wind ? It weets the grass ; it slokens the yowes ; and it's God's Will." That for him was final. He learnt that from John Knox, the outstanding man who has left his lasting mark for good on Scottish religion. And Knox learnt it from John Calvin, the Frenchman, when a refugee in Geneva.

There is a certain congruity in this Congress of the Reformed Churches holding its meetings in Scotland at this time, and in making the topic of its study and discussion " the Reformed Faith and its Ethical Consequences." It is in line with the great movement, at present in progress, of the Scottish Recall to Religion, a movement in which all the Protestant Churches in the land are united. It is in truth a recall of the people and of the Church to God. What led to the Recall was concern awakened, for one thing, by the definitely Anti-God movement which was actively and aggressively displaying its hostility to the Christian Faith and Ethic in some lands. In a less blatant, but more insidious, way Humanism and Behaviourism were doing the same thing in other lands. These things had led to a decline in spiritual life and to indifference to sin and responsibility to God. Light-hearted materialism and engrossment in the things of this world begat a practical atheism which thought that ethical interests could stand by themselves without religion. It was soon found out, however, that without a religious foundation, the morals of a people are among the things that can be shaken. It is to a people in this case, and alive to the needs of the hour, that there comes this Congress. At it, the place and importance of the fundamental principle of the Reformed Faith " In the beginning—

God " has been faithfully set forth in one sphere of life after another ; the Individual, the Family, the Church, Society, the State, Economics, and so on. Again and again the great answer to the first question of the Shorter Catechism has been quoted : " Man's chief end is to glorify God and to enjoy Him for ever." Wherefore if we are to receive a kingdom, in this land or any land, which cannot be moved, we must have grace—that dominant word in the Reformed vocabulary— whereby we may serve God acceptably with reverence and godly fear, for our God is a Consuming Fire. It is a fearful thing to fall into the hands of the living God ; but, as Dr. Matheson used to say, " it is a more fearful thing not to fall into His hands."

ANNOUNCER.—As this Congress is in every sense international, it is appropriate that our three other speakers should all be drawn from other countries than our own. First, speaking for Calvinism in France, the country of its origin, is Professor Auguste Lecerf, of the Protestant Faculty of Theology in Paris.

PROFESSOR LECERF.—France is the cradle of Calvinism. It was in the French language that the Calvinistic theology found its expression for the first time. The *Institutes* is the first monument of theological thought in French literature, and that book has had a powerful and decisive influence in the moulding of modern French. Nevertheless, the Word of Scripture has been, till this time, sadly fulfilled in Calvin : " No one is accounted a prophet in his own country." France, as a nation, has rejected the Gospel of the Reformation. At present there is no more than one Protestant out of forty souls in our people, and, till the first year of our century, even the so-called " Reformed "—the very spiritual sons of Calvin in France—had become almost utterly unfaithful to the creed of their own Reformer.

But, by a quite unforeseen miracle of the grace of God there is, at the present time, a powerful revival of Calvinistic faith and theology in our recently united Reformed churches. Great numbers of the young ministers and students of other branches of human culture are Calvinists. Calvin's *Institutes* and Catechism, long ago forgotten, are read and studied with the zeal of the first days of our glorious Reformation.

In the beginning of this revival Calvinism in France was thought to be only a religious and theological system. We did not realize at first that Calvinism is much more than a system of dogmatics ; that it is, in fact, a universal principle.

In order to fathom the mind of John Calvin in all its depths we needed the help of men bred in countries moulded by Calvinistic influence ; of men who had already fought battles on other fields than that of theology. That help came from Holland. Abraham Kuyper, that theologian of genius, who was also a very great statesman and a first-class writer, taught us his lesson. Then we realized that Calvinism had to exert its influence in all departments of human activity and thought.

Our brethren of other Reformed countries were already aware of that, and so it came to pass that at our last meeting at Geneva it was resolved that the present Calvinistic Congress in Edinburgh should deal, as a general topic, with the ethical consequence of Calvinism in Society, in the State, in Economics, in Art, in Secular Knowledge, and so forth.

" All things belong to you, and you belong to Christ, and Christ belongs to God." That idea of St. Paul, who has been termed by a German theologian " The Guardian Angel of Protestantism," is the motto, not only of the Congress but in the different activities of those attending. They are determined to make it true in the Church and for the benefit of the whole world. So help us God !

ANNOUNCER.—Throughout the centuries in different parts of the world, Calvinists have had to struggle for the rights of their faith. This was perhaps nowhere so much the case as in Eastern Europe. Dr. Alexander Nagy of the Reformed Church of Hungary has travelled from Budapest to attend the present Congress.

DR. NAGY.—Calvinism as a spiritual power had its mission and its famous history in the land of the Magyars too.

It came to the country in a very early period of the Reformation. That period was the most critical in the life of the nation as well as of the race.

In the beginning of the sixteenth century the Hungarians had two yokes to bear :

The one was the Germanizing policy of the Habsburgs, who occupied the throne of the Hungarians. The Habsburg kings had for their dangerous policy a very obedient instrument in the Roman Catholic Church. Their programme was to make the Hungarians first poor ; second, Roman Catholic ; and then German. But their endeavour was thwarted by the simple and strong faith of the Calvinist ministers, who endured imprisonment, death, and some of them even the unimaginable sufferings of the galleys as pure slaves sold by the Austrians. They were faithful to the end, and their glorious sufferings are still a living source for the furtherance of the Calvinistic ideals of Christianity.

The second yoke was that of the Turks.

Hungary had been the bulwark of the Christianity of Western Europe since the early period of the fifteenth century against Moslems. No country or race ever defended Christian civilization and religion more than the Hungarians. There was a century when they had to fight for the sheer existence of their race against both the Austrians and the Turks. From the enormous loss of manhood and blood our race has never fully recovered. The country was almost depopulated. This is a main reason why Hungary received a Germanic coloration. This was a sacrifice that Europe has never properly realized and the Hungarian race is waiting still in vain to be recompensed by the cultured West.

In this great struggle for her life and existence, the Calvinistic elements of the race have distinguished themselves. They were able to keep strong and healthy their racial eminence and virtues because they were Calvinists; their secret was their trust in God. As far back as the sixteenth century in the Principality of Transylvania the Calvinists created a State in whose atmosphere it was possible to have religious and civil liberty, freedom of conscience and peace between diverse peoples—an object lesson for the world of to-day.

We Hungarian Calvinists are imbued with the same spirit of willingness to struggle for such rights and liberties, in the conviction that hereby the World at large may come to enjoy these blessings under the Providence of Almighty God.

ANNOUNCER.—To-day the Churches of the Reformed Faith are to be found in all parts of the world. And in the New World the influence of Calvinism has always been a force in the life of the people. The Reverend Dr. Stewart M. Robinson, Editor of *The Presbyterian*, comes to Edinburgh from Philadelphia.

REV. DR. STEWART M. ROBINSON.—The United States of America were settled principally by men and women strongly influenced by Calvinism. Early immigration included the Pilgrims to New England, the Dutch and Scoto-Irish to the Middle Colonies, New York, the Jerseys, Pennsylvania, and North Carolina, and the English to Virginia, South Carolina, and Georgia. All these groups were Calvinistic in their theology although their political and ecclesiastical views differed.

The only ordained minister of religion to sign the Declaration of Independence in 1776 was the Calvinist, John Witherspoon, President of Princeton. It has been stated that in the thirteen original States about one-third of the inhabitants were Presbyterians and an even larger proportion were children of Calvinism.

The Constitutional Convention of 1787 was meeting in

Philadelphia at the same time and but a few squares away from the Assembly of the Presbyterian Church which formulated the basis for the first General Assembly, the One Hundred and Fiftieth Anniversary of which we have just celebrated and to which was welcomed, as a guest of honour, a former Moderator of the Church of Scotland, the Very Reverend Daniel Lamont, D.D., Honorary President of this Calvinistic Congress now in session.

Theodore Roosevelt called the Scoto-Irish, *i.e.* Calvinists, the spear-head in the winning of the great West which occupied the first 125 years of our national life. These brave men and women were moved by the heartening belief that God had given them a place and a calling. They believed in Divine Vocation and were not discouraged by savage inhabitants, dense forests, lofty mountains, mighty rivers and boundless plains.

Almost a million people, whose ancestors settled in the mountain area of the Southern States in America, reveal a type of mind strongly built on those traditions, which came to them from their Calvinistic forebears who first fled from Scotland in the eighteenth century, that they might live under the sovereignty of God.

Lord Tweedsmuir once pointed out the fact that five of the greatest military leaders of our Anglo-American history were all Cavalrymen and all Calvinists, namely, James Graham (the Marquis of Montrose), Oliver Cromwell, Robert E. Lee, T. J. Jackson more commonly known as Stonewall Jackson, and Earl Haig. Of these Jackson was one of the greatest strategists of all time. There is preserved the copy of a Commentary on the Epistle to the Romans, which he always carried through his campaigns, and he is as well known for his devotion to Christ as for his military genius. He lived and died a humble believer in his salvation through the shed blood of his Saviour. He was a staunch Calvinist and an ordained office-bearer in the Presbyterian Church. It was he who said that he felt as safe on a battlefield as in his bed, because he knew that God would spare him as long as God needed him here below. To-day the bulwark of constitutional government—friendly international relations, and a decent consideration for the opinions of mankind—runs through those lands where the Calvinistic tradition still has influence.

APPENDIX *B*

INTERNATIONAL COMMISSION ON CALVINISTIC CONGRESSES

AFRICA . . .	Professor Besselaar.
AMERICA . . .	Dr. Stewart Robinson.
	Professor Childs Robinson.
CZECHOSLOVAKIA .	Dr. J. B. Souček.
FRANCE . . .	Professor Lecerf.
GERMANY . .	Dr. W. E. Langenohl.
HOLLAND . .	Dr. Kromsigt.
	Dr. Rutgers, *Vice-Chairman.**
HUNGARY . .	Professor Sebestyen.
	Reverend Alex. Nagy.
SWITZERLAND . .	Pastor Saussure.
	Pastor W. Vischer.
BRITAIN :	
ENGLAND . .	Rev. S. Leigh Hunt.
	Rev. W. J. Parker.
SCOTLAND .	Professor Burleigh.
	Professor Henderson.
	Dr. Hector Macpherson.
	Rev. W. H. Hamilton.
	Rev. David H. C. Read.
	Principal Macleod.
	Professor Davidson.
	Rev. W. J. Moffett.
	Rev. Professor Donald Maclean, *Chairman.**

* Address of Chairman and Vice-Chairman, for correspondence, is as given in " Who is Who," pp. 7-16.

16. XII. 38